THE EMPLOYEE RETENTION HANDBOOK

Stephen Taylor is a senior lecturer in HRM at Manchester Metropolitan University. Formerly, he taught personnel management and industrial relations at the Manchester School of Management (UMIST). Prior to these appointments he held a number of personnel management posts in the hotel industry and the National Health Service.

Stephen is the CIPD's national examiner for the managing in a business context paper. His research focuses on management practice in the fields of employee retention, recruitment and remuneration. He teaches employee resourcing, reward management and employment law.

Other titles in the series:

Appraisal (2nd edn)
Clive Fletcher

Benchmarking for People Managers
John Bramham

The Competencies Handbook
Steve Whiddett and
Sarah Hollyforde

Development and Assessment Centres
Charles Woodruffe

Employee Attitude and Opinion Surveys
Mike Walters

Empowering Team Learning
Michael Pearn

Flexible Working Practices
John Stredwick and Steve Ellis

From Absence to Attendance (2nd edn)
Alastair Evans and
Mike Walters

HR Forecasting and Planning
Paul Turner

HR Know-How in Mergers and Acquisitions
Sue Cartwright and
Cary L. Cooper

The Job Evaluation Handbook
Michael Armstrong and
Angela Baron

Learning Alliances
David Clutterbuck

Managing Redundancy
Alan Fowler

New Dimensions in Pay Management
Michael Armstrong and
Duncan Brown

Performance Management
Michael Armstrong and
Angela Baron

Project Management
Roland and Frances Bee

Recruitment and Selection
Gareth Roberts

Strategic HRM
Michael Armstrong and
Angela Baron

Stress and Employer Liability (2nd edn)
Jill Earnshaw and Cary L. Cooper

Turbo-Charging the HR Function
Paul Mooney

The Chartered Institute of Personnel and Development is the leading publisher of books and reports for personnel and training professionals, students, and for all those concerned with the effective management and development of people at work. For details of all our titles, please contact the Publishing Department:
tel. 020–8263 3387
fax 020–8263 3850
e-mail publish@cipd.co.uk
To view and purchase CIPD titles: www.cipd.publishing.co.uk

THE EMPLOYEE RETENTION HANDBOOK

STEPHEN TAYLOR

Chartered Institute of Personnel and Development

Design by Paperweight
Typeset by Fakenham Photosetting
Printed in Great Britain by
The Cromwell Press, Trowbridge

British Library Cataloguing in Publication Data
A catalogue record for this book is available from the
British Library

ISBN 0–85292–963–3

The views expressed in this book are the author's own, and
may not necessarily reflect those of the CIPD.

CIPD Enterprises Ltd has made every effort to trace and
acknowledge copyright holders. If any source has been
overlooked, CIPD Enterprises would be pleased to redress
this for future editions.

Chartered Institute of Personnel and Development, CIPD House,
Camp Road, London SW19 4UX
Tel: 020-8971 9000   Fax: 020-8263 3333
E-mail: cipd@cipd.co.uk Website: www.cipd.co.uk
Incorporated by Royal Charter. Registered charity no. 1079797.

CONTENTS

ACKNOWLEDGEMENTS

In writing this book I have been greatly helped by the experience of working with several research students (all practising HR managers) who have completed projects on staff retention under my supervision in recent years. Some have contributed chapters to this book, while others have shared ideas, experiences and research findings on which I have been able to draw. Particular thanks are thus due to Claire Barnes, Nick Bellis, Noel Burton, Lynn Cross, Lindsay Pettit, Claire Redpath, Victoria Royle, Graeme Semple, Claire Sweeney, Roya Taylor, Valerie Thornborrow, Mary Veitch and Lauren Worth. I have also had the privilege, for a number of years, of working closely with Shirley Jenner on retention-related issues. Many of the views put forward in this book were originally generated from work we carried out together on graduate employment issues. I would also like to thank Alex Evans and Allan Macpherson for making very useful suggestions as I was completing the book. I have also been fortunate in having the support of an excellent publishing team at CIPD. Thanks are due to Matthew Reisz (who helped well beyond the call of duty), Rob Foss and Rebecca Evans for their efforts and encouragement.

PART I

ANALYSIS

1 MANAGING EMPLOYEE RETENTION

Let's start with a success story ...

Over the last five years Asda – the UK's third-largest super-market chain – has brought its staff turnover rate down each year. In 2001 it stood at 23 per cent, which would be very high in some industries, but was a good deal lower than the rates achieved across most of the UK's retailing sector. Indeed, Asda can now boast that it has a better record on staff retention than all the other major UK retailers. What is more, this reduction in staff turnover has been achieved at a time when job mobility in the economy as a whole has been increasing. It has also coincided with a year-on-year growth in the number of people employed by Asda as the company has expanded its operations. What is especially interesting is the way the company has managed to lower its wastage rates without increasing its pay rates vis-à-vis those of other employers. Rival chains pay more, but still have higher staff turnover rates.

According to IDS (2000a), a range of policies have been introduced by managers at Asda which explain its success on the staff-retention front. What they have in common is a focus on what happens internally rather than on what other companies are doing. Benchmarking is carried out to allow comparisons to be made, but it is the results of the company's staff attitude surveys, leavers' surveys and focus groups which have informed the practices that have reduced turnover. Key factors which the company believes account for its success include the following:

☐ a share option scheme in which over half of staff participate. Employees have to have a year's service to join the scheme, and stay for three further years in order to be able to cash in their option rights.

□ several flexible working initiatives aimed at helping staff to achieve the right balance between their home and working lives. These allow employees to take periods of unpaid leave and to return to their jobs afterwards. They include 'Benidorm leave' of up to three months a year for the over-fifties, a group who tend to remain in their jobs for longer than their younger colleagues.

□ drives to promote hourly-paid staff up the supervisory ladder. The company now aims to fill 70 per cent of managerial posts internally through very structured centrally run training programmes. All employees with service of a year or more can apply to join one of two career development programmes, entry being dependent on the satisfactory achievement of defined competencies.

Asda's approach to the management of employee retention is very much that which is advocated in this book. Success follows when managers refrain from making assumptions about the way forward and instead try to find out what is actually causing people in different groups to resign voluntarily. This ensures that initiatives aimed at improving staff retention rates are targeted carefully and precisely at the source of the problem. This is a field in which there is no easily defined 'best practice' approach available. Different occupational groups have different needs. Their members come to work each day and are attracted to particular types of employment for different reasons. The key to retaining them is to understand the main 'turnover drivers' that affect each group and to respond appropriately.

In recent years recruitment and retention difficulties have moved to the top of the human resource management agenda in most UK organisations, displacing performance management and employee relations issues as those which consume most management time (IRS, 2000).

There are several plausible explanations for this trend:

□ We have seen a tightening of labour markets as the economy has grown in the past decade. Since the early 1990s, in most parts of the country, unemployment has fallen steadily to create a situation in which there are considerably fewer people out of work than there are jobs being advertised. This means that it is harder to replace leavers quickly with able successors than was the case in the recent past. It also means that there are more alternative job opportunities around, leading to more voluntary resignations.

☐ We have seen the development of particularly serious skills shortages in certain industries and in particular regions of the country. The problem has been most acute in the south-east and in London, where job growth has been strongest. Finding people with specialised skills has been especially tough, but the shortages have affected most industries and most labour markets to a greater or lesser extent. Intense recruitment and retention problems in the public services have been especially well documented.

☐ Demographic trends are beginning to have an impact. The working population has been ageing for some years now, which means that fewer young people are coming on to the job market than there are people retiring each year. This 'demographic time-bomb' was expected to explode in the early 1990s, but in the event failed to go off thanks to the intervention of a recession. Instead, its effects have been delayed and are only now really becoming apparent, and being exacerbated to an extent by later entry on to the job market as more young people are opting to attend university.

☐ There has been a steady growth in the proportion of jobs that are knowledge-based or that require the possession of some kind of professional qualification. There is less low-skilled work around and more that is high-skilled in nature. Moreover, most of the supposedly 'low-skilled low-paid' jobs that are being created in the service sector require relatively well-developed social skills. This makes it harder to fill the jobs appropriately and means that employee turnover is more damaging to the organisation. The loss of an employee who has been trained up over months or years is a bigger problem than the resignation of someone who is more readily replaced.

☐ In the skilled trades and professions people appear to be becoming less loyal to their employers and less prepared to view their jobs as likely to last for a long period of time. This has occurred partly because there are more job opportunities available, but there are other reasons too. For example, employers have tended (at least in their rhetoric) to show less loyalty to their employees. Although many still chant mantras such as 'Our staff are our biggest asset', they appear to be simultaneously creating a type of workplace that is more insecure. Endless reorganisations keep people continually worried about their futures, while moves towards greater flexibility breed further insecurity as employers experiment with outsourcing, subcontracting, casual/agency working of various kinds and the employment of people on a fixed-term basis. Final salary pension schemes fast disappear down the corporate plughole, while memories of redundancies in the two last recessions stay fresh in our collective memories. As a whole, the workforce is no more fickle than it ever was, but we are seeing less by way of long-term psychological commitment on the part of professional groups who have traditionally remained in jobs for the long haul. Employee loyalty, it seems, is increasingly conditional on the receipt of a good deal in return.

The upshot, from an organisation's perspective, is greater staff turnover or, in some cases, the development of an 'employee-retention problem'. It is increasingly hard and more expensive to find suitable replacements quickly when people leave, leading to inefficiencies and lost business opportunities. Moreover, because people are occupying more highly skilled jobs, greater potential damage is done to organisations when people leave. Precious accumulated knowledge and experience leaves through the front door with them when they go.

Despite these truths about our contemporary business environment, many managers seem to find it hard to adjust. There remains a tendency to run organisations in quite an autocratic, inflexible, controlling kind of way. Unwanted staff turnover results because attractive, alternative job opportunities are more readily available, yet this rarely seems to lead to any kind of critical self-appraisal of the way we manage our people. Managers seem loath to accept that tighter labour market conditions require a style and set of policies which take greater account of what employees want and need from their work. One consequence appears to be a tendency (whether deliberate or subconscious) to blame employees themselves when they choose to leave. They tend to be seen as being disloyal or are thought to be making a mis-judgement in resigning. Alternatively, the decision to leave is said to have been wholly unavoidable ('Sad to see him/her go, but we just couldn't provide him/her with what he/she wanted,' etc). Sometimes these are fair comments – but more often they are devices used to mask the fact that the depar-ture could have been avoided had more care and professional-ism been put into the management of the employment relationship.

The truth is that most times when there is an unwanted resignation it *should* be seen as an organisational failure. A valued asset in which the organisation has invested time and resources has been lost. This should lead us to reflect on the causes, to think about how things could have been made to turn out differently, and to adjust our practices so that the chances of its happening again are reduced. However, such a response is rare. Instead, we brush aside the departure, blame everything and everyone but ourselves, and cheerfully resist the need to change the way we operate. In tight labour markets this just results in higher levels of unwanted staff turnover.

Aims and objectives

The main purpose of this book is to provide material that will help forward-thinking pragmatic managers to start tackling their employee-retention 'problems' in a creative and effi-cient manner. I have basically set out to help answer the fol-lowing three straightforward questions:

□ Why do people choose to leave organisations?
□ Why does this matter?
□ What can be done to reduce its occurrence?

In completing the book I have tried to write in an engaging and readable style. I have also set out to provoke readers into questioning some of my ideas and assumptions by stating views in a rather starker manner than I am used to when writing for student and academic audiences. Moreover, I have also drawn extensively on my experience working as a human resource manager first in the hotel industry and later in the NHS. In these jobs I observed the problems associated with competing in tight labour markets at first hand and was involved in initiatives designed to reduce turnover levels. I saw many mistakes being made, as well as a few examples of sustained success. I have also drawn on anec-dotal evidence gleaned from conversations with friends, family and people I have met more recently in my work as a university lecturer. The result, I hope, is a book which con-tains highly practical, workable suggestions on how to improve an organisation's employee turnover record over the long term.

At the same time I have sought to ensure that wherever possible the book is also based on the most robust and up-to-date research findings I have been able to find – including many of my own and those of my students. Unfortunately, given its significance in many organisations, staff turnover and retention has not been a well-researched topic in the UK. The amount of published research available on which I have been able to draw is thus relatively meagre. What has been published has been of good quality and is most useful, but there is, as yet, not enough of it. However, this is not the case in the USA, where there are now hundreds of studies to draw on and good, strong evidence available either to back up or cast doubt on the validity of most of the assertions that people make about turnover and retention. I have thus made full use of the major US research studies published in recent years, and hope that this book will serve to bring them to the attention of a wider audience. I accept, of course, that care must be taken in assuming that labour markets in the USA work similarly to those in the UK. Average American employee turnover rates are always a bit higher than those in the UK (in booms as well as recessions), which means that average US workers hold more separate jobs during the course of their careers than is the case for equivalents in the UK. More people are dismissed by

American corporations too, creating workplaces which are more prone to personnel changes and often feel less secure. However, the research work that has been carried out in the UK shows that in nearly all respects our labour markets operate in a very similar fashion to American ones. We give the same reasons for leaving our jobs, go through the same processes when thinking about resigning, and respond in the same ways to policy initiatives designed to encourage us to stay longer with our employers. When it comes to improving retention rates, UK employers are thus safe to assume that what works there will also work in the UK.

The book is divided into three Parts. Part 1 – entitled 'Analysis' – assesses the major contemporary debates about employee-retention issues before going on to review the various tools available to managers seeking to understand both the causes of staff turnover and its effects in their organisations. A major aim here is to give readers the raw material needed to develop a strong business case for investing time, effort and resources in tackling employee turnover. Part 2 – headed 'Prescriptions' – focuses on the different kinds of initiative and policy change that can be considered when seeking ways to reduce staff turnover in different organisations. Here we look at the approaches that are commonly used, and also at those that have some merit but which feature more rarely in retention-management plans. Finally, in Part 3, is a series of six cases are presented which look at the causes of and appropriate responses to unwanted staff turnover among different occupational groups. Each case has been written by a different author and draws on the results of her own research. In many respects these chapters break new ground, focusing as they do on the reasons people give for leaving organisations when asked confidentially about actual recent resignations or planned 'intentions to resign'. While there are some similarities between the six groups, what is most striking is how different factors are more or less prominent in different cases. What has to be done in order to retain new graduates is very different from what is needed in the case of call-centre employees, police officers or engineers. The labour market dynamics and turnover drivers vary greatly in each case, reflecting the different types of people who are attracted to these jobs, their long-term ambitions, and the occupational structures and cultures in which they work.

Perspectives

My final task in this opening chapter is to set out briefly the major perspective I have adopted in researching employee turnover and in writing about it here. This differs slightly from the perspectives that have generally been adopted by other authors.

Most existing prescriptive writing on employee retention approaches the topic from one of two angles. The first, which is the longest-established, tends to view staff turnover in the round. An organisation-wide perspective is taken, the focus being on rises and falls in corporate attrition rates. All unwanted turnover is viewed as being equally undesirable and of the same significance to employers. A reduction in the turnover rate for the organisation as a whole is thus seen as desirable and forms the aim of initiatives in the area of employee retention. It follows that improving retention/ turnover rates *in general* is or should be a central objective of human resource management policy. High turnover rates tend to be taken as evidence of poorly managed organisations with failing human resource functions, whereas low turnover is associated with well-run organisations and successful human resource functions.

In recent years a different perspective has emerged and has become a standard fixture in much writing on employee turnover. This stems from a belief that in 'the new world of work' rising staff turnover rates are inevitable and probably desirable too. The more flexible our labour markets are, the more people will move, retrain and put their experiences at the disposal of new employers. The national economy benefits as a result because it is more dynamic, productive and responsive to change. Higher tunover is thus the price that has to be paid for greater adaptability and the move away from the 'job-for-life' mentality. The result is an abandonment of concern with overall turnover rates or the retention of typical employees. Instead it is argued that organisations should focus their efforts on the retention of their most out-standing performers – the 'few' in each part of their operations who have the capacity to 'make a real difference'. This perspective is associated with the use of such terms as 'the war for talent', which sum it up pretty well. It is about identifying the very best people (the queen bees) and acting with some aggression to ensure that competitors do not get their hands on them.

Both these approaches to employee turnover are appropriate in some organisational situations. Neither is wholly wrong – but I prefer to adopt a rather different frame of reference. First, it is my view that virtually all employee turnover is damaging from an organisation's perspective, whether or not the people concerned are excellent performers or have outstanding potential. The truth is that most organisations are staffed mainly by average achievers who, without making a huge personal impact all the time, keep the show on the road and ensure that core objectives are met. Their loss is not inevitable and should be regarded as negative for the organisation. Moreover, it is my contention that we should resist viewing the departure of below-average performers as a positive occurrence. It may bring some relief to managers and it provides an opportunity to bring in a more effective successor, but there is still a cost attached. As a 'staffing episode' it remains undesirable and should be a situation to avoid in the future through the development of more robust recruitment and selection techniques.

However, although the focus should not be exclusively on the most highly talented individuals, it is also naive to assume that all staff turnover is of equal significance for organisations. The truth is that losing people from some groups is potentially more harmful than is the case when members of other groups leave. There are three major reasons for this:

☐ Some labour markets are tighter than others. Members of some groups are thus easier and less expensive to replace than others.

☐ Some groups of employees take longer to become fully effective when they start than others. The effect of high staff turnover is a great deal worse where it takes a replacement several months to reach full effectiveness than where it takes a few days.

☐ Members of some groups, because of the nature of the work that they do, represent a greater loss to the organisation than is the case with members of others. This is especially so where the individual customer–employee relationship is central to an organisation's market reputation.

My view is that effective management of employee retention is focused primarily on those groups of staff you employ whose resignations are the most problematic from the organisation's point of view (ie those in the above categories). The loss of an average performer in one of these groups is often more damaging for the organisation than the loss of someone outstanding from some other group. It follows that retention efforts should be targeted on these 'high-risk groups' rather than on those among whom turnover rates are highest. A 15 per cent turnover rate in a high-risk category of staff is often a considerably greater cause for concern (and often of expense) than a 30 per cent, or even 50 per cent, rate in a low-risk category.

The key is thus to start by establishing which groups of employees in your organisation you most *need* to retain. This can be established systematically by calculating the cost implications of each voluntary resignation. The next step involves working out what *in particular* drives staff turnover among these people. The final step is to start putting in place management practices which stand a good chance of improving their rates of retention. It is about understanding what exactly makes specific labour markets tick, and going on to forge policies which directly address these issues.

Lastly, I want to state my belief that tackling staff turnover issues in organisations is in most cases a long-term project. There are few quick fixes available to managers, and no easy answers. People resign from jobs for many different reasons. Sometimes it is because they are dissatisfied with their current job. On other occasions the attraction of an alternative is too good to miss. Usually it is a mixture of these types of reason and others too (time for a change, relocating to another area, wanting some time out of the workforce, etc). However, it is possible to observe patterns of reasons among different sets of employees. Each labour market that an organisation taps into tends to be populated by people who have a similar career agenda and who tend to leave for similar reasons. This is illustrated effectively in the case studies provided in Part 3 of the book. What is needed, therefore, is a strategic approach. Measures must be appropriate to the group being targeted, carefully thought through, and then applied over a sustained period.

2 STAFF TURNOVER: MYTHS, FACTS AND DEBATES

In this chapter many of the themes that we return to later in the book are introduced and discussed. However, the main purpose is to set out my position on three fundamental issues that are frequently debated by managers when topics related to employee turnover and retention are raised. In each case the main contours of the debate are described and evidence put forward to justify my conclusion. To a large extent this analysis sets out the assumptions on which the book's subsequent chapters are based.

☐ The first debate concerns the extent to which staff turnover is or should be seen as a significant organisational problem at all. For some, turnover is simply an avoidable cost, while for others it has rather more negative consequences. An alternative view stresses the potential benefits that can accrue from a modest level of turnover.

☐ The second debate relates to job-tenure trends in the economy as a whole. Some argue that changes in the nature of the commercial environment mean that employee turnover is bound to rise whatever managers do, and that increasing rates should not therefore worry them unduly. Others dissent, believing that claims made about fundamental changes in the world of work are exaggerated and that there is no discernible long-term trend towards higher employee turnover rates.

☐ Thirdly, we examine the claim that staff turnover is inevitable for most organisations and that there is little in practice that managers can do to reduce it.

Staff turnover: wastage or opportunity?

The most fundamental debate that managers have about employee turnover and retention concerns the extent to which the issue should be a matter of concern. While most would agree that too high a level of turnover has negative implications for an organisation, there is disagreement about how significant these implications are. For many HR specialists, rising staff turnover is seen as being an important organisational problem *per se*. It follows that improving retention rates should be high on the management agenda, and that it is proper for resources to be devoted to achieving this aim. Others disagree. For them staff turnover is at most an irritation, well down their lists of priorities for action. Moreover, a certain amount of turnover is actively welcomed by many managers. There are no right or wrong answers in this debate. In the end the extent to which staff retention difficulties constitute an important organisational problem depends entirely on the type of organisation and its particular business circumstances.

The view that staff turnover has essentially negative implications derives first from an appreciation of the costs that are associated with it. We examine this issue in some detail in Chapter 3, but it is useful to point out at this stage just how costly to an organisation excessive turnover can be. Nine times out of ten when someone leaves, a vacancy is created that is subsequently filled externally. A range of different costs are necessarily associated with this process. In many cases the most significant element is the cost of recruiting a new person. It may be necessary to place an advertisement in the press, to pay agency fees, or both. At the very least there is a cost in terms of management time involved in administering the recruitment process, shortlisting candidates and selecting a replacement. For some types of job several interviews may be arranged or some kind of assessment centre. Interview expenses are often paid, and recruitment literature is printed and posted to candidates. Then there is the cost of inducting and training the new employee, the cost of administering the entry of a new starter (payroll, personnel records, offer letters, issuing contracts, etc). In addition, while all this is going on there is a vacancy. This may mean that the organisation is less productive or effective for a few weeks, or it may result in further expenditure on overtime or temporary staff employed at a premium hourly rate. In any case there is likely to be a loss of productivity in the last weeks of the resignee's period of work and during the first weeks or months after his or her replacement arrives. The final cost is difficult to calculate accurately and varies substantially from job to job, but has to be absorbed by the organisation in virtually every case of voluntary turnover. Most often the cost is not especially high for one individual leaver. However, when assessed cumulatively across an organisation, the total cost associated with staff turnover can mount to hundreds of thousands or even millions each year. Very substantial savings can thus be achieved by reducing turnover levels even by a few percentage points.

In addition to direct costs such as these, a voluntary resignation also represents a waste of organisational resources in other ways. This is particularly so when someone is given intensive or extensive training at the organisation's expense and then leaves before a proper return on the investment is attained. The situation is made worse when one of your organisation's employees resigns in order to take up a post with a rival organisation. The training and experience gained at your expense is then not just lost but can actively be deployed in competition with you. The more extensive and commercially useful the knowledge that resignees take with them when they leave, the more significant is the potential damage done.

The other major negative consequences of voluntary turnover result from its impact on the staff who remain employed. The resignation of a colleague often means more work for those left behind. New duties have to be taken on and project work taken forward. Some see this as an opportunity, but others find it difficult to cope and become resentful. They are also typically required to help train the new employee in addition to their existing duties. Taking on this kind of extra burden is not a problem when it occurs occasionally. The consequences in terms of lost morale and commitment can be a great deal more damaging where there is high turnover and where a near-continual shortage of staff results. High turnover is also bad from the point of view of labour market competition. A reputation for being unable to keep people rapidly translates into a poor reputation as an employer generally. The result is a disinclination on the part of good people looking for jobs even to consider applying. This effect is strongest where an employer relies heavily on recruitment from a defined geographical area and the local job centre or newspaper always seems to be advertising its vacancies.

Finally we can point to the negative perceptions that staff turnover can present from the perspective of customers. The impact here is in jobs where familiarity with the individual needs or preferences of a customer on the part of employees is central to an organisation's reputation. This is the case wherever professional services are being provided on an ongoing basis – it is as true of hairdressing and restaurants as it is of schools and firms of solicitors. Too much chopping and changing of personnel in such workplaces tends, at the very least, to diminish customer loyalty. At worst it leads to a genuine reduction in perceived standards of customer service, which translates, in turn, to the development of a poor reputation in key markets.

The case against staff turnover and for retention initiatives is thus strong and has considerable resonance in most types of workplace. However, we can also construct an alternative argument which serves to downplay the negative impact of turnover from a management point of view. First, it is important to acknowledge that a good employee retention record is not necessarily needed in order to achieve substantial commercial success. McDonald's, for example, is by anyone's standards a highly successful international corporation. Yet it has reportedly managed to grow spectacularly over recent decades despite having a staff turnover rate of over 300 per cent (Ritzer, 1996, p130; Cappelli, 2000, p106). Average length of service of just four months has not been so great a handicap as to stop McDonald's becoming the dominant player in its industry. The reverse is also true. Some public sector corporations in the UK, which by common consent provide a dire service, have some of the highest rates of staff retention in the country. We must thus recognise from the start that other variables (ie apart from staff turnover) very often have a more significant role to play in determining business success.

A second argument concerns the need for organisations to have regular infusions of fresh blood from time to time. Too high a retention rate can lead to organisational decay because new ideas are barred from entering and circulating. New people bring with them alternative perspectives and varied types of experience on which organisations can profitably draw. They also frequently bring to their jobs a burst of enthusiasm and idealism which reliable old-stagers have lost over their many years of service. The fresh blood argument in favour of employee turnover is especially true of senior people in an organisation. Although there are clearly many exceptions, as a general rule there is little more damaging to the interests of an organisation than leaders who have run out of new ideas or have outstayed their welcome in other ways. Unless senior teams get periodically rejuvenated with suitable people from outside, they can very easily stagnate or become essentially self-serving. Moreover, of course, it is only because of turnover at senior levels that more junior staff get an opportunity for promotion. Where turnover rates are too low, not only can fresh blood not get in but existing blood cannot circulate healthily either.

The third strand of the argument in favour of a measure of staff turnover simply reflects the fact that some resignations are welcomed by managers because they result in the replacement of a relatively weak performer with a better one. This is the most common example of a resignation which is 'functional' rather than 'dysfunctional'. Others include the departure of people who did not fit in particularly well, whose attendance was poor, who had ceased to enjoy their work, or who had developed destructive relationships with colleagues. Griffeth and Hom (2001, pp6–7) quote research evidence gathered in a US bank which showed that over 40 per cent of voluntary turnover was appropriately classed as 'functional'. The precise proportion varies from workplace to workplace, but it is reasonable to assume that 40 per cent is a good estimate for most workplaces. This is because a fair number of all resignees quit because they are dissatisfied with some aspect of their work, which in turn is likely to be reflected in their relative work performance prior to the resignation.

Finally, we must acknowledge the fact that in some situations relatively high staff turnover allows managers to exercise greater control than would otherwise be the case over their wage bills. This is particularly true of organisations whose business levels are subject to regular fluctuation. It means that when the level of income drops for a few weeks or months, wage costs can be made simultaneously and painlessly to fall simply by holding back from recruiting replacements. Profitability is thus maintained without the need to lay people off at a cost to the organisation.

With strong arguments on either side of the debate it is reasonable to conclude that the significance of turnover varies from organisation to organisation. There are some situations in which it matters a great deal and can have a real impact on the employer's competitive position, but also others in which the impact is neutral or even positive. A third type of situation is one in which staff turnover is acknowledged to have a damaging effect but where the costs associated with its reduction outweigh those being created by the turnover itself.

By and large, if the following apply it is fair to argue that you should be concerned about turnover levels which are higher than those of your competitors or which are rising significantly:

☐ Labour markets are tight, making it hard to recruit the people with the skills your organisation needs.

☐ Recruitment costs are substantial (eg agencies or press advertisements are used or sophisticated approaches to selection).

☐ Training has to be provided to new starters at some cost to the organisation.

☐ A new starter takes several weeks or months to reach full effectiveness in the job.

☐ Patterns of business are reasonably stable on a week-by-week and month-by-month basis.

☐ Leavers take with them (in their heads) knowledge which would be very useful to a competitor.

☐ The organisation is growing and does not anticipate a need to make compulsory redundancies in the foreseeable future.

In these kinds of situation staff turnover over and above 5 per cent to 10 per cent is rightly seen as a management issue that must be tackled. It is likely that substantial resources are currently being wasted as a direct result of excessive voluntary resignations. There is thus a strong business case for investment in retention initiatives. Conversely, in the following situations relatively high rates of turnover are more likely to be sustainable:

- Labour markets are loose, making it easy to find replacement staff of the required quality when someone resigns.
- New staff can be hired at relatively low cost (eg via a job centre or through word of mouth recruitment).
- Selection can be carried out easily and cheaply (eg via a simple interview with one or two managers).
- Training costs for new starters are low.
- New starters can become fully effective in their jobs within a few days or weeks.
- Patterns of business are reasonably unstable or unpredictable on a week-by-week or month-by-month basis.
- It is likely that compulsory redundancies will have to be made in the coming months.
- Leavers do not generally walk out of the door in possession of knowledge that would be of use to a competitor.

Of course, it is quite possible for different groups of employees to fit into each of the above two categories. Some are readily and cheaply replaced when they leave, others hard to substitute with effective successors. Some are highly skilled knowledge workers, others relatively low-skilled employees whose replacements are trainable to a good standard within a week or two of starting. For these reasons there is a good case for treating each major staff group differently as far as employee retention is concerned. Efforts (and investment) should be focused on those whose resignations are the most problematic or costly, even if their raw turnover rate is not the highest in the organisation.

UK turnover trends: up or down?

The second commonly held view worth subjecting to critical analysis derives from a belief that employees are steadily becoming less loyal to their employers and vice versa. Once upon a time, it is argued, employers offered something known as 'lifetime employment' – an offer which employees happily took up. The unpredictability of today's business environment means that long-term relationships of this kind are no longer possible. The result is a more fickle type of association which both parties view, from the start, as being of a temporary nature. Whereas we used to view our employment relationships as something akin to marriages (entered into with a view to permanence), we now see them as being more like one-night stands (short-term and liable to be ended as soon as one of the parties has no more to gain). In some quarters this 'new' world of impermanent employment is welcomed. Our labour markets are now more flexible, it is said, making the economy more dynamic. Employers gain because they become more efficient and better able to compete in changing times, while employees have the opportunity to trade dull old 'employment' for the more exciting concept of 'employability'.

Management gurus who make a good living out of predicting the 'future of work' sometimes go a great deal further in anticipating with some excitement the imminent 'death of the job'. As the twenty-first century unfolds, they argue, the twin forces of globalisation and information technology will create a business environment in which we all become 'portfolio workers'. Instead of occupying jobs, we will undertake a series of short-term assignments for different employers on a self-employed or temporary basis as and when required. To survive we will all need to reinvent our working personas every few years, leading to a situation in which we will have several different careers during our working lives.

It is possible to make a number of assertions about employee turnover and retention from this kind of analysis:

□ Rising staff turnover rates are inevitable, given the nature of 'the changing world of work'.

□ Staff turnover rates are going to rise a great deal more as the 'new world of work' unfolds in the years ahead.

□ General staff turnover should not concern employers too much – it is the price that has to be paid in order to gain the flexibility needed to achieve competitive advantage.

□ Employers should focus their efforts on retaining the services of those top performers and key personnel who add considerable value and whose resignations constitute a loss of competitive advantage.

All this would make perfect sense if the assumptions on which the analysis was based were reliable. Unfortunately, the evidence does not stack up. Important trends are discernible, but they tend to be hugely overstated by commentators peddling a 'change now or die' message in books, in articles and in speeches from conference platforms.

First, let's look at the historical trends. Were we to be fast entering a new world of short-term working, we would expect to see this reflected in the staff turnover figures reported in the major annual surveys. We would also expect to see evidence of a decline in the average length of job tenure among UK workers. What we actually find is evidence of rather modest trends for which other explanations are readily available.

The truth is that for most people working in the UK there never has been anything approaching 'a job for life', and where one was on offer, the vast majority chose not to take the offer up. The most authoritative recent analysis of UK trends in staff turnover and job tenure is provided by Gregg and Wadsworth (1999). Their analysis of data from the General Household and Labour Force surveys shows clearly that the average length of job tenure has changed only modestly over the past quarter of a century. It stood at four years and nine months in 1975, and at four years and 10 months in 1998. In between these dates the figure rose during economic recessions and fell during the booms. Throughout the period, between 45 per cent and 54 per cent of employees had over five years' tenure in their jobs, while the proportion who had served for less than a year fluctuated between 18 per cent and 20 per cent. There was some decline in the number of people with more than 10 years' service in the one job during the

1980s and 1990s, but this was modest. Moreover, it appears to have begun to reverse again over the last few years. In 2000 32 per cent of employees fell into this category, as many as 12 per cent of us having stayed with our employers for more than 20 years (*Labour Market Trends*, 2001a, p92).

The same story is reflected in the staff turnover figures produced in annual surveys commissioned by the government, the CBI and the CIPD. Here too we see rates fluctuating according to economic conditions but little evidence of any long-term underlying trend towards greater turnover. The Skill Needs in Britain Survey (which has now stopped including turnover data in its reports) reported annual average staff turnover in 1990/1991 to be 16 per cent. This then slipped to 10 per cent in 1992 before climbing steadily over the next two years. Since 1995 the annual figure has been 20 per cent or 21 per cent in all but one of the years. A similar story is told in the figures derived each year from data submitted to the CIPD survey, although caution is required here because in its first years no overall national average turnover figure was calculated. As the UK came out of recession in the mid-1990s, turnover rates increased from around 14 per cent in 1994 up towards 19 per cent or 20 per cent in the late 1990s. The CIPD survey reported a substantial leap up to 26 per cent in 2000. This could be a statistical blip (the sample sizes being relatively small) or it could simply reflect the tightest labour market conditions in decades. Unemployment in 2000 fell below its 1975 level, creating a situation in which there were more job vacancies than there were people claiming unemployment benefit (IRS, 2001). Rather lower figures were reported by the 2001 CBI survey, suggesting a more modest increase from 17.3 per cent in 1999 to 17.9 per cent in 2000 (CBI, 2001, p31). Further evidence of a close link between staff turnover rates and economic conditions is provided by the regional breakdown included in the Skill Needs in Britain Survey series. This shows that turnover tends to be lowest in those parts of the country which suffer the highest rates of unemployment and highest where there are most job opportunities.

The evidence on turnover in the workforce as a whole thus suggests that very little has actually changed over the past

30 years. However, the overall figures for the UK mask the presence of two separate trends that operate in opposition to one another:

☐ a marked reduction in male average job tenure, especially among older men

☐ a counter-trend among women, whose average job tenure has risen.

The major trend, as is shown by Gregg and Wadsworth (1999, p116) is in the position of women with dependant children. Job tenure among women without children is not far short of that of men and has followed a similar trend pattern over the years, but the average length of time that women with children remain with each employer has increased quite dramatically. In 1975 their average tenure was only 20 months, since when it has more than doubled to 46 months. Over the same period, average male job tenure fell from 78 months (six years, six months) to 69 months (five years, nine months). So the figures reflect widely observed and important social trends. Career jobs are no longer the preserve of men, while the majority of women are taking up the rights extended to them in law to return to the same employment following a period of maternity leave.

We also see the increased propensity to take early retirement reflected in these figures, job tenure rates among men over the age of 50 falling by 14 per cent between 1985 and 1998.

What we do not see in the statistics is any evidence of a paradigm shift, or indeed any evidence at all to support the view that we are entering a 'new world of work' in which people move from job to job or career to career more readily than they have in the past. The picture portrayed is overwhelmingly one of continuity in respect of turnover rates and average job tenure. Moreover, far from falling dramatically, there are actually good grounds for expecting job tenure to increase in the future. Three strands come together to make up this case:

☐ We can expect to see a continuation of the trend towards higher average female job tenure as maternity rights are further extended after April 2003.

□ Because tenure is considerably higher among older people than younger colleagues, we can expect to see reduced turnover rates as the workforce ages in years to come.

□ We can reasonably surmise that economic conditions were close to a cyclical peak in 2001, and that average tenure will start to increase again as the economy weakens again in years to come.

Only time will tell whether or not these factors turn out to affect future turnover and tenure statistics in this way. Either way, we can conclude this section by rebutting the four common assertions listed a paragraph or two above. Rising staff turnover rates are not inevitable, and will not be in the future. If your turnover rates have risen faster than national trends, you should not be tempted into dismissing the matter as an inescapable product of the 'new world of work'. Except in certain industries which have seen wholesale restructuring, the advent of this 'new world' is greatly exaggerated. High turnover rates (or low job tenure rates) are thus likely to signify either growing dissatisfaction on the part of your employees or a failure to compete effectively in the labour market vis-à-vis your competitors. They should therefore be a matter of management concern.

Voluntary turnover: avoidable or unavoidable?

Our third debate concerns the extent to which an organisation's management *can* take action which serves to reduce staff turnover rates. It is common for the issue to be identified as a concern by those working in an HR function or by the line managers whose staff are hardest to retain, but for little action to be taken in practice. This often occurs because other managers see employee turnover as something of an occupational hazard about which little can actually be done. The attitude is particularly prevalent in the sectors which suffer from the highest rates of turnover (ie IT, retailing, sales, pubs, leisure, call centres and hotels). Here it is typical for poor retention rates simply to be accepted as forming part of the business environment in which the organisation operates.

Linked is the widely held belief that it is all a question of money. Turnover rates could be reduced, it is argued, but only by increasing pay rates to a higher level than is paid by competitors. Because this would result in reduced profit margins it is not considered worthy of discussion. The organisations concerned thus continue to 'live with' high turnover rather than focusing on what they might do to reduce it.

This book is based on the premise that such views are profoundly mistaken. Of course, some staff turnover is always going to occur, but a sizeable proportion of voluntary resignations are avoidable. In addition, in the case of a large number, pay is either an irrelevant factor or a secondary consideration in explaining voluntary resignations. Most people are not naturally inclined to move jobs all the time. Indeed, their preference is for stability. Those employed in roles which they find boring will move from time to time in search of change, while others will not wished to get 'trapped' in one job for too long for fear that this may hold back their career development. People who are genuinely underpaid will be inclined to move in search of a higher rate, but this situation is relatively uncommon. The same is true of resignations that originate in a desire to relocate to another part of the country. In fact, most voluntary resignations occur when the following two conditions are in place:

☐ The employee is unhappy in his/her work, with his/her organisation, with his/her manager(s) or with his/her colleagues.

☐ The employee is able to find alternative employment which he/she anticipates will give him/her a greater level of long-term job satisfaction.

It follows not only that managers by their actions can improve staff turnover rates but that management actions (or inactions) are frequently a major cause of voluntary departures.

There is a natural reluctance to recognise these truths because we all have a tendency to want to convince ourselves that we are not primarily responsible for an organisational failure. We are thus inclined to blame the business environment, or factors outside our control, or even the employees themselves. In the case of staff turnover our sense of blamelessness is often bolstered by the presence of the statistics we collect on 'reasons for leaving' in our organisations.

Few employees, when asked at an exit interview, state that they have been unhappy in their jobs, and even fewer admit to dissatisfaction with management. Most cite their pay as their reason for leaving or simply state that they are 'ready for a change'. Unfortunately, the research evidence suggests that reasons for leaving given by employees at the time of their departure are highly inaccurate in very many cases. As will be shown in Chapter 4, there is a strong tendency for staff to avoid giving full and honest answers about their true reasons for resigning. The result is a situation in which managers genuinely perceive staff turnover to be a phenomenon that is largely unavoidable and outside their control.

Various types of research evidence can be marshalled to back up the assertion that most turnover is avoidable. First, we can draw attention to the now sizeable volume of 'good practice' research which has been published in recent years on both sides of the Atlantic. This principally comprises large-scale questionnaire-based studies that seek statistically significant correlations between different types of management practice and defined business outcomes. The aim is to prove or disprove hypotheses about links between human resource activities and business success. The results of most studies suggest that organisations which have in place 'best practice' human resource policies are more likely to be successful against a range of commercial indicators than those that do not. What is more interesting for our purposes is the use, in many such studies, of employee turnover as a key variable in the analysis. We can now therefore point to robust research evidence which backs up the long-held view that good people management practice is associated with low rates of employee attrition. The most frequently quoted study is that of Huselid (1995) who found strong evidence to suggest that US organisations which had in place 'high-performance work practices' enjoyed turnover rates that were substantially below the average for his 1,000-strong sample. Other studies have reached broadly similar conclusions. Arthur (1994) in another American study found that 'the commitment model' of HR practice was associated with relatively low staff turnover, while Chadwick and Cappelli (1998) concluded that turnover rates averaged 5 per cent below the mean in organisations which had 'investment-oriented' HR systems. In UK-based studies Fernie and Metcalf (1996) found that employee involvement was associated with relatively low resignation rates, while Gallie *et al* (1998) found that effective performance management systems and well-communicated fringe benefits substantially reduced the extent to which employees stated that they intended to leave their jobs. Although each of these authors (and many others who have conducted similar studies) start out with a somewhat different idea of what exactly constitutes 'good practice' in HR, they are in broad agreement about the kind of approaches that merit this title. The key features are:

☐ a high degree of employee involvement
☐ investment in training and development
☐ the opportunity for employees to develop a career internally
☐ formal selection procedures
☐ teamworking/devolved decision-making
☐ performance-based reward systems.

Later in the book we will investigate which of these is more or less likely to have a major impact on employee retention, in what circumstances, and in what ways. At this stage the following points are all that need be made:

☐ Authoritative research shows that employee turnover levels vary substantially between employers across industries.
☐ Organisations with relatively low turnover are a great deal more likely to employ effective people management practices than those which do not.

A second type of research is case study-based. Here, examples are found of organisations that have managed to reduce their staff turnover rates substantially or hold them at a low level, their methods subsequently being assessed and written up. Management texts are full of examples of employee-retention success stories of this kind, many identifying as central factors particular management decisions. Some of the most convincing are described by Pfeffer (1998), Bramham (2001) and

Michaels *et al* (2001), all drawing on the experience of American organisations. Some good examples from the UK were described in a recent publication by Incomes Data Services (IDS, 2000a). The experience of five private sector employers was explored, all of which had reduced staff turnover levels, in some cases quite dramatically, during the late 1990s – a period when rates were rising across the economy as a whole. Each organisation used different approaches. In the case of Makita Manufacturing recruitment, selection and induction processes were improved, whereas Glaxo Wellcome focused on flexible working and childcare support. At Asda, by contrast, the main changes made were in the area of career development opportunities. At PriceWaterhouse Coopers it was work–life balance issues that needed most attention, while Plan-Net Services reduced turnover using a range of separate initiatives. What is similar in each of these five cases is the way that managers identified a problem, investigated its underlying causes and put in place new human resource management policies as a result. In all cases retention rates improved substantially and reasonably quickly.

Thirdly, I would like to draw attention to my own research on employee retention issues and to several studies carried out in recent years by my research students. Our focus has been on finding out, through interviews and questionnaire studies, why people left their former jobs. The total number of in-depth interviews we have carried out now numbers over 200. Much of this research is described in the case studies at the end of the book, so for now it is necessary only to make a few general conclusions about our findings:

☐ We have found numerous examples of organisations (in both the public and private sectors) in which staff turnover rates vary very substantially from one department or business unit to another. This is true of chains of supermarkets, of directorates within the same hospital, of call centres operating in different areas, and of private nursing homes owned by the same group and operating in the same city.

☐ Many more people leave a job because they are dissatisfied with it or with the employer than because they are positively attracted to other employment. Pay is a far less significant factor, according to our research, than many people believe. We found many examples of people taking a pay cut in order to move to another job, and precious few examples of people stating that money was any kind of a factor in their decision to switch jobs.

☐ We found that dissatisfaction with an organisation, and particularly with supervisors, is very often the root cause of decisions to quit. This is particularly true of the service sector (retailing, catering, nursing, professional services, etc) where the quality of supervision appears to be particularly poor. We have been given dozens of examples of unprofessional or incompetent practices – all manifestly avoidable – perpetrated by inexperienced, unqualified or plain bloody-minded supervisors.

☐ We found that many organisations were losing staff largely because they were making quite fundamental mistakes in terms of their human resource practices. The main examples were poor management of expectations when people first started, a failure to provide any kind of career development opportunity, a failure to address work–life balance issues, and a refusal to assist employees in managing the tension between their work and domestic responsibilities.

In nine cases out of every ten, even though the 'official' reason for leaving was sometimes different, the core problem was the approach taken in the organisation concerned to the management of its people. On many occasions it seemed as if managers were refusing, almost as a matter of principle, to consider the needs and ambitions of staff. The prevailing attitude in many UK workplaces appears to be summed up as:

> This is the way we do things around here. There is no room for flexibility. If you can't meet our requirements, you might as well leave.

This is by no means the position sanctioned by the organisations concerned, nor is it usually expressed in such stark terms – but it is the reality as perceived by many employees, who subsequently resign.

It is therefore fair to conclude this section by asserting strongly that managers can do a great deal to reduce staff turnover levels. The use of sophisticated people management practices will help a great deal, but often it is a question of getting the fundamentals right first. It is not by any means simply a question of pay. There is substantial evidence from different sources showing beyond question that major inroads can be made without increasing pay rates, or indeed without spending extensive amounts of money at all.

3 MEASURING, COSTING AND PREDICTING EMPLOYEE TURNOVER

In this chapter our focus is on the range of tools used by managers to gain an understanding of turnover in their organisations. Some are well-known and commonly used, others are rarer but interesting and worth considering. All are designed to help map the turnover and retention terrain and hence form the basis of subsequent interventions designed to reduce the number of voluntary departures.

I am convinced that managers do not generally appreciate the full extent to which their organisations are held back by unnecessary and preventable turnover. As a result, by many it is seen either as not being a major organisational problem or else simply as part and parcel of doing business. The idea that successful turnover reduction might lead to significant competitive advantage is not therefore a widespread point of view.

This chapter aims to supply the instruments that can be used to change such perceptions.

First, it describes the methods available for measuring labour turnover levels accurately and usefully. Second, it sets out how the cost absorbed by the employer each time an individual employee leaves can be worked out. Taken together, these types of analysis will help the reader to calculate credible and reasonably accurate figures for the cost of employee turnover for his or her organisation as a whole in past years. The final section focuses on predicting tomorrow's turnover rates and patterns. Such activities should help to identify likely future costs and build a case for expenditure on programmes aimed at improving retention rates.

Measuring turnover

Finding a satisfactory way of measuring staff turnover in your organisation is important because it allows you to:

□ compare turnover rates between different departments, business units or occupational groups

□ benchmark turnover rates against those of your competitors or norms for your industry

□ track over time the success or failure of interventions aimed at reducing turnover

□ draw on past data in order to predict likely future turnover rates

□ estimate the cost of turnover to the organisation over a specific period of time.

Approaches used to measure turnover differ somewhat, there being no single perfect instrument. The most straightforward method involves calculating 'crude turnover rates' (also known as wastage rates). The basic formula is simple:

$$\frac{\text{Total number of leavers in the year to date}}{\text{Total number of employees at date}} \times 100$$

A crude turnover rate of 30 per cent thus indicates that 30 out of every 100 people employed left during the course of the past year. It provides a good rough 'rule of thumb' guide but can be criticised for being too blunt an instrument to facilitate effective management action. This is because it fails to reveal the detail of the comings and goings in an organisation (or part of an organisation), characterising all turnover as being of equal significance. For example, it acknowledges no distinction between the loss of someone after two days' service and of someone who has left after five years. It also fails to distinguish between the functional and dysfunctional, avoidable and unavoidable, or voluntary and involuntary varieties of turnover. It is particularly misleading for organisations who employ people on a seasonal basis or whose headcount tends to fluctuate markedly at different times in response to commercial opportunities. For such organisations the crude rate is heavily influenced by the time of year at which the measurement is taken. An organisation that employs large numbers in the summer months but then reduces its head-count in the winter will be shown to have a far higher turnover rate if the year-end date is 31 December than if the date chosen is 1 July when the number of employees is high. For this reason it makes sense to use a modified formula which includes an average annual figure for total headcount:

$$\frac{\text{Total number of leavers in the past year}}{\text{Average total number employed in the past year}} \times 100$$

Adjusting the formula in this way cannot capture the distinction between early turnover and turnover of relatively long-serving employees. This can be important when thinking about what prescriptions are most appropriate to help reduce turnover. It also makes meaningful comparisons between different units difficult. For example, two regional divisions of a bank might both report crude turnover rates of 20 per cent, yet be experiencing very different kinds of turnover. In one the vast majority of the turnover could be accounted for by people leaving after a few weeks of employment, the majority of employees having much longer service. By contrast, in the other, the 20 per cent could represent the loss of a fifth of the most experienced staff. While it is possible to argue about whether or not the second situation is more damaging than the first, it must be conceded that the two regions are experiencing different patterns of turnover with different effects and requiring different types of management action.

The most common approach used to deal with this defect in the crude turnover rate is to calculate a stability rate. Some organisations use this instead of the crude turnover rate, but most see it as an additional tool of analysis. The commonly used formula is:

$$\frac{\text{Number of staff with service of a year or more}}{\text{Total number of staff employed a year ago}} \times 100$$

Effectively, this gives you the proportion of staff in the unit concerned who have more than a year's service. The result is an index which removes early leavers from the equation. It is thus possible to have a high crude turnover rate (eg 60 per cent) while also having a high stability rate (eg 90 per cent). Nine out of every ten employees in such a situation have been employed for over a year, but there is also very substantial turnover of staff in the first months of their employment. The same situation would be true of an organisation that employed a substantial number of employees on fixed-term contracts of less than a year. The stability index does not allow their departures to 'contaminate' the overall picture of a stable workforce.

It is possible, of course, to carry out analyses of the stability index using any number of years as the basis (ie the proportion of staff with two years' service, five years', ten years', etc). This type of calculation can then form the basis of cohort analysis – a third commonly used approach. This is a more complex method of measuring turnover, but one which gives a richer picture and which can be used as a predictive tool. It can be applied to the whole workforce or to a particular grouping. Either way, the aim is to assess what happened in turnover terms to a defined group of employees who started working at around the same time. It could be all new recruits in a particular year, a group of graduate trainees commencing at the same time, or the employees who were recruited when a new unit first opened. The cohort analysis reveals what proportion was still employed after one year, two years, three years, four years, and so on. The analysis is readily illustrated graphically with the production of a 'survival curve'.

Another feature of cohort analysis is the calculation of a 'half-life' figure. This is the number of months it takes for half the members of a defined cohort (ie people who started at the same time) to leave. Because it is a single figure (eg 10 months, 30 months, 60 months) it allows ready comparisons to be made between different groups and over time. In this way an organisation which takes action to reduce turnover among graduate recruits can usefully judge its effectiveness by calculating the half-life for successive cohorts. A rising figure shows that turnover rates are declining.

A more complex approach to stability analysis – but one that has a good deal to offer – is defined by IDS (1995, p3). This could be labelled a 'grading' approach because it effectively awards a mark out of 100 to an organisation or part of an organisation on its performance as far as employee turnover is concerned. Central to it is the notion that turnover among long-standing staff is more damaging than that among new entrants, presumably on the grounds that experience is being lost. The method skews the calculation accordingly. The formula is:

$$\frac{\text{Total length of service of all employees at date}}{\text{Total length of service had no turnover occurred in the year to date}} \times 100$$

Its effect is best understood by means of a simple example. Assume that there is a company which employed nine people one year ago. At that time the newest member of staff had one year's service, the longest-serving had nine years', while each of the others started working for the company in successive years. The total number of years' service a year ago was thus 45. If nobody was to leave during the subsequent year, the total number of years' service at the date under consideration (the 'date' in the equation) would be 54 years. This is illustrated in Table 1. However, what in fact happened was that three people left at the start of the year (those with five, six and seven years' service respectively), each being replaced by a new employee. This means that the total length of service at the 'date' was actually 36 years. This is illustrated in Table 2. This gives us a figure for the index of 67 per cent (ie 36 divided by 54 and multiplied by 100). Had no one left at all, the score would have been a perfect 100 per cent. Had the three most junior employees left instead of those who did, the total number of years' service at the 'date' would have been 48, giving an index score of 89 per cent.

Table 1

Employees	Length of service a year ago	Length of service now (the 'date') if there has been no turnover
Alison	1 year	2 years
Ben	2 years	3 years
Carol	3 years	4 years
Deborah	4 years	5 years
Emma	5 years	6 years
Fiona	6 years	7 years
Gill	7 years	8 years
Hamish	8 years	9 years
Irene	9 years	10 years
TOTAL	45 years	54 years

Table 2

Employees	Length of service a year ago	Actual length of service now (the 'date') following turnover
Alison	1 year	2 years
Ben	2 years	3 years
Carol	3 years	4 years
Deborah	4 years	5 years
Emma	5 years	–
Fiona	6 years	–
Gill	7 years	–
Hamish	8 years	9 years
Irene	9 years	10 years
John	–	1 year
Kieron	–	1 year
Laurie	–	1 year
TOTAL	45 years	36 years

There are clearly disadvantages as well as advantages to this approach. First, there is its complexity – although getting access to the required information is not difficult where a good personnel information system is in operation. Second, it can be criticised for over-egging the significance of turnover among long-standing staff vis-à-vis those who are less experienced. The differential between them in practice is often a good deal less than is supposed in the method of calculation. For this reason it is particularly important to remove retirees from the analysis. A couple of retirements of long-standing staff, even though wholly unavoidable, can badly affect a department's figure if this is not done.

Despite the possibility of using all these other approaches in addition, it remains the case that the crude turnover rate (or one of its closest relatives) continues to be the central index of turnover in organisations. This is partly because it is so readily understood and partly because it facilitates necessary costing exercises such as those described below. It is also the standard unit of measurement used in most of the published turnover surveys, so it has to be calculated to allow meaningful benchmarking with other organisations.

The best approach is to measure turnover in more than one way. The crude turnover (wastage) rate has to be calculated for the reasons given above, but the other calculations outlined in preceding paragraphs can add useful additional information and provide the basis for more sophisticated comparisons between internal units. On the same grounds there is also a good case for calculating wastage indices which omit some types of departure and are thus no longer properly characterised as 'crude'. The following are those that are most commonly excluded from the analysis:

☐ temporary contracts coming to an end
☐ redundancies
☐ dismissals
☐ retirements
☐ ill-health-related resignations
☐ deaths in service
☐ other resignations regarded as unavoidable.

This last category is often mainly made up of people who resign in order to relocate to another area, usually in order to follow (or join) a spouse or partner. In fact, our research indicates that such resignations are often anything but 'unavoidable'. What often happens is that the partners make a joint decision about who is to relocate. In making such decisions, those who are less happy in their jobs or perceive themselves to have the poorer career prospects are usually the ones who end up moving. By recording these decisions as unavoidable organisations are often reducing their avoidable turnover rates unjustifiably.

Griffeth and Hom (2001) suggest that there is merit in removing from the analysis all turnover which is functional as well as that which is clearly unavoidable. The term 'functional' is used to describe resignations that are welcomed by the organisation because they result in the replacement of a relatively poor performer by one who is stronger. The upshot is a final figure a good deal lower than the crude turnover percentage, which measures only that turnover which is both damaging from a corporate perspective *and* which it is in the organisation's power to avert. Ultimately, it can be argued, this is the only figure that really matters – the true measure of how effectively an employer is managing to compete in key labour markets.

There is merit in this point of view, but it must be remembered that all turnover, functional or dysfunctional, avoidable or unavoidable, voluntary or involuntary, carries a price-tag. It is in the interests of organisations to reduce all forms wherever possible as a means of avoiding the costs, as well as the more general disruption which occurs to workplace relationships and staff morale when too many posts are being emptied and refilled again at short intervals. Moreover, many instances of functional turnover – as well as many dismissals – are in truth examples of management failure. Avoidable departures occur when the wrong people are selected for the wrong reasons or where supervisors fail to inspire effective levels of individual performance. Early retirements can certainly be seen in this way, as can situations in which someone leaves on the grounds of ill health when he or she could, if he or she really wanted to, continue to work. If turnover levels are to be used as an index of organisational effectiveness on the people-management front, then all types with one or two clear exceptions should be included in the figures. These probably only include normal-age retirements, genuine redundancies, very serious ill-health-related resignations and deaths in service.

LEVELS OF TURNOVER MEASUREMENT

In their article entitled 'Unweaving leaving', Morrell *et al* (2001, p223) distinguish between three distinct 'levels' of turnover measurement. Level 1 involves developing a basic awareness of the problem. A general turnover rate for the organisation is calculated and benchmarked in a broad-brush way against national figures or industry norms. At this level managers can be said to be doing little more than monitoring turnover in their organisations.

Level 2 involves planning, predicting and controlling turnover. Rates are calculated for different departments or units within the organisation, and targets set for reducing them. There is a move away from a reliance on crude turnover (wastage) rates as measures are developed to take account of voluntary and involuntary leaving in working out the figures. Figures are compared with those of direct competitors, especially those competing in the same local labour markets.

> At Level 3, turnover can be said to be truly managed. Measurement is much more sophisticated. Account is taken of functional and dysfunctional turnover as well as that which is avoidable and unavoidable. Moreover, an 'ongoing dialogue' is established with staff and with leavers to develop the most effective retention measures.

Costing turnover

People have different ideas about the cost that an organisation bears each time an employee leaves. Even when asked to estimate the costs associated with the loss of the same types of staff, managerial estimates can vary hugely. An example is a recent survey of retention issues in the NHS which asked respondents at different hospital trusts to estimate the costs associated with filling 'a typical vacancy'. Respondents suggested figures ranging from £150 up to £9,500 (Health Service Report, 2001, p6). The average figure was £2,300 which is similar to the £2,500 quoted by an Audit Commission study of turnover costs for local government employees (IRS, 1996, p4). Yet these figures fall way below estimates of the total turnover cost calculated by academic researchers and consultants who have looked at the issue in greater detail. Most put the lowest figure at around 50 per cent of the annual salary for the job in question, upper figures climbing as high as 200 per cent or even 250 per cent (Cascio, 2000, pp23–24; *The Economist*, 2000).

Much depends, of course, on the type of job that a person is leaving. Where it is easy to find a replacement quickly and inexpensively, and where it takes a matter of days to train them up fully, costs are going to be low. At the other end of the scale there is the loss of highly-skilled employees who go to work for competitors, taking their expertise and organisational knowledge with them. When such people's skills are in short supply or where they have been developed over some years at the organisation's expense, the costs can easily run into hundreds of thousands of pounds. The other key variable is the method used to calculate the cost associated with the resignation. Several different approaches can be used here. One is simply to tot up the most obvious direct costs (eg recruiting and training a replacement); another is to try to estimate the total real cost in terms of staff time spent administering the resignation and covering while there is a vacancy. The most sophisticated approaches seek to quantify matters such as lost productivity and unrealised opportunities that result from resignations.

In the case of public sector turnover, a distinction has to be made between situations where staff move from unit to unit within the same service (eg hospital to hospital, school to school, police force to police force) and those where people leave altogether to take up other work or to withdraw from paid employment. In the former case there is a cost to a particular unit, but skills and experience are retained for the taxpayer. In the latter these are lost to the service, which means that the total cost of resignation is considerably higher. As long ago as 1989 it was calculated that the total cost of losing a qualified nurse to the private sector or to another line of work was £30,000 for the NHS (IDS, 1989, p8).

The truth is that it is very difficult to estimate the overall total cost of turnover within an organisation. Many of the elements are not easily quantified, and in any case organisations may not record data which enables the ready quantification of the more basic, direct types of cost. Further complexity is added when trying to distinguish between functional and dysfunctional turnover or trying to add in cost savings associated with staff turnover as well as financial losses. Examples are redundancy payments that no longer have to be made, salaries saved during a 'quiet period', and fewer contributions needed for the company's final salary pension scheme. In short, no absolutely accurate figure will ever be reached. But this does not mean that there is no point in making reasoned estimates. Staff turnover in most organisations does have an expensive price-tag attached, such that there are substantial savings to be achieved from its reduction. Measuring these allows progress to be tracked in financial terms but also greatly enhances the chances that funds will be made available by finance directors to help tackle the issue. Your chances of success are a good deal higher if you can say 'We calculate that avoidable resignations cost the company £3.8 million last year' than if you make some vague claim about the benefits that could accrue if turnover levels were lowered.

Several approaches can be taken to the costing of turnover. The most straightforward involves focusing solely on the basic, direct costs that result when an individual leaves the organisation either voluntarily or involuntarily. This approach has the virtue of accuracy as far as it goes, but is likely to underestimate the actual total cost by a considerable margin. The results are believable and easily justified to a sceptical audience – but do not usually reflect the reality. The proportion of the total cost reflected in basic, direct costs is a matter of opinion, but several American studies have estimated 'hidden' or 'indirect' costs to account for as much as 85 per cent of the total (Douglas Phillips, 1990). There is thus a good case for trying to make a reasonable estimate of indirect costs, accepting that here accuracy is a good deal harder to achieve. Beyond this, it is possible to opt for an 'all-singing-all-dancing' approach which takes into account all matters that impact on the cost of turnover including cost savings. The aim is to achieve accuracy in estimating *both* the hard direct *and* the soft indirect costs. Calculations of this kind are complex and involve detailed research. By their nature they require in-depth analysis of factors that relate to particular jobs, making them impractical to carry out for all types of role in larger organisations. However, there is a case for carrying out focused analysis of this kind in the case of groups of employees who are highly valued, costly to replace and prone to leave a good deal more often than is good for the organisation. Where you want to target retention drives at such people and need funds to bring about a marked reduction in turnover, it makes sense to make use of the most sophisticated form of cost analysis as a means of convincing doubters that substantial investment is worth making.

Identifying the costs

Over the years analysts have developed a range of different checklists setting out the different types of cost that organisations sustain when staff leave. Some lists are more

ESTIMATES OF TURNOVER COST

Each year since 1995 the CIPD has carried out an extensive survey on labour turnover in the UK. In 2001 the number of respondents was 629 from across the various industrial sectors. They were asked to estimate the cost of labour turnover in their organisations during 2000 for each of a range of job types. Some guidance was given in the survey notes about how to calculate turnover costs, but the figures reported must be treated as broad estimates rather than accurate calculations.

The average cost of turnover per employee across the whole survey in 2001 was £3,933. This figure tells us little in itself, but it is interesting to note that it is 28 per cent higher than the figure quoted in the 2000 survey. Evidence of substantially rising turnover costs (or at least the perception that the costs were increasing) was thus found. The range of estimates given for different kinds of job ranged from £895 in the case of 'routine unskilled manual occupations' up to £6,086 for managers. Other leavers who are seen as being costly to replace are professional staff (£5,206) and sales people (£4,591).

It is worth noting that these figures are somewhat lower than those quoted by other organisations who have participated in recent UK-based surveys. IDS (2000a), for example, reported estimates made by a number of companies. In this survey, Glaxo Wellcome stated that turnover costs in their research and development division were equivalent 'at least' to one year's salary, while PriceWaterhouse Coopers calculated that the cost shouldered by them every time a management consultant leaves is over 150 per cent of the salary. A year or two earlier IRS (1998) also reported the results of costing exercises in other UK firms. One2One estimated the cost to be equal to 100 per cent of the departing employee's salary for 'key posts', and 30 per cent to 50 per cent for others. An NHS study derived figures for nurses, estimating £4,900 per head.

comprehensive than others, and different terminology is used, but all focus broadly on the same areas. Reading this work serves to concentrate the mind by revealing the magnitude of potential savings when turnover levels are reduced in larger organisations – even by a just few percentage points. The following 'super-checklist' has been compiled with reference to the work of Douglas Phillips (1990), Fair (1992), Hom and Griffeth (1995), Cascio (2000), Joinson (2000), IDS (2000a), Bramham (2001), Pinkovitz *et al* (2001) and successive IPD/CIPD Labour Turnover surveys, while also taking account of my own management experience.

Potential direct costs

- ☐ redundancy pay
- ☐ pay in lieu of holidays not taken
- ☐ advertising the vacancy
- ☐ recruitment agency fees
- ☐ recruitment literature (paper-based or web-based)
- ☐ overtime payments while there is a vacancy
- ☐ temporary cover while there is a vacancy
- ☐ interview expenses for candidates
- ☐ cost of psychometric tests
- ☐ assessment centre costs
- ☐ relocation allowances
- ☐ induction programme
- ☐ initial training programme
- ☐ literature provided for new starters
- ☐ sign-on bonuses/employee referral bonuses
- ☐ uniforms for new starters
- ☐ litigation costs when tribunal applications are made
- ☐ security badges/car-parking permits/keys issued, etc.

Potential administrative costs and management time

- ☐ administration of the resignation (filing, personnel information system, etc)
- ☐ payroll activity associated with the resignation/dismissal
- ☐ pension fund transfers
- ☐ conducting exit interviews (manager and departing employee)
- ☐ writing references
- ☐ meetings to discuss vacancy/job description and person specification

- liaising with external agencies (eg job centres, head-hunters, advertisers)
- direct recruitment costs (eg employer presentation at a job fair)
- sending out documentation to potential candidates
- shortlisting
- arranging interviews
- chasing up references
- management preparation for selection interviews/assessment centres
- time spent interviewing and assessing potential replacements
- pre-employment medical examinations
- issuing contracts
- personnel administration associated with new starters
- payroll administration
- pension fund administration
- orientation of new starter
- company car arrangements
- informal training of new starter by experienced staff.

Potential efficiency-related costs

- inefficiency prior to termination (ie absence, slackness, failure to meet deadlines, etc)
- inefficiency while there is a vacancy (ie temporary cover less effective)
- inefficiency of new starter vis-à-vis experienced employees
- inefficiency of colleagues affected by the resignation/with responsibility for the new starter.

Potential lost opportunities

- business lost due to lower standards of service from new starters
- impaired standards due to low morale of staff left to cover
- knowledge, skills and experience developed now made available to a competitor

□ investment in ex-employee (training, experience, etc) wasted

□ restrictions on/delays to growth due to shortages of skills, knowledge and experience.

There are some 50 different potential sources of cost listed here. Not all, of course, will apply in every case. Moreover, most larger organisations will find important economies of scale by advertising several posts together at the same time and subsequently providing 'joint' induction sessions for all people starting in a particular week or month. It is, none-theless, sobering to read through the list and to reflect on how much actual and potential income can be saved by creating a workplace which people want to stay in rather than leave.

Rudimentary approaches to turnover costing

There is a real danger, thinking about how to put a figure on some of the items listed above, that the analysis of turnover costs could itself be seen as an inefficient activity. Better use, it could be said, can be made of management time than developing very sophisticated models to estimate the true cost of turnover. There is truth in this observation. Some of the attempts described in the academic literature are hugely involved and would be difficult to justify in many organisations. This is especially true of those undergoing sustained periods of change which mean that organisational activity and job content is continually being altered. In such circumstances calculating the cost of turnover among a particular group of staff can be meaningless 12 months later when skills shortages are faced elsewhere in the organisation.

So there are many circumstances in which the only need is to get a broad handle on turnover costs by making rough but credible estimates.

The most straightforward approach is to focus solely on the costs that can readily be measured. For the most part these would be those items listed above under the first two headings that are applicable to your own organisational context. It is not necessary to measure staff and management time down to the last minute. Instead, rough estimates should be made as to the number of hours spent in total on recruitment, selection and induction activity, as well as on administration linked to the resignation. The direct costs are by their nature straightforward to compute. For an experienced personnel manager with responsibility for the key activities, estimates of this kind need only take a few minutes to carry out.

It is wise to focus on the major staff groups that are employed, and particularly on those which suffer the highest level of turnover. However, some companies try to work out an estimate for the whole organisation (ie all types of staff) by calculating an estimate of turnover costs for 'the typical post'. This is then multiplied by the annual overall turnover for the organisation to reach a final 'total turnover cost' figure. The following example (Table 3) illustrates how the costs mount up, even in the case of quite junior low-paid jobs. The organisation here is a chain of clothing stores employing 240 retail assistants at several UK locations. The aim of the exercise is to estimate the total cost of turnover among that particular staff group in a typical year. There is an annual turnover rate of 28 per cent.

Table 3

Estimate of basic turnover cost for a retail assistant		
Staff time administering the resignation	2 hours	£13
Management time on exit interview	1 hour	£9
Other resignation-related management activities	2 hours	£18
Holiday not taken by the resignee	7 days	£308
Management time writing and placing ad	1 hour	£9
Recruitment ad in local paper		£720
Postage and application forms sent to candidates		£22
Management time shortlisting	1 hour	£9
Staff time administering interviews	3 hours	£20
Management time interviewing (two managers)	10 hours	£90
Interview expenses		£50
Staff time administering new starter	2 hours	£13
Management time on new starter	1 hour	£9
Induction day for new starter	6 hours	£33
Management time on induction/orientation activities	4 hours	£36
Staff time for on-the-job training	12 hours	£66
TOTAL COST PER INDIVIDUAL TURNOVER EPISODE		£1,425
TOTAL NUMBER OF TURNOVER EPISODES IN A YEAR	67	
TOTAL TURNOVER COST FOR THE YEAR		£95,760

An alternative approach simply involves estimating the total costs incurred by the organisation (or part of it) on resignation, recruitment, selection and induction activities over the course of a year. This is readily done by working out, broadly, the percentage of each player's time that is spent on these activities in a typical week before adding in recruitment costs (ie advertising, agencies, etc). The next step is to estimate the percentage of recruitment activity that results from expansion and not from turnover. The final figure is reached by deducting from the total that element. It is then very straightforward to work out the cost incurred each time a 'typical' employee leaves.

This process is illustrated in the following simple example (Table 4). Here we have a hotel employing 150 people. There is one personnel manager employed (total annual employment cost £18,000) and a part-time personnel assistant who deals with payroll matters (cost £8,000). Line management salaries (plus on-costs) average £15,000, while the average staff salary cost is £10,000. The hotel has an annual turnover rate of 35 per cent. It has not expanded or contracted at all in the past year, so every recruitment episode has resulted from a resignation or dismissal. No redundancy payments were made, no overtime payments were made, and no temporary cover was hired while there were vacancies.

These approaches have the virtue of being simple to carry out, but the results can only amount to rough estimates. Moreover, of course, they underestimate the total true cost of turnover considerably because they do not take account of the 'soft' costs incurred such as loss of productivity or lost customers due to poorer service levels than could have been

Table 4

Percentage of time spent on resignation, recruitment, selection and induction activities		Cost
Personnel manager	30	£5,400
Personnel assistant	40	£3,200
Line managers (7 of them)	5	£5,250
Staff (150 of them)	2	£30,000
Annual recruitment advertising bill		£15,750
TOTAL ANNUAL TURNOVER COST		£59,600

achieved with a more stable staff. There are two alternative approaches to take in acknowledgement of these deficiencies. First, it is possible to present the figures to managers on a 'not less than' basis. This is what the Audit Commission does when it carries out assessments of turnover costs in public sector organisations. In other words, you state that the figure represents a minimum estimate of the likely total cost incurred in the year. Alternatively, you can accept the judgement of researchers who have sought to quantify the percentage of total turnover costs that are 'soft' costs and gross up the figure accordingly. As stated above, estimates vary, but most suggest that for average non-managerial jobs soft costs account for half to two-thirds of total costs. The figure is rather higher for management and professional occupations in which efficiency losses deriving from resignations are higher.

In recent years a number of consulting firms have set up free web-based turnover costing tools which anyone with Internet access can use. Some do no more than add up a total figure using headings such as those in the above examples. However, others are more sophisticated, building in assumptions about soft costs to give a more accurate estimate of total costs. There are numerous tools of this kind on the Web now, most originating in the USA. Several dozen can be discovered simply by typing 'employee turnover cost' into a search engine.

Sophisticated approaches to turnover costing

The sophisticated approaches to turnover costing include the types of analysis in the rudimentary approaches but they examine each item in greater detail. Broad assumptions are avoided so that at each stage a figure is reached that is as accurate as possible. In addition, an attempt is made to put a figure on the 'hidden' or 'soft' costs. Some of the methods that have been evolved are quite intricate, but are necessary if any kind of accurate estimate is to be made.

An important component of hidden turnover costs is reduced efficiency or productivity. The most significant chunk relates to the performance of new starters as they learn their new jobs, but it is also important not to forget impaired productivity on the part of co-workers and supervisors who have to devote time to the initial development of the new employee. Then there is lower productivity on the part of the leaver in the weeks leading up to his or her departure. When someone is working the notice period out, productivity can dip very substantially as he or she slows down, completes existing projects and is not involved in new ones. In the few jobs where individual performance is measured easily and objectively, costs of this kind are easy to calculate. Examples would be roles in which efficiency is gauged according to the number of tasks completed successfully, such as piece-work in manufacturing and agricultural environments, some types of call centre work, and sales-based jobs. For most, however, efficiency measurements have to be a matter of personal judgement.

In his influential article, Douglas Phillips (1990) sets out, with worked examples, methods that can be used to quantify reduced productivity in such jobs. His suggested method draws on two detailed research projects. It is not by any means perfect, but it does provide a method of making a convincing calculation of these types of costs. He suggests that 'incoming employee inefficiency' is best estimated by asking employees in particular job groups (or their supervisors) to estimate the number of weeks or months it took when they started in the role before they were able to work at full efficiency. The method recommended involves estimating productivity during the learning-curve period.

The approach is best understood by means of two simple examples. First, let us assume that a new junior manager arrives to start a job with relevant technical experience but no prior knowledge of how the organisation operates politically, culturally or structurally. A year and a half later she is asked to estimate how many months were required before she was working at 25 per cent efficiency, 50 per cent efficiency, 75 per cent efficiency and 100 per cent efficiency respectively. Thinking back, she says that it took a year to reach 100 per cent efficiency in the job. She estimates that she was 25 per cent proficient after two months, 50 per cent proficient after six months and 75 per cent proficient after nine months. These figures allow the following analysis to be undertaken (Table 5):

Table 5

Efficiency level	Average efficiency		Months required		Months of full productivity
0 to 25 per cent	0.125	×	2	=	0.25
25 per cent to 50 per cent	0.375	×	4	=	1.5
50 per cent to 75 per cent	0.625	×	3	=	1.875
75 per cent to 100 per cent	0.875	×	3	=	2.625
TOTALS			12		6.25

For the first two months our manager was working, on average, at 12.5 per cent efficiency. This translates into 0.25 months of full productivity. She then works for four months at an average efficiency of 37.5 per cent (equivalent to 1.5 months), and so on, until she reaches full efficiency at 12 months.

We thus estimate that during the first year she was fully productive for a period equivalent to 6.25 months. The remainder of the time (5.75 months) represents 'lost' productivity or the difference between the efficiency level of an experienced long-term employee and that of a new starter moving up the learning curve. It is then straightforward to convert this figure into a percentage and to work out a total 'cost of lost efficiency' that can be accounted for because the post is held by a new starter. In this case, with an annual employment cost of £20,000, the cost recorded would be £9,600 (48 per cent of £20,000). For jobs with a faster learning curve it is best to set the unit of calculation at weeks or days rather than months.

The same approach can be used to calculate a cost associated with the declining productivity of a departing employee. Here, though, the estimates have to be made by supervisors and work colleagues. The following example (Table 6 overleaf) focuses on the declining productivity of a clerical worker who costs his employers £1,000 to employ each month.

In this case our worker's efficiency took eight weeks to decline from 100 per cent to zero. During this time we estimate that he was averaging 87.5 per cent efficiency for three weeks, 62.5 per cent efficiency for two weeks, 37.5 per cent efficiency for two weeks and 12.5 per cent efficiency for one week. Over the eight weeks we thus calculate that he was

Table 6

Efficiency level	Average efficiency		Weeks required		Weeks of full productivity
100 per cent to 75 per cent	0.875	×	3	=	2.65
75 per cent to 50 per cent	0.625	×	2	=	1.25
50 per cent to 25 per cent	0.375	×	2	=	0.75
25 per cent to 0	0.125	×	1	=	0.125
TOTALS			8		4.775

fully efficient for a period equivalent to 4.775 weeks or around 60 per cent of the time. The lost efficiency due to his impending departure is thus 40 per cent of £2,000 (the cost of employing him during the eight weeks). That is £800-worth of work that is 'lost' because of an impending resignation.

Clearly, these figures can only be broad estimates, but the method represents a credible and reasonably straightforward way of assessing losses sustained due to reduced operational effectiveness when people leave and are replaced with relatively inexperienced successors.

The same approach could be used to calculate losses sustained by impaired productivity on the part of co-workers and supervisors when new starters are climbing the learning curve. However, it is a great deal easier to ask them simply to estimate the number of hours or days they spend attending to the new starter's needs rather than engaging fully with their own work. This can then be translated into a percentage of their time and a cost figure worked out according to their respective hourly rates.

When carrying out this kind of project the most effective method involves focusing in detail on actual 'turnover episodes' experienced in your organisation. You will probably want to carry out at least three or four separate analyses for each major job group. Resulting costs can then be averaged to give a credible 'typical' figure for lost efficiency each time someone leaves that type of job.

It is a great deal harder to estimate costs associated with lost business opportunities when people leave – the fourth category in the list set out above. There are no standard approaches available here, because these factors affect each organisation very differently. For many jobs the effect in these terms is negligible when one person leaves. No customers are lost and no business opportunities are passed up. However, the impact can be significant when a particularly effective performer leaves. Examples would include a solicitor whose personal reputation attracts clients to a law firm, a well-known and respected head teacher, or a particularly success-ful sales executive. In each case the departure of the individual can be seen, in practice, to have a measurable negative impact on the organisation. Where this is the case it would be negli-gent not to include some kind of damage estimation in any calculation of turnover costs. The only way it can be done is to examine, in detail, what happened when such an individual left. Reasoned costings are then applied and totalled up.

The final feature of sophisticated approaches is the inclu-sion of the pluses as well as the minuses. There is thus a rec-ognition that some turnover in some circumstances can lead to cost savings. Examples are:

□ where new starters enter employment at the bottom of an incremental scale, replacing leavers who had reached the top (this is a very common situation in the public sector)

□ where the opportunity is taken, when there is a vacancy, not to recruit for a few weeks (ie by freezing the post)

□ where employer pension fund contributions are lower for a new recruit than for the leaver (eg where entry to a final salary scheme is barred for new starters)

□ where a particularly unproductive employee is replaced by a highly productive new starter.

Predicting turnover

Predicting turnover is basically about estimating the prob-ability that existing employees will stay or leave during a defined future time period. Looking forward a year is common, but in larger, more stable organisations which carry out relatively sophisticated human resource planning exer-cises the time-scale can be 10 years or more. Predicting future levels of turnover is a useful activity for several reasons:

□ It allows future costs to be estimated, thus providing a robust basis for bids for funds to reduce turnover rates.

☐ It provides a rationale for the setting of future training and recruitment budgets.

☐ It allows realistic targets to be set, unit by unit, for turnover reduction.

☐ It helps managers to flag up, ahead of time, possible future skills shortages or tightening labour market conditions which require an organisational response.

At root there are two types of approach that can be used. The first is essentially quantitative and involves using data collected in the past to make forward projections about the numbers and types of staff likely to leave. The second relies on managerial judgement to establish what is likely to happen in the future. This can involve taking account of changing labour market conditions (for example, if a recession is expected, turnover is likely to go down) or can involve thinking at a micro-level about the probable intentions of individual members of staff. These are not mutually exclusive. The most accurate forecasts draw both on quantitative analyses and management judgement, the latter being used to adjust the former in the light of knowledge and experience.

The quantitative approaches are those that have long been used by human resource planners. The most basic method is a simple projection of existing trends in crude turnover rates, making modifications to take account of wider labour market trends. An example is shown in Figure 1 using maintenance engineers employed in a manufacturing company by way of illustration. Here, the bold line represents past turnover levels and the lower dotted line (Projection 1) represents an estimate based on a continuation of past trends. The upper dotted line (Projection 2) is a modified estimate taking into account the age of the existing workforce and a perceived increase in the number of alternative job opportunities that will become available locally over the next two or three years.

A more sophisticated approach involves analysing *patterns* of existing turnover as well as the rate. Most organisations can identify a number of variables that influence the propensity of employees to resign from their jobs. Age is a common example, younger employees being more likely to leave than older colleagues, up until the age at which retirement

Figure 1

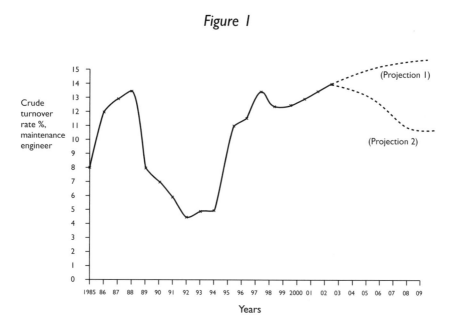

becomes possible. Gender can be a factor too. Historically, job tenure has been lower among women than men, although the gap has narrowed somewhat in recent years. Another key variable is length of service itself. Many organisations can identify patterns of turnover here, in that there is likely to be a higher propensity for employees to quit after certain periods of time. Typically there are three points at which turnover levels are high:

□ in the first three months of employment (ie the induction crisis period)

□ at around two years' service (ie when the employee has remained in an unloved job for a period respectable enough not to worry a subsequent employer)

□ after five years (ie when the employee fears that remaining any longer in the one employment might hold back his or her future career development).

If historically one or more of these 'high points' has been observed, it makes sense to use that information when making projections about likely turnover levels in the following year. Turnover may be expected to rise, for example, where a large proportion of a particular employee group is coming up to five years' service. It can be expected to fall if the five-year mark, for a majority, was passed last year. The same is true of age profiles. If high turnover in past years was explained, in large part, by retirements, lower future turnover may be expected, depending on the age of those who replaced the retirees.

Bramham (1988) recommends the use of a census analysis to help make accurate projections – an approach that is really suitable only for larger organisations with hundreds of voluntary terminations each year. The method involves examining the major attributes of employees who left during a defined 'census period'. Essentially, this involves recording basic data about leavers over the course of a year. All manner of variables could be included in the analysis. The most important are age, gender and length of service, but others of relevance could include:

□ qualifications
□ whether or not the employee was a pension scheme member
□ the original recruitment source (advertisement, employee referral, agency, etc)
□ scores achieved on selection tests at the recruitment stage
□ performance appraisal ratings
□ the employee's absence record.

Indeed, anything may be included that is perceived to be a possible factor in explaining a higher propensity to leave – and hence which might be used as the basis for future predictions of turnover. The results of a census analysis might, for example, be:

□ Employees in Job A are most likely to leave after one year and six months' service.
□ Employees in Job B are twice as likely as employees in Job C to take retirement between the ages of 55 and 60.
□ Pension scheme members have twice the average job tenure as non-members.

□ On average, male employees remain in their jobs for a year longer than female colleagues.

□ Staff in Job B recruited via employee referral stay on average for three years; those recruited via newspaper ads stay on average for two years; and those recruited via agencies for one year.

The information recorded by the census is then applied to the current workforce to gain an accurate estimate, job group by job group, or department by department, of what turnover is likely to be next year. There are now a number of software packages available on the market to assist in these types of exercise. Examples are successive versions of the *Prospect* software produced by the Institute of Employment Studies, and a package known as *Pyramid*.

For smaller employers these types of analysis can be useful in helping to gain an understanding of turnover patterns, but cannot form the basis of a statistically meaningful forward projection.

An alternative approach is to use management judgement combined with knowledge of individual employees to predict likely turnover levels in the coming year. There is no science here, just informed guesswork, but the process helps to focus the mind on the likely impact of voluntary turnover ahead of time. It also helps with budgeting processes. A very simple approach can be used that involves every supervisor's ascribing to each of his or her employees in a particular job group a grade which indicates how likely he or she is to leave in the coming year. An example of the system follows (Table 7 overleaf).

Putting it all together

A number of different tools and techniques have been described and evaluated in this chapter – some very straightforward, others complex and sophisticated. Used where appropriate and in combination they should help you to:

□ gain an appreciation of the levels and patterns of turnover in different parts of your organisation

Table 7

Grade	Definition	Team member	Grade
A	*Is highly unlikely to leave during the coming year*	Meg	A
		Nigel	A
B	*Is more likely to stay than to leave in the coming year*	Ozzy	D
		Pat	C
C	*Would not be surprising if he/she leaves in the coming year*		
		Rod	A
D	*Is very likely to leave during the coming year*	Tony	D
		Val	B

LIKELY NUMBER OF LEAVERS THIS YEAR: 3 or 4

□ benchmark your organisation's performance, in terms of turnover, against that of other organisations in your industry

□ calculate with a reasonable degree of accuracy the total cost of turnover for your organisation (and parts of it) during the past year

□ predict the likely level of turnover and its probable cost during the coming year

□ identify information on which to base plans for interventions designed to reduce staff turnover.

TURNOVER ANALYSIS AT W H SMITH

In the mid-1990s the W H Smith group employed over 33,000 staff in the UK. Its overall staff turnover rate was 40 per cent, but turnover was a great deal higher in some of its larger stores. The main problem was high turnover among sales assistants. The company calculated that it shouldered an average cost of £2,485 each time a sales assistant left – a figure mostly accounted for by induction and training time, as well as the 13 weeks that it took new sales assistants to become fully productive. In 1993 the company calculated that the annual cost of turnover was equivalent to 10.8 per cent of its pay bill. For every 1 per cent by which turnover rates could be reduced, the company worked out that it would save £250,000 per year. Millions could be saved if a target rate of 15 per cent turnover could be reached.

Detailed analysis showed that stability rates were increasing, despite the high levels of turnover. This indicated that turnover was especially high in the first months of employment. Once people remained in post for a year, they were likely to stay for some time. Wastage rates were found to be much higher among younger staff than older employees, and higher among women than men. A particular issue identified was the relatively small numbers of women choosing to return after a period of maternity leave.

As a result of these different analyses the company put in place several policy initiatives designed to reduce turnover. They included:

☐ targeting recruitment at older potential employees
☐ basing selection on tests of ability rather than on educational quali-fications
☐ encouraging older people to take up training opportunities
☐ establishing a mentoring scheme for school-leavers and other new recruits in younger age-ranges
☐ providing a clear internal career path for sales assistants
☐ flexible working arrangements (such as termtime working) to encourage women returners.

Turnover rates at Smiths did not fall to 15 per cent, but they were sub-stantially reduced without the need for major new expenditure.

Source: IDS, 1994

4 IDENTIFYING THE CAUSES OF EMPLOYEE TURNOVER

Self-evidently, it is necessary to find out why people are leaving your organisation before you can put in place measures to improve the employee-retention record. Individuals may choose to resign their jobs for many different reasons, but there is a tendency for some to be more significant than others among specific groups of employees or in certain organisations. Particular professions have evolved their own labour market dynamics, with the result that the leaving behaviour displayed by some occupational species differs from that of others. Moreover, departures take different forms and occur in different patterns according to prevailing organisational circumstances, much depending on culture, management orientation and competitive position.

The fewer reasons employees are given to feel dissatisfied, insecure or uncommitted, the less likelihood there is that they will even consider handing in their resignations. But the sources of serious discontent can vary greatly. Another key variable is the extent of attractive alternative job opportunities. The greater the number of these there are available to staff, the more likely they will be to take them up.

In the light of all these factors it is useful for managers who seek to increase retention rates to take the time and trouble to understand the real drivers of turnover in different parts of their organisations. Only then can effective, targeted interventions be developed that stand the best chance of success. Our focus in this chapter is thus on the tools that can be used to diagnose the true causes of staff turnover.

Most UK organisations either fail altogether to record the reasons people leave or do so in such an unsophisticated way as to provide little by way of a useful platform on which to build robust employee-retention practices. The typical approach involves managers' talking briefly and formally to their departing staff to confirm the reason for leaving and to ask the identity of their new employer (if there is one). The commonly used name for these encounters is 'exit interviews' – but they are often too short and peremptory to justify such a title. Their content is frequently driven either by a standard questionnaire or by the requirements of the computerised personnel information systems used to record their outcomes. A list of a dozen or so possible reasons for leaving is given, one of which has to be identified by the manager at the end of the interview as being the most salient in the case of each leaver. Sometimes there is an opportunity to record a few lines of information in addition, but the main aim is to gather data in as brief and easily manipulated a form as possible. Periodically, this is then used by the organisation to generate reports which claim to set out the reasons that staff left in the previous months.

All too often, of course, the manager does not find time to conduct an exit interview at all, or forgets to do so. The forms (or computer-screen fields) are then completed by them alone using their personal knowledge of the employee who has just left.

It is my contention that such approaches serve little purpose, particularly when used in isolation, because the two major assumptions that lie behind them can be shown to be unreliable. These are that:

☐ departing employees give their managers full and accurate accounts of their reasons for leaving at exit interviews

☐ it is possible to identify, for each departing employee, a single 'most salient' reason to explain his or her resignation.

Neither of these statements is correct. Employees commonly have good reason to withhold the whole truth from their managers when it comes to explaining their departures, and even if they don't, are often economical with the truth when accounting for them. Furthermore, even when they are wholly frank about what has led them to quit, in many cases the real reasons are so mixed-up, involved and intricate as to defy simplistic categorisation.

More sophisticated approaches are thus called for if managers are to gain a genuine and useful understanding of the 'turnover drivers' operating in their organisations.

Reasons for leaving

The major causes of employee turnover fall into four categories: 'pull-type' causes, 'push-type' causes, unavoidable causes, and situations in which the departure is initiated by the organisation rather than by the employee. Each is fundamentally different from the others and demands a different type of organisational response when it is identified as the major explanation for turnover among members of particular occupational groups.

Pull factors

Pull-type resignations occur when the major cause is the positive attraction of alternative employment. The employee concerned may be wholly satisfied with his or her existing organisation and happy in the job, but nonetheless decides to move on in search of something even better. It may be a higher rate of pay, a more valued benefits package, more job security, better long-term career opportunities, a less pressured existence, the opportunity to work overseas, a shorter journey to commute or more convenient hours of work. Alternatively, it may be the desire to work with particular colleagues or for a particular management team. People also move in order to spend some time working for a high-profile or well-respected employer so as to build, over the years, a portfolio of such experience. CV-fashioning is necessary in some professions as a means of getting on, there being a tendency for employers to prefer candidates with a breadth of experience to those who have built their careers in just one organisation.

Where pull factors are at work, the organisation seeking to reduce quit-rates will gain little by seeking to enhance job satisfaction. This may delay the inevitable for a few months, but will not in itself serve to deter resignations. Instead, it is necessary to find out what employees really value, what they are looking for in their careers, and to enhance the organisation's ability to provide it.

Push factors

By contrast, in the case of push factors the major underlying cause of resignations is the perception that something is wrong with the existing employer. The person concerned may move in order to secure a 'better job', but he or she is as likely to join another organisation without knowing a great deal about it just because he or she no longer enjoys the current one. In doing so the hope is that working life will improve, but there is no guarantee that it will. A range of different push factors can be identified, ranging from a dislike of the prevailing organisational culture to disapproval of changed structures and straightforward personality clashes with colleagues. Perceptions of unfairness often underlie these types of departure, but they can also occur simply because the employee is bored or generally fed up with the day-to-day work. He or she thus starts looking for something (or anything) different, and leaves on finding a suitable alternative. In the more extreme cases of dissatisfaction people leave *before* securing another position.

Where push factors are pre-eminent, the required organisational response is to address the root causes of dissatisfaction. This may mean selecting supervisors with greater care, providing them with better training, and appraising them more effectively in terms of their supervisory skills. It may mean examining organisational policy with a view to improving the fairness of its operation. Or it may mean simply paying greater attention to enhancing the quality of working life.

Above all, it requires the creation of what Freeman and Medoff (1984) characterise as an employment relationship of 'voice' as opposed to one of 'exit' – it requires providing a structure (both collective and individual), as well as a culture, which encourages the resolution of disaffection internally before it generates unwelcome resignations. If people are given the opportunity to express their dissatisfaction or to air their grievances, and to have them heard, they are less likely to see leaving as their first option.

Unavoidable turnover

This category comprises reasons for leaving which are wholly or mainly outside the control of the organisation. The resignation does not occur because of dissatisfaction with the job, or the perceived opportunities provided elsewhere, but for reasons that are unconnected to work in any direct sense. The most common is retirement, which affects almost everyone at some stage, but there are many others too. Illness is often a cause, because it incapacitates either the employee or a relative for whom he or she has caring responsibilities. Maternity is another – women often preferring not to return to the same job after their leave, either to take a break from work altogether or in order to secure a job that makes it easier for them to combine work with childcare arrangements. A fourth common reason is relocation – usually in order to follow or join up with a spouse or partner. Finally, there is the desire to take a career break for a period in order to travel, re-enter full-time education or pursue some other interest.

Organisations often conclude that nothing can be done to reduce turnover of this kind. This is only partly true, because in many situations the employee who leaves for an 'unavoidable reason' could choose to continue working in the same job if he or she really wanted to. People choose to take a career break, choose not to return to work after maternity leave, and often choose to retire. This suggests that if the job was more valued and attractive they might choose not to exercise the option of leaving. Similarly, when two people decide to set up home together in one place, a choice has to be made about which of the partners is going to relocate and which is going to stay put. In practice, this decision is very often based on work-based factors. The one who is least satisfied in his or her job or who is perceived to enjoy the poorest career prospects is usually the one who resigns and relocates.

Involuntary turnover

Our final major category includes departures which are involuntary and initiated by the organisation. The employee would have remained employed had he or she not been asked or required to leave. Redundancies clearly fall into this category, along with short-term layoffs, the ending of fixed-term contracts and other dismissals of one kind or another. Many resignations are also in fact largely involuntary because people often prefer to 'jump before they are pushed'. Someone who knows she is to be made redundant in a few months therefore seeks alternative employment ahead of time, while a colleague who believes his employment will soon be terminated on grounds of poor performance secures another job before being formally dismissed.

Although such turnover can sometimes be characterised as 'functional' rather than 'dysfunctional', it still carries a cost and is thus best avoided where possible. The main aim should be to prevent the situations which cause it to happen from arising in the first place. Except in the case of some dismissals on grounds of illness, measures can be taken to reduce the incidence of involuntary turnover. These largely focus on recruitment and selection practices, the aim being to ensure as far as is possible that a large pool of potential candidates comes forward and that poor decisions are avoided when deciding who to offer jobs to. However, good supervision plays a role too. Well-managed employees tend to 'give of their best', resulting in fewer examples of poor performance and hence fewer dismissals.

Exit routes

For some employees the decision to leave is taken on the spur of the moment, an incident occurring or a management decision being confirmed that leaves little room for second thoughts. These episodes occur regularly, but account only for a minority of voluntary departures. In most cases the process is drawn out over a longer period of time. There may well be months or even years separating the actual resignation from the first thoughts about the possibility of leaving. In between there are a series of stages, some more complex in nature than others, at which the decision to quit comes a step closer. At each of these stages an organisational intervention of some kind may have the effect of halting progress towards the resignation either temporally or permanently.

Researchers specialising in the study of employee turnover have long debated the nature of the multi-staged decision-making process which precedes the final decision to quit. Some have put forward universal models which claim to cover all turnover scenarios, while others have specified different types of exit route. One of the most influential approaches has been that of William Mobley (1977) who found evidence to support the validity of the following 10-stage model:

☐ Evaluate existing job.
☐ Experience job dissatisfaction.
☐ Think of quitting.
☐ Evaluate expected utility of search for a new job and the cost of quitting.
☐ Decide to search for alternatives.
☐ Search for alternatives.
☐ Evaluate alternatives.
☐ Compare best alternative with present job.
☐ Decide whether to stay or quit.
☐ Quit.

Mobley's was the first academic work undertaken in the modern business environment to draw proper attention to the complexity of most resignation decisions. His model includes both push and pull factors, suggesting that in practice the former come before the latter. In other words, his view is that in most cases dissatisfaction occurs first and that this precipitates the search for a new job.

While few would argue with the items Mobley includes in his model, there is doubt about the extent to which the 10 stages tend, in practice, to follow one another in linear sequence. It is plausible to argue, for example, that employees who perceive themselves to enjoy plenty of alternative job opportunities enter a workplace with a wholly different mindset than those who believe their career options to be severely limited. The first group will judge their employers harshly, will be quicker to criticise and more likely to feel discontented. They are also less likely to seek to develop feelings of commitment. From the start they know that as soon as they cease to enjoy their jobs, they can and will move on. By contrast, the second group will instinctively seek (literally) to make the best out of a bad job. They will be prepared for knocks, will expect to go through periods of dissatisfaction, and will put up with poor treatment from supervisors. Their lack of alternative job opportunities makes them inclined to seek accommodation with their organisation and to develop a degree of attachment towards both it and their colleagues. In both cases, these employees are, at least in part, reversing the stages set out in Mobley's model. The evaluation of alternatives comes first, the experience of dissatisfaction afterwards. The employer seeking to reduce staff turnover is thus well-advised to develop different strategies for tighter and looser labour market conditions.

More recent models, such as those put forward by Steers and Mowday (1981) and Price and Mueller (1986), identify the different elements that can combine to bring about a resignation, but remove the concept of linear stages. Their purpose is to identify all the different types of factor that lead to employee turnover and to suggest how each relates to each other. The Steers and Mowday model is illustrated in Figure 2.

Figure 2

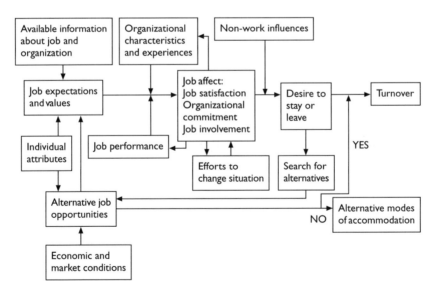

Source: Steers and Mowday, in L. Cummings and B. Straw (eds) (1981), *Research in Organizational Behavior.* Greenwich, CT. JAI Press. p242. Quoted in Hom and Griffeth (1995)

A useful feature of the Price and Mueller model is the clear separation of the notions of 'job satisfaction' and 'organisational commitment'. In separating them they are asserting that it is possible to be broadly satisfied in your job and yet simultaneously uncommitted to the organisation you work for. Reduced commitment leads to turnover – but this can be brought about as a result *both* of dissatisfaction with a job *and* of other factors such as a disapproval of company policy or the growing importance of issues in one's non-work life. This is a vital distinction for managers who want to get a better grip on turnover in their organisations to take on board. You need to find out, as far as is possible, which antecedents of turnover are operating among key groups of employees and how they interact. For some it may be job dissatisfaction, for others a more general underlying lack of commitment to the organisation, and for yet another group the lure of alternative employment. It may be two of these acting in combination, or all three. It is only after finding out that remedial action can be taken which will have the best chance of making an impact.

The most recent developments in this field have been advanced by Thomas Lee, Terence Mitchell and their colleagues (Lee and Mitchell, 1994; Lee *et al*, 1999). Their 'unfolding model' is notable for its suggestion that employee turnover rarely occurs after careful, rational consideration on the part of employees. Drawing on image theory, these researchers have found that what actually happens in many cases is that individuals experience some kind of 'shock' which jolts them very quickly into thinking about leaving when they have not seriously given it much thought previously. Far from weighing up alternatives and thinking carefully about the advantages and disadvantages of quitting, employees tend often to make the decision very quickly. Shocks do not always lead to resignations, but they set off the kind of process described by Mobley. Someone who is happy in his or her job and has not even considered leaving is jolted overnight into thinking about the possibility of alternative employment. The term 'shock' can refer to any event, personal or organisational, which has the effect of bringing continued employment with the current employer into question.

Because it need not, by any means, be an unpleasant experience, the term 'trigger' is perhaps more appropriate.

Common examples of 'shocks' or 'triggers' are:

- a call from a head-hunter
- pregnancy
- divorce/splitting up with a partner
- mergers
- reorganisations/allocation of new job duties
- the appointment of a new supervisor.

The great contribution of the unfolding model from a management perspective is the finding that some event or new occurrence usually has to galvanise an employee into evaluating his or her level of job satisfaction and considering the utility of moving to other employment. If the employer can stop these 'triggers' from occurring in the first place, the chances of retaining employees are substantially enhanced. Some, of course, are genuinely outside the organisation's control – but many can be influenced. It is possible, for example, in very competitive labour markets, to build defences that are hard for head-hunters to penetrate (see Chapter 5). It is also within the employer's power to lessen the extent to which the trigger has 'shock impact'. There are no one-off easy answers to these predicaments. It is a question of managers' knowing what makes their staff tick, understanding the nature of the most common exit routes, and anticipating possible turnover triggers ahead of time.

THE AUTHOR'S JOB MOVES

In my career to date, since leaving university, I have had seven separate jobs. The shortest lasted four months, the longest so far has been five years. The first three were hotel management jobs, the next two in the NHS, and the final two in higher education. I have thus resigned on six separate occasions. Some are easily explained, others resulted from a mix of separate factors. Together they illustrate the range of different reasons that lead to voluntary turnover.

Job 1

The company I was working for started losing money and decided to curtail its management training scheme six months early. We trainees were given a few weeks to find jobs within the organisation. I was offered a new post, but it was unexciting and less senior than I had been hoping to secure on completion of the training scheme. I was approached by a head-hunter at this time and interviewed for a bigger and more interesting job in a smaller company. I was also offered 40 per cent more than the salary being offered by my existing employer. So I left.

Job 2

This resignation occurred pretty quickly when I was told by my employer that I could not appoint anyone who was not white to a front-of-house role. I thus resigned on a matter of principle and not in order to take up an alternative job. A period of unemployment followed. Had this instruction not been given, I would certainly have remained employed in the organisation for longer – but if I am honest I think other factors were also operating that made me more willing to resign than fight to keep the job on my own terms. The hours were long and the location distant from friends and family. I had also become ill and would soon need to have two operations.

Job 3

I resigned my third position in order to return to university to study for the (then) IPM qualification. It was a temporary job which I greatly enjoyed and which provided very useful experience, but it was never intended to last for more than a few months.

Job 4

The part of the NHS I was working in was undergoing rapid downsizing, and future employment was far from guaranteed. The job itself was largely enjoyable and stimulating, with pleasant colleagues. I would have stayed longer had I not feared future redundancy. Several of my most valued colleagues had already left when I started looking for a new job. Push factors were the major cause, and I eventually accepted a position on a lesser rate of pay. However, there was a positive attraction towards the new job too. It promised to be interesting and challenging, and it provided the opportunity to work with very agreeable people.

Job 5

This was a hard decision – to leave a permanent job in the NHS, which

I loved, to take up a temporary teaching post in higher education. The salary offered by the university was marginally higher, but this was not a factor in the decision. It was a close call and I tried to have it both ways by seeking to delay entry into the new job for 12 months. In the end I decided to try academia for a year or two because I thought that I would not get another opportunity. This job-move decision was the only one of the six that was largely rational and based entirely on a clear-headed weighing up of the pros and cons.

Job 6

Push and pull factors operated together here. My new employers were able to offer a permanent contract and an attractive job, but the move would entail some reduction in salary and lower long-term earning potential. The search for job security was thus the most significant factor. But I had also become unhappy in my existing job and for the first time in my life found that my unhappiness was affecting relation-ships outside work. The stress was partly caused by a fear of unem-ployment, partly by discomfort with the direction the organisation was taking, and partly by a serious personality clash with a colleague with whom I was obliged to work closely. I could have stayed and fought harder to secure more job security, but deep down I knew I was ready to go, and left with a feeling of relief.

Exit interviews

Most books on employee retention and related issues recom-mend that managers carry out exit interviews with departing employees. The aim is first and foremost to establish (and record) the main reasons for the resignation. Ideally, the man-ager will also discover if the organisation could have done anything to postpone or prevent the resignation, with a view to avoiding others in the future. For those employers who re-hire ex-employees from time to time, a third aim will be to leave a favourable impression of the organisation in the leaver's mind. There is nothing wrong with carrying out exit interviews, especially if they are the only diagnostic tool being used in turnover management, but managers must be mindful of their weaknesses as well as their strengths. It is wise both to treat data collected in this manner with some caution and to search out alternative sources of information about reasons for leaving.

Researchers investigating the accuracy of exit interviews have generally given them a poor press, the main finding being that they constitute a highly unreliable source of information about why individuals have resigned from their jobs. This is particularly the case when such interviews are carried out by the immediate supervisor or by someone who has exercised managerial authority over the resignee. Several American studies (Griffeth and Hom, 2001, pp206–216) have sought to validate information given at exit interviews by:

☐ following them up with questionnaires about reasons for leaving that are returned on a confidential basis to researchers based outside the employing organisation

☐ using independent consultants to carry out further interviews on a confidential basis *after* the individuals have left.

The results of these studies suggest consistently that many employees fail to tell the whole truth about why they have resigned to their managers at the time of leaving. Firstly, there is a tendency for resignees to give equivocal answers in interviews when they actually have clear and definite reasons for going. Secondly, employees tend to down-play push factors and play up the pull factors and 'unavoidable' reasons when explaining their departure to their managers. Thirdly, it is the case that departing employees are a great deal more likely to cite pay levels as the main reason for leaving when asked by managers than is the case when the interview is conducted by a neutral party. In a widely quoted study by Zarandona and Camuso (1985), 38 per cent of employees in one organisation claimed that they left to secure a higher salary package when interviewed by management, while only 12 per cent stated that this had been their main reason in a postal questionnaire returned to independent researchers some months later. Conversely, only 4 per cent cited poor supervision in exit interviews carried out by managers, a reason given by 24 per cent in the subsequent questionnaire survey.

It is reasonable to state that the likely explanation for the discrepancies is a reluctance on the part of most departing employees to come clean about the true extent of any dissatisfaction when asked by their supervisors to explain the decision to quit. It is not difficult to speculate on why this should be the case:

☐ a reluctance on the part of the employees to criticise managers who they have worked closely with and may personally like

☐ fear that the manager will take criticisms personally and will rebut them in the interview

☐ a wish not to 'burn bridges' because a favourable reference may be sought in the future

☐ a wish to leave wide open the possibility of returning to work with the employer at a later date – anything that might prevent this from occurring is thus avoided

☐ embarrassment that the true reason for leaving will seem trivial or pathetic when articulated to a manager

☐ a reluctance to reveal that what the manager may see as weaknesses were the genuine reasons for leaving

☐ a wish to protect colleagues who are not leaving

☐ in cases of resignations in anger or frustration, a desire not to be helpful to the organisation in question

☐ feelings of generosity and goodwill towards colleagues who are marking the employee's departure with leaving cards, presents or parties

☐ an insistence that the true reasons for leaving are personal and therefore confidential

☐ the perception that the real reason for leaving would make the employee appear ungrateful for opportunities given and exercised while in the job.

For all these reasons it is easier for departing staff (whose real reasons for leaving are complex or which imply criticism of their managers) to state that they are leaving to gain more pay, or because they are relocating to move in with a partner, than it is to set out the genuine causes of the resignation. In fact, a good case can be constructed for actively advising people not to tell the whole truth at exit interviews – a line convincingly argued in a recent *Financial Times* article by Adrian Furnham (2001).

In order to maximise the likelihood that leavers will talk frankly in their exit interviews a number of steps may be taken. Firstly, the interview should not be carried out by the individual's immediate line manager, or by any manager who has exercised direct authority over him or her.

Instead, the interviewer should be someone with whom there has been no prior reporting relationship and who will not be required to give a reference in the future. Human resources personnel are often ideally placed to carry out the role, but it can equally well be performed by managers based elsewhere in the organisation. The less contact the manager concerned has had with the leaver, the better. However, very senior personnel should not be used simply because people can be overawed when talking to them ('the headmaster syndrome'). Some organisations go as far as to outsource the exit interviewing function entirely to a consultant, while others simply apply common sense and ask the employee concerned who he or she would prefer to conduct the interview. Both approaches significantly increase the chances that valuable information will be obtained.

Secondly, as far as is possible, confidentiality must be ensured. If the real reason for the resignation is some perceived failure on the part of management, few employees will come clean for fear of burning their bridges unless they believe that any comments they make will not subsequently be relayed to the individuals of whom actual or implied criticism is being made. Confidentiality can never be 100 per cent guaranteed, but steps can be taken to reassure leavers:

☐ If an organisation ensures that its exit interviews are confidential, the practice will be seen as such by existing employees. When their turn comes, they are more likely to have confidence in the system.
☐ Explaining that maintaining confidentiality is as much in the interests of the employer as the ex-employee enhances the leaver's belief that what he or she says will not get back to those he or she criticises.

Thirdly, the timing of exit interviews is important. Avoid the last day or two of employment. This is because they are abnormal days for the leaver, tending to be a more pleasant and exciting experience. The imminent prospect of a break between jobs or of new employment naturally weighs heavily in our minds on our last days. To this is added the tendency for leaving events of one kind or another to be organised and anticipated, at which cards and presents are given and generous speeches made. The messages conveyed are often designed by co-workers to be both touching and memorable. They thus have the effect of engendering in the leaver feelings of generosity towards people and towards the job that he or she may actually have detested and couldn't wait to leave a week or two earlier. Conversely, where these rituals do not occur or are apparently organised under some suffrance by colleagues, the leaving employee will often be disappointed. Overly negative perceptions of the organisation can then be generated ('The bastards couldn't even be bothered to send me off in style!' etc) which tend to lead to an unduly poor assessment of the organisation emerging at the exit interview. The emotions generated in the final days are thus too strong to make this a good time to carry out the interview.

In theory, exit interviews are best carried out as close as possible to the date of resignation when the reasons are clearest in the leaver's mind and best articulated. The problem here is that the resignation may occur some weeks before the physical departure because of notice provisions. This means that there are plenty of working days still to go, and hence a reluctance to jeopardise working relationships by voicing criticism of managers or colleagues. So a balance has to be struck. The best time is probably a week or so prior to the last day. There are a few days of work left – not enough to worry about the fallout associated with critical remarks, but a sufficiently long period before the more emotionally charged atmosphere of the last days begins to kick in.

The final point to make about exit interviews concerns their content. Here too the traditional approach involving the use of standard questionnaires should be avoided. This is because they tend to prejudge the responses that departing employees will give through the presence of prompts. In many cases a list of reasons for leaving is given and the resignee required to state which one was the most significant in their case. Such approaches make for easy analysis and collation of data, but they are unlikely to reflect the true picture. Prompting must therefore be avoided, as should any attempt to simplify for data collection purposes the complex reality of the decision to leave.

For most people a number of factors come together, often over a long period, to cause a resignation. Some will be pull factors, others push factors; some will be work-based, others rooted in personal circumstances. Each will interact with others in different ways and at different times. It is only via unstructured exit interviews that the employee will be able to articulate his or her reasons properly and in his or her own words. The interviewer must explain the organisation's purpose in completing exit interviews with leavers before asking the departing employee to explain step by step and in his or her own words why he or she is resigning. Supplementary questions can then be asked as a means of clarifying points made and of probing a little more deeply, or to encourage the interviewee to keep talking. At the end the interviewer should sum up what he or she thinks has been stated and check with the employee that this represents a fair summary of his or her words. After this has been done, a further question can be asked along the following lines:

> What, if anything, could the organisation have done differently which would have led you to remain an employee?

Here again the leaver should be left to answer in his or her own words without prompting. Supplementary questions should be asked only to clarify points, to ask for something to be repeated or to probe for more detail. The urge to contradict or to enter into any kind of discussion about the answer given to the question must be suppressed. What matters, after all, in terms of retention management (as in customer retention) is what ex-employees actually perceive – not what managers hope that they should perceive.

Alternative diagnostic tools

Exit interviews are by far the most common method used by organisations to establish why their employees leave, but there are plenty of other tools available. None is perfect by any means, but all have a role to play. Used in combination they help to build up the most effective and comprehensive picture possible – and thus the best foundations on which to build robust employee retention strategies.

Staff attitude surveys

Questionnaire-based attitude or opinion surveys circulated among all employees are a widely employed communication mechanism in the UK. They are used to gauge morale in the workforce generally as well as to help managers pick up on specific issues that need attention. In many organisations the results are quantified to allow progress to be tracked over time and comparisons to be made between different business units. Increasingly, attitude surveys are used as a method by which the performance of the human resource management function is evaluated and its value to the organisation judged. Such surveys can also be employed as an effective technique for establishing the major reasons underlying staff turnover among different groups, although how this can be done is not immediately apparent.

The problem with attitude surveys, as is made clear by Levin and Rosse (2001, pp115–116), is that in order to be effective they must be anonymous. In other words, if you want your employees to answer the questions in the survey frankly and fully, their completed forms must not be traceable back to them. However, anonymity in a survey prevents the organisation from identifying individual problems and acting upon them. It also means that it is not possible to compare the answers given by people who subsequently leave with those of colleagues who stay. Yet from a retention management perspective it is this kind of data that is most valuable. Attitude surveys often reveal general dissatisfaction with some aspects of an organisation and general satisfaction with others. This information is useful to know but does not allow a scrutineer to establish which types of dissatisfaction lead to turnover and which do not. Nor does it indicate what forms of positive assessment of the organisation are associated with people who stay a long time and what forms have no impact on the propensity to leave. For example, a survey may well reveal that 50 per cent of the staff are dissatisfied with their pay level whereas 50 per cent are satisfied. But it is impossible to tell from this data alone whether or not there is a higher turnover rate among those who are dissatisfied with their pay. Such judgements could easily be made if staff were required to identify themselves on the survey questionnaire – but that would compromise the accuracy of the survey. So it is impossible to tell whether or not an increase in pay would or would not have any actual impact on staff retention rates.

For attitude surveys to be useful as a tool for diagnosing the causes of turnover, ways have to be found around this conundrum. Four approaches are worth considering:

□ Issue an attitude survey to all staff on a regular basis, but also ask leavers to complete the questionnaire before they depart. The leavers' forms can then be compared with those of the staff as a whole. The problem here is the same as for exit interviews – namely, a tendency to inaccuracy. However much the organisation guarantees confidentiality, departing employees will perceive their answers to be traceable back to them.

□ Use an independent, external body to issue the attitude survey and to collate the results. Provided employees trust the consultancy concerned to protect their confidentiality, this can work well. Employees write their name and job title on the attitude survey form and, hopefully, go on to give full and honest answers. A list of leavers is then given to the consultants on a regular basis and comparisons made in their report between the attitudes of leavers and those of stayers. The disadvantage, of course, is the cost.

□ Ask leavers to complete a confidential attitude survey (as above) and then administer the same survey to a group of stayers from the same job groups. Ideally, try to find pairs of people (one leaver and one stayer) with broadly the same characteristics in terms of job tenure and job duties.

□ Include in a confidential attitude survey a question about intention to leave (eg: 'Are you actively seeking alternative employment at present?' or 'Do you intend to leave your job in the next 12 months?'). The American research suggests that such questions are good predictors of actual resignations, making it useful to compare attitude survey responses to questions about job satisfaction/dissatisfaction of those who express an intention to leave with those who do not (Griffeth and Hom, 2001, pp121–124).

It is beyond the scope of this book to discuss the content of attitude surveys in general terms. Readers interested in the topic are referred to another book in the CIPD's Developing Practice series, *Employee Attitude and Opinion Surveys* by Mike Walters, which covers all the issues very effectively.

Surveys of former employees

One way round some of the the problems associated with exit interviews is to survey staff some weeks or months after they have left. This can be done using a standard questionnaire, but is better able to tap into the mix of factors and their interaction with each other if it is conducted as an interview. The assumption here is that ex-employees will be both more willing and more able to identify and articulate their real reasons for leaving once they have successfully settled into a new job. They are less emotionally involved in the affairs of the organisation than is the case at the time of leaving, and may well be more inclined to give a clear-headed, considered response to questions about their reasons for leaving. Moreover, because they are able to compare their new organisation with their previous one, they are in a better position to give advice about how retention rates could be improved in the future.

However, a number of the problems associated with exit interviews remain in the case of surveys of ex-employees. There endures in many cases a reluctance to appear to criticise a former employer or individual managers for whom one has previously worked. References may still be needed in the future, while in some cases there is a wish to keep open the possibility of a return in the future. In many industries, of course, managers move regularly too, leading to a situation in which people find themselves working with or for ex-managers in new workplaces. For all these reasons assurances of confidentiality are necessary and best guaranteed through the employment of an independent consultant to carry out the survey.

Stayers' surveys

Bramham (2001, p73) suggests that organisations have much to gain from looking at the other side of the coin and investigating what makes people stay rather than what makes them leave.

Any of a number of approaches could be taken, each of which is attractive in theory but does not appear to be widely used in practice. Each starts with the identification of a sample of employees who are *both* long-serving *and* above-average performers.

The first approach involves issuing an attitude survey to the members of this group. A few days later the same survey is issued to another group of staff, in similar jobs but with below-average length of service. The responses are then compared and a report written identifying how characteristics or attitudes differ between the two groups. An alternative approach is less systematic but could be just as useful. This simply involves establishing a focus group made up of long-stayers and asking them why they have remained employed for so long. Each member should be asked to describe a time when he or she thought about leaving, and to articulate the reasons for his or her eventual decision not to quit. A third type of 'stayer' survey' is interview-based. This is more time-consuming but may induce some long-stayers to be more frank about their 'near-leaving experiences' than they would be in a focus-group situation.

Stayer's surveys do not explain exactly why people leave your organisation, although the long-stayers may well have an informed and accurate view about this issue. The surveys do, however, provide information that can be used to shape retention initiatives. For example, stayers might state that a major reason they chose not to leave when they had the opportunity was because of the relatively generous pension scheme or the flexible working arrangements or the crèche – and in this way you learn that these features are key to your organisation's competitive position in its labour markets. Communicating their value to the workforce should then form part of the retention strategy. Alternatively, you may discover that long-stayers share certain competences or attitudes which are present to a lesser extent in other employees.

If so, this can help inform future selection exercises. More ambitious employers seeking to develop a full-blown employer-branding exercise will also find the information gained by these means to be a useful contribution.

Last-job-move surveys

Useful if less directly relevant information can be assembled by asking new employees to talk frankly about their last job moves (ie the decision to leave their former employer and to join your organisation). This is not going to tell you much about what you are doing right or wrong as an employer, but it will help to build a clear picture of the dynamics that operate in your key labour markets. You may, for example, find that your more recent employees applied not because of any positive attraction to your organisation but simply because they hated their previous jobs and needed to work somewhere. This information suggests that push factors are more significant than pull factors in the particular labour market concerned. Alternatively, you may be told that the main reason employees left their previous jobs and joined you was because you offered them 50p an hour more for their efforts. This informs you that your labour markets are highly pay-sensitive – and that it is important to keep a close eye on what competitors are paying if you are to retain people.

As with the other methods, surveys of this kind can either be questionnaire-based or interview-based. The former is less expensive and yields data that is readily quantified, whereas the latter provides a richer seam of information which serves to deepen your understanding of what makes your key labour markets tick. In either case, timing is important – unless independent consultants are to solicit the information on a confidential basis. Asking employees about their last job moves is problematic if it is attempted too soon after their initial interviews. This is because all of us seek to give the best possible impression at job interviews, a process which can often involve putting a positive gloss on our reasons for leaving our previous employment. If we perceive that stating our real reasons may reduce our chances of securing the new position, we cover these up and put forward instead a plausible alternative explanation (which may or may not contain large grains of truth). If subsequently our employers ask us to talk candidly about our reasons for leaving we are going to be inclined to repeat the same explanation given at the selection interview. This is particularly the case if we feel insecure in our new job and have yet to establish frank and relaxed working relationships.

For these reasons it is probably best to conduct last-job-move surveys around a year after employees join. This is long enough for people to feel secure in the new job and also long enough for them and their managers to have forgotten exactly what was said when they were first interviewed. It is also short enough to ensure that employees can remember clearly why they left their previous employment and how they felt in responding to the events leading up to their resignation.

PART 2

PRESCRIPTIONS

5 IMPROVING RETENTION RATES

In this and the following five chapters the focus shifts to the different types of measures that employers can take in order to improve their rates of employee retention. The major human resource management interventions and issues surrounding them are each covered in a separate chapter. Chapter 6 focuses on reward management issues, Chapter 7 on training and development, Chapter 8 on working conditions, Chapter 9 on action to take in the fields of recruitment and selection, and Chapter 10 on the crucial relationship between supervisors and subordinates.

It is in these areas of activity that most employers will find the best route to cutting unwanted turnover. Most in their different ways ultimately involve giving employees a 'better deal'. Which area forms the focus of a drive to reduce turnover must depend on the structure of your particular labour markets, the preferences of your employees, and the relative strengths of your major labour market competitors. However, 'giving employees a better deal' is only one type of approach that is available. Perhaps less powerful in terms of their effect, other strategies may also have an important role to play – and it is on these that we concentrate in this chapter. Firstly, we assess the extent to which employees can be 'tied in' or at least discouraged from leaving using contractual terms. Secondly, we look at steps that can be taken to deter people who are intent on poaching your staff. Finally, the focus shifts to public relations and branding exercises which are concerned with improving an organisation's image as an employer and hence strengthening its appeal in key labour markets.

Terms of contract

In theory it is possible to include terms in your employees' contracts of employment which deter them from resigning. A far as the courts are concerned there is a broad acceptance of the notion that contracts are negotiated and freely entered into. They are reluctant to rule that a clause is unreasonable and therefore unenforceable, although this is an option open to them. They sometimes rule that an employer has been unreasonable in the manner he or she has applied (or activated) a term of contract, or in the way he or she has exercised any discretion allowed under the contract. But it is relatively unusual for a court effectively to strike out a term an employee has freely signed up to. This means that it is possible, within reason, to use contracts of employment as a staff-retention device.

The difficulty, of course, is getting people to sign up to such terms in the first place. If the contract is too restrictive in its approach to voluntary resignation, people will be deterred from accepting posts that you offer, and may well prefer to work for a competitor instead. So care must be taken when using the following approaches:

Notice periods

Courts have rarely been asked to rule on the reasonableness of notice periods set out in employment contracts. Employers are obliged to give departing staff at least the notice laid down in statute for a given length of service, but statute says nothing about requiring employees to give longer periods. It is thus possible, if people will agree when starting a job, to require three or six months' notice from employees. Courts can rule such terms to be unreasonable, but tend not to. In one case, according to Leighton and O'Donnell (1995, p223), it was accepted that an employer was reasonable in requiring one of its managers to give a full year's notice.

Enforcing contracts which contain long notice periods is another matter. Where employees refuse to work their full periods of notice there is usually little point in pursuing the matter through the courts. Except in the case of particularly highly paid employees whose individual contribution is truly substantial, damages are going to be relatively small and may well cost less than the legal fees spent taking the matter to court. There is also the potential problem of a dissatisfied and demotivated worker on your premises who wants to be working somewhere else. It is usually better to let such people go and find a more enthusiastic replacement.

Restrictive covenants

A more promising avenue involves requiring employees to sign restrictive covenants or restraining clauses which can serve to limit the number of alternative job opportunities that are open to them. The purpose of such terms is to prevent employees from damaging your business by taking up a position with a direct competitor or setting up in business themselves in competition with you. However, restrictive covenants are a possibility only where the individuals concerned would be in a position to do definite damage to your business using knowledge gained while in your employ. In other words, the covenant must be in place for a legitimate business reason if it is to be valid in law. One which is overly restrictive or which exists for a reason other than the protection of business is likely to be judged unreasonable. The leading case in this field is *Greer* v *Sketchley* (1979). Here, Mr Greer resigned from his job as a manager in a dry-cleaning business to take up a similar job with a rival firm. He was sued for breach of his restrictive covenant which forbade him from associating with 'any other person, firm or company' engaged in dry-cleaning anywhere in the UK for a period of 12 months following his resignation. He won his case on the grounds that the clause was unreasonable.

Nonetheless, it is possible to require employees to agree to restrictive covenants that are more limited, especially people in senior positions. It is possible, for example, to restrict their right to work for a direct competitor in a particular geographical area or in a specific line of work for 12 months. Had Mr Greer's restrictive covenant related to dry-cleaning businesses in a particular London borough, it may well have been valid. Provided genuine damage could be done to your business as a result of an ex-employee's taking up such a post, you are acting entirely reasonably, as far as the law is concerned. Although the purpose should not be improved staff retention, the effect can nonetheless be a strong disincentive for people to move on in certain circumstances. There will often be a psychological effect even if you would not in fact normally consider suing someone who broke a covenant.

Pay-back clauses

We will look in more detail at pay-back clauses relating to training later on, in Chapter 7. All that is necessary at this stage is to flag up their existence and to define them as requirements on staff to reimburse the employer for any genuine costs of training met prior to a resignation. In principle such approaches are entirely lawful and do in practice act as a deterrent to voluntary resignations in the months during and immediately following participation on a defined training programme.

The other common type of pay-back arrangement concerns maternity pay. Where employers pay higher rates of maternity pay or for longer than is required by the statutory scheme, it is possible for them to do so on condition that the additional sums are repaid should the employee concerned choose not to return to her job following her period of leave. Such arrangements are very effective in practice.

Golden handcuffs

The major types of golden handcuff arrangement are discussed in Chapter 6 in the context of pay. Many have a limited impact because they can be matched so easily by a truly determined competitor who is prepared to pay a little extra to secure the services of one of your employees. However, they can have a psychological effect, dissuading some employees from looking for alternative work for a period. The schemes do not have to be particularly ambitious. The simple payment of a bonus at the end of a defined period of time is all that is required. Provided employees know that they will forfeit this if they leave earlier, it will serve to retain some people at least for a bit longer than they otherwise would have stayed.

Building effective defences

In the tighter labour markets, the poaching of staff can be common and very problematical from the perspective of the employer seeking to retain employees. Sometimes rival employers go on 'poaching raids', deliberately targeting strong performers in other organisations and making them attractive offers to switch jobs. In many cases they use the services of head-hunters as a means of opening up confidential channels of communication with your people. Another scenario involves head-hunters' operating alone, seeking out the more able employees in particular fields, and then acting on their behalf either with or without explicit consent. These types of activity are particularly damaging because they tend to result in the loss of the better performers. They are also infuriating from the point of view of employers on the receiving end because of the way that juicy alternative opportunities are dangled in front of people who are entirely happy in their jobs and would not otherwise even consider moving on.

Alec Reed (2001, p26) suggests that head-hunters should be thought of as resembling heat-seeking missiles in that they are able to target potential candidates very precisely and to do so without creating a great deal of prior noise. The only way to deal with them is therefore to build more effective defence systems. Not only does this make it harder for them to penetrate your organisation, it should also crucially deter them from trying. Like the burglar who stalks a neighbourhood at night, recruiting agents are going to prefer entering premises which offer them the least resistance.

Useful advice on how to develop better defences of this kind is provided by Reed (2001) and also in a fascinating article by Timothy Gardner (2002). Reed describes the activities of an organisation called Anti-Headhunting UK, which specialises in advising companies and training staff in the skills of repelling recruitment agents. Gardner, by contrast, reports the results of an extensive US-based academic study focusing on the responses of companies who are the subject of 'talent raids' by competitors or agents acting on their behalf. These and other publications/websites offer useful suggestions, which include:

- training receptionists and telephonists to spot calls from head-hunters and to avoid giving out any useful information
- guarding lists of internal e-mail numbers as securely as possible – these are highly desirable possessions for head-hunters and rival organisations to get their hands on
- refusing to do business yourself with any head-hunter who you discover has been poaching your staff
- simply asking your rivals to stop 'raiding your talent'

  Gardner (2002) records an instance of one chief executive calling another and requesting that he stopped his people from poaching. It worked. The second chief executive did not know that the poaching raids were going on and did not approve of such approaches.
- entering into pacts with other employers in your industry not to poach one another's staff via direct approaches
- retaliating – if you suffer a 'talent raid', employ the same tactic quite deliberately against the offending competitor
- litigating or threatening litigation – there is scope for head-hunters and poaching organisations to be sued for inducing breach of contract

  In 2002 the City of London broking firm Cantor Fitzgerald took its competitor Icap to court following its successful poaching of three Cantor brokers.

Employer branding exercises

'Employer branding' is a term that has entered the human resource management vocabulary in recent years and that represents an attractive idea. Essentially, it is about applying the tools and techniques of consumer branding to the employment relationship. In the main it is an activity which serves to boost an organisation's recruitment capabilities, but it can also play a role in reducing staff turnover. This occurs because one outcome of an employer branding exercise should be a greater appreciation of the organisation on the part of the people who work for it.

Developing a strong and recognisable employer brand involves taking the same basic steps as are carried out when building product market brands. The aim is to develop an association in the minds of existing and potential employees between the experience of working for your organisation and certain positive values or psychological responses. Ultimately, it is a public relations type of exercise, the result of which is to make people feel more positively about your organisation as an employer and more appreciative of what it offers vis-à-vis other employers. Just as customers become loyal to their preferred consumer brands, the idea is that employees can be encouraged to stay loyal to an employer brand.

A common misconception is the idea that an employer brand can be built simply through the construction of advertising images and messages. This is not the case. As in the consumer field, you can say what you like about a product, but this will not help to build it as a brand if the claims made are untrue. Indeed, making false claims is often shown to have a negative effect because it generates cynicism and mistrust on the part of consumers. So the starting-point must be the actual, living experience of working in your organisation. Perceived reality has to form the basis of a successful employer branding exercise. The key is to find out:

□ what your employees like about their experience working for you

□ what differentiates you as an employer from your labour market competitors.

Armed with this information you can move on to the second stage, which involves finding language and images that are appropriate for broadcasting these messages. Ideally, you want to come up with certain key 'value propositions' which can be articulated repeatedly using different platforms or types of media. Every opportunity available should be taken to help build your brand. Fields (2001, pp101–102) describes four basic types of employer brand identified by the McKinsey consulting group. These are by no means the only possibilities, but they give a good idea about the type of brand values that can be identified and grown:

□ prestige (ie we have a great reputation in our business –

working for us will enhance your long-term career opportunities)

□ cause (ie we undertake work which is meaningful and socially important – working for us will provide you with the opportunity to help humankind)

□ high risk/big potential (ie we are a small but growing organisation – working for us will enable you to grow alongside us to reap big long-term rewards)

□ work–life balance (ie we will provide you with a good job, but also allow you plenty of time to spend doing other things).

Running focus groups with employees and job applicants is probably the best way of working out which of these, or other possible brand propositions, best matches your organisation. It is then possible to start finding the most effective ways of putting the message over to your staff.

6 PAY AND BENEFITS

Common sense tells us that the link between pay and staff turnover is both clear and significant. Most people, we suppose, work in order to earn money. Payment considerations must therefore play a major role in guiding their decision-making about which employer to work for. It follows that low-paying employers will suffer most from staff shortages. People will avoid working for them if they can, and will quit to take up better-paying positions at the earliest opportunity. These are the basic laws of supply and demand in a material world. It is therefore assumed that staff turnover is highest where pay is lowest, and that a sure-fire way to retain staff for longer is to pay above the market rate.

This is a commonly held view – but it is not an accurate one. In practice, things are a great deal more complicated. There is plenty of evidence to suggest that employers can enjoy high rates of retention among their staff without paying particularly well. Conversely, we know that high-paying employers can by no means guarantee the long-term commitment of their employees. Raising pay rates will not therefore *necessarily* bring about reduced levels of turnover. In some situations there will be a marked effect, but in others, especially where there are other sources of discontent, there will be no impact at all.

However, that does not mean that pay policy more generally cannot play a role in improving your staff-retention record. The reconfiguration of reward packages can be important, as can the development of a valued benefits package. A great deal can be done in these areas, but making them work is as much about perceptive and creative management as it is about increasing rates of pay.

In this chapter we explore all these issues, outlining the relevant research evidence and pointing to a range of reward strategies which have the potential to reduce the number of voluntary departures.

The major recommendations are:

☐ Focus activity on those staff groups who you know are the most likely to leave in order to secure higher base pay.

☐ Always try to ensure that payment systems are perceived by your staff to operate equitably.

☐ Wherever possible look for ways of making the total reward package you offer hard for your labour market competitors to replicate.

Debates about pay and employee turnover

There is a big divide in the academic literature between writers who see remuneration as central to an organisation's ability to retain staff and those who downplay its importance vis-à-vis other areas of management practice. It is thus impossible to reach firm conclusions. As a rule, the role of pay is stressed by economists and researchers whose focus is on pay policy, its importance being under-emphasised by occupational psychologists and by those whose research concentrates on employee retention in more general terms. The messages that emerge are thus very divergent – as is illustrated by the following quotations:

> External equity refers to setting wage rates for jobs that correspond to those prevailing in external markets – markets from which the employer hires. An employer that ignores the external market will not survive for long.

> Wallace and Fay (1988, p49)

> These are minimum requirements to attract and retain people, yet they are fundamental in that if the organisation is unable to attract and retain people, all other human resource activities are meaningless.

> Hills *et al* (1994, p60)

Research suggests that, by and large, rewards succeed at securing one thing only: temporary compliance. When it comes to producing lasting change in attitudes or behaviour, however, rewards like punishment are strikingly ineffective ... They do not create an enduring *commitment* to any value or action.

Kohn (1993, p55)

As far as they [graduate employees] are concerned, while challenging work will compensate for pay, pay will never compensate for having to do boring, unstimulating work.

Sturges and Guest (1999, p19)

Research evidence on this issue is of three major types. First there are studies carried out over decades on human motivation, job satisfaction and the factors that influence employee decision-making at work generally. These tend to suggest that payment is a good deal less powerful as a positive motivator than intrinsic rewards (ie the 'pleasures' people gain from doing the job itself). The conclusion reached is that raising pay rates buys only short-term job satisfaction. If there are underlying problems causing unhappiness among employees, these will not be 'bought off' in most cases. In terms of employee turnover and retention this suggests the following:

☐ Employees who are dissatisfied and minded to look for another job will only be deterred from doing so in the short term if they are given a pay rise.
☐ Employees who are otherwise happy in their jobs are unlikely to leave purely in order to secure a higher hourly rate.

However, this same body of research points out that while pay rarely motivates positively, its capacity to demotivate is substantial. Herzberg (1966) famously described pay, along with other extrinsic rewards, as a 'hygiene factor'. It is something that people tend only to act upon if it is absent – like the cleanliness of a house. In practical management terms this suggests that the capacity of pay to act as a push factor in employee turnover terms is a great deal more powerful than its capacity to work as a pull factor. It is therefore helpful to see these as two separate types of situation. In the first, employees are unhappy either with the level of pay they are receiving or with the distribution of rewards in the organisation. The issue of what other employers are paying is a second-order consideration. Whatever the market rate, the dissatisfaction is likely to lead to voluntary departures. The second situation is one in which employees are content with their rate of pay in terms of the living standard it buys, and regard it as being broadly 'fair' vis-à-vis co-workers, but in which a higher rate could be secured by moving jobs. Voluntary turnover, according to the research evidence, is a good deal less likely to occur where such conditions apply.

The second type of evidence derives from studies which look at turnover rates across industries, seeking patterns that link high pay with low turnover and vice versa. Here the evidence seems to point both ways. Mobley (1982) reported that most US studies found only weak correlations between pay and voluntary resignations, but this contention has been questioned by other researchers (Hom and Griffeth, 1995, p222). Gustman and Steinmeier (1995) studied three separate large American data sets looking for a relationship between pension coverage and employee turnover. They found that turnover in non-pensionable jobs was three to six times higher than in pensionable jobs, but that this was almost entirely explained by the higher levels of base pay that were provided by companies alongside the pension. Another study, looking at the reasons for voluntary employee turnover in Singapore (Khatri *et al*, 2001, pp68–69), concluded that income levels influenced turnover rates in two industries studied (food and shipping), but that there was no observable relationship in a third (retail).

The third source of evidence comes from surveys which ask employees about why they have left or why they intend to leave their jobs. Some of these suggest that pay is a reasonably important factor, though by no means able to account for a majority of voluntary departures. Studies based on exit interview or exit survey data often reach this conclusion, but as was shown in Chapter 4, considerable caution has to be exercised in the interpretation of such results. Employees commonly seem to prefer to give 'pay' as their reason for leaving even when other factors are of greater salience.

The biggest UK surveys are those carried out regularly on behalf of the government and published in *Labour Market Trends*. Here employees are asked two separate questions:

☐ Are you currently looking for another job?
☐ What is your main reason for looking for another job?

The data collected persistently shows that over 20 per cent of women and nearly 30 per cent of men cite 'pay unsatisfactory in present job' as their main reason (*Labour Market Trends*, 2001b). This confirms the importance of dissatisfaction with pay as a cause of turnover but does not help to establish whether or not people tend to leave purely to secure higher pay. Moreover, this data does not tell us whether the people looking for a new job actually found one, and whether or not they did ultimately leave for a higher rate of pay.

Other survey-based studies point to a different conclusion. Bevan *et al* (1997, p25), for example, found that people leaving jobs only rarely gave dissatisfaction with pay as their main reason and that attitude surveys found relatively little difference in terms of pay satisfaction between people who leave and colleagues who stay in the same organisation. My own research, carried out with colleagues at Manchester Metropolitan University, has led me to reach the same conclusion. In 2001 we interviewed 80 people from three professions (retail, engineering, and professional services) in depth about the reasons for their last job move. We found only three people who stated that the main reason for their move was to secure a higher rate of pay. In fact, we found several more examples of people taking a pay cut when they switched jobs. (Further findings from these case studies are described in Part 3.)

It is difficult to reach firm conclusions about these issues because the research evidence is both inconclusive and relatively scanty. However, it is possible to advance a number of conclusions based on such evidence as has been published. These provide the assumptions on which the rest of this chapter builds.

Firstly, it is reasonable to assert that dissatisfaction with payment arrangements is a major potential cause of staff turnover. In some cases this may originate in a sense of injustice about pay levels vis-à-vis those being paid by other employers – but it is more likely to relate to perceptions of unfairness about internal distribution of rewards between people employed in the same workplace. In such situations it is not the *level* of pay *per se* which is the source of the discontent but the way that one person is paid more than another for doing work that is perceived to be equally valuable. Ultimately, it is far more irritating to discover that the person sitting at the next desk is paid more than you than it is to find out that an equivalent employee in another firm is paid more.

Linked to this are perceptions about 'effort reward bargains'. Here too dissatisfaction derives not from the rate of pay but from the amount and type of work put in to secure it. Employees may be perfectly happy working for a set rate of pay (however much rival firms are paying) provided they perceive that it is a broadly just reward for the amount of effort they expend. The problem comes when the employer demands more in terms of hours, work intensity or responsibility while not offering simultaneous compensation by way of a pay rise. The result is a sense of injustice and an increased likelihood of a voluntary departure.

Secondly, if rather more tentatively, it is fair to assert that some groups of employees are more likely to resign in order to secure a higher rate of pay than others. The research evidence suggests that most people (probably 75 per cent or so) are unlikely to quit a job in which they are broadly happy purely in order to secure a higher rate of pay. They only leave or think about leaving when some other matter intervenes which serves to reduce their job satisfaction (eg a reorganisation, new responsibilities, growing boredom, personality clashes, etc). But this leaves a sizeable minority who are more money-oriented and will leave jobs voluntarily mainly to enhance the size of their pay packets. From a management point of view this matters because it means that raising pay rates can potentially increase retention rates among these groups – even where it will have less effect for the majority. Moreover, where the pay-focused people are concentrated in certain types of work, relevant managers are likely to find that a majority of *their* employees fall into this category. For these organisations, therefore, paying at or above market rates is a crucial ingredient of any policy aimed at improving retention records.

In my view the groups most likely to fall into this category are:

□ *the insulted* – workers who are very poorly paid vis-à-vis contemporaries in equivalent professions

   Several groups of public sector workers fall into this category (teachers, nurses, midwives, social workers, prison officers, etc) all of whom are paid well below the levels enjoyed by many of their friends and relatives in other lines of work. This situation tends to breed dissatisfaction with pay rates and creates a situation in which people will leave, even though happy with other aspects of their jobs, simply in order to secure more money.

□ *needs-musters* – the lowest-paid workers of all (mostly employed in agriculture and the private services sectors)

   These are people who cannot afford the luxury of being able to opt for a job which they enjoy over one which pays more. In order to make ends meet, even if it means taking up less satisfying employment, they are prepared to move as a means of securing a higher hourly rate. More-highly paid people can suddenly find themselves propelled into this category by some event that increases their need for money. Examples are the birth of a child and a steep rise in mortgage rates.

□ *yawners* – workers employed in jobs which give little or no job satisfaction

   Tedious work falls into this category (eg some clerical or call-centre roles, assembly-line work, etc) as does work which is stressful or unpleasant in a significant way (eg telesales, hard manual labour, etc). Here, especially where internal career development opportunities are few and far between, people might as well move to gain some extra cash. Why not? There is no other reason for working.

□ *get-rich-quickers* – people employed in relatively well-paid jobs that are typically entered because of the high rates of pay they provide

We are talking here about professions which attract people whose prime motivation in choosing their line of work is the making of money. The workers concerned are often intelligent and well-qualified, but are not doing their jobs because it gives them much personal satisfaction. Some will be hoping to make sufficient money early in their careers to allow them to downshift in their forties or even retire completely. Some high-pressured roles in the City of London attract these types, as do many IT jobs. If these people are denied the opportunity to maximise their earnings, they will move on.

☐ *cash-lovers* – workers who enjoy the process of making money for its own sake and who are in jobs which permit them to achieve this aim

I am thinking here about people who derive real personal satisfaction from enhancing earnings on a day-to-day basis, not because they need the money for any particular purpose but just because they are motivated by their ability to acquire more of it. The major examples would be sales staff and financial dealers whose skills lie in clinching deals and who are happy to be rewarded through the payment of commission. Such people often end up running their own businesses and speculating on their own account, but where they remain employed it stands to reason that pay is central for them. They will readily quit in order to gain bigger earning opportunities.

☐ *high-flyers* – genuine high-flyers, people in all fields who are outstanding at what they do, and know it

Such individuals tend to have a keen sense of their own worth to an organisation and naturally wish to secure a fair return for their individual contribution. Crucially, they also tend to be well-known in their industries and are hence courted by a range of hopeful employers. We can describe these people as belonging to a 'head-hunted class'. They move a great deal, despite being satisfied with their jobs, because they have the opportunity to do so and because they are in a position to negotiate their own 'personal terms'.

The final point to make in this section is to distinguish between current pay and career earnings/income. In this chapter we are focusing on the interaction between current rates of pay and employee retention, not on other causes of quitting which have an economic dimension. People often leave jobs for reasons which are money-related but which do not concern the desire to earn a higher hourly rate or a better annual salary in the next job. The major example is a job switch that occurs for career development purposes, an aim of which is to help secure longer-term earning potential. Alternatively, some departures derive from a desire to move to an area of the country where housing is cheaper or to a job which permits less income to be spent on childcare arrangements. In each case the motivation to leave has an economic dimension but does not derive from a desire to enhance today's take-home pay. These other types of departures are important for managers to think about, but are dealt with in later chapters. Our focus here is solely on pay and benefits in the sense of the 'here and now'.

The importance of fair dealing

The research evidence strongly suggests that dissatisfaction with payment arrangements in an organisation is a bigger cause of employee turnover than the simple desire to earn more money. The amount of pay that is given to individual employees is seen by them as a powerful indicator of their individual worth to the organisation. It can also be a significant status symbol and acts as an important form of tit-for-tat compensation when burdens are shouldered by particular employees. For the majority of people these are far more salient issues and have greater capacity to affect their behaviour than concerns about the purchasing power of their pay packets. Perceptions of unfairness or injustice in payment matters are thus the big turnover drivers when it comes to reward policy. Eliminating these, as far as it is possible to, must therefore be a priority for organisations wishing to improve their staff-retention records.

In my view this is one of the main explanations for why staff turnover rates are lowest in those public sector organisations that are widely considered to pay poorly vis-à-vis comparable roles in the private sector (eg NHS workers, teachers, police, civil servants, etc). They may pay you badly for the work that you do, but they have in place payment systems that are transparent and rational, and that by and large operate fairly. People know what each other earns in the public sector and are clear about the rationale that underlies decisions about who is paid what. The systems are cumbersome and bureaucratic, making the organisations concerned slow to embrace change, but they have the advantage of acting to reduce avoidable turnover.

Conversely, in most private sector organisations, particularly for the more highly skilled jobs in non-union firms, the opposite situation tends to prevail. Pay levels are individually negotiated and then kept secret. You are paid what your manager thinks you are worth and can afford to pay you. A huge amount thus hinges on what you ask for on joining the organisation and can persuade the organisation to pay you subsequently. External market rates have to play a greater role when such approaches are used than concerns about internal differentials. Hence in many private sector organisations a situation is created in which people working together and undertaking roles of broadly similar value are paid differently. The result is high turnover rates, despite relatively high rates of pay.

From a management perspective the non-union, private sector approach makes perfect, rational sense. It means that people are paid a market rate and are rewarded for their individual contribution. In many cases individual performance-related pay systems are used either as means of determining base pay increases or annual bonus payments. While formal systems are becoming more common, in the majority of workplaces rather informal merit-based systems operate which involve pay increases (or upgrades) being awarded primarily on the basis of supervisor judgement. The great problem with these kinds of approach is that while they may be set up to look objective and scrupulously fair, it is common for them to work rather differently in practice – or at least to be perceived to operate unfairly from the employee's point of view. There are two major reasons for this:

☐ When formally rating their employees' performance, managers tend to be swayed by a range of subjective factors (eg who they personally like most, recent events, concerns about how the employee will react to the rating). As a result, payment arrangements are perceived by employees to lack objectivity.

☐ Employers are naturally inclined to pay as little as they can get away with paying. As a result, a situation is created in which people doing the same jobs, or undertaking similar roles, are paid different amounts of money. Typically, this occurs simply because Employee A had to be offered more than Employee B when he or she started in order to secure his or her services. A great deal thus hinges on what was asked for at interview, what was being paid in a previous job, and the timing of the appointment. Employee A may have been unemployed prior to joining or looking for a job in a recession, while Employee B was poached from a competitor at a time when the labour market was tight. The difference in pay then becomes permanent as each subsequent rise is in addition to the original starting salary.

These kind of approaches are sustainable where pay levels are kept confidential. If nobody knows exactly what his or her colleagues are getting, no sense of injustice can develop. The problem is that pay levels rarely do stay confidential in practice. People want to know and thus find ways of finding out what their colleagues are paid. Where the differences are more (or indeed less) marked than they think they ought to be, the result can be dissatisfaction or a seething sense of injustice. Finding out about how your pay measures up to that of your colleagues can even be sufficiently 'shocking' (using the terminology described in Chapter 4) to set in motion the process which leads to a resignation. Worse still are situations in which false information about what individuals are paid gets spread around by means of a rumour-mill. Where pay is kept confidential this happens a great deal, misinformation frequently originating from the mouths of employees who think that their status will be enhanced among colleagues if they are believed to be earning more than they are.

Employees who know that they are being paid less than a colleague who is engaged in a similar role are not the only people for whom payment arrangements are perceived as unfair. Severe dissatisfaction can also result from a situation in which employees consider differentials to be too small. This also results from informality and subjectivity in payment arrangements. Situations therefore arise in which a supervisor is paid only a tiny amount more than her subordinates or where an employee of many years' service who carries major responsibilities is paid the same as younger, more recent appointees who he is responsible for training. Here the problem is one in which a genuine individual contribution is not being sufficiently recognised in the relative remuneration that is being paid.

In terms of improving staff retention it is most important that managers do not underplay the significance of these kinds of issues by dismissing them as trivial. From a management perspective things tend to look a great deal more rational, objective and fair than they do from the employee perspective. You may well have a good, clear rationale in your mind to explain and justify what each of your employees is paid and what their rise is going to be in the coming year. But this is an irrelevance when it comes to reducing dissatisfaction and turnover levels among your staff. What matters is that *they* perceive the payment arrangements to be fair. It is my contention that this is very difficult indeed to achieve where the systems used are closed and informal.

At base, the problem that all organisations inevitably face is a difference of opinion about the worth of individual contributions. Most employees genuinely believe that they:

□ are above-average performers
□ contribute as much as, if not more than, their colleagues
□ deserve to be recognised accordingly.

This is particularly true of employees who are seen by their managers as good, solid, reliable, but also unexceptional performers. Dissatisfaction thus occurs whenever the employees are told or reminded of the fact that their managers consider their contribution to be only average. Pay rates and pay rises are the most powerful ways that an organisation communicates these kinds of judgement. Hence their importance as a potential driver of staff turnover among the groups of staff on whom organisations rely (ie solid, reliable performers).

For those who accept the main thrust of this analysis there are two types of response to choose from. The first involves sticking with informal and flexible payment arrangements but bending over backwards in an attempt to ensure that pay levels are kept confidential. I know of several employers who go to quite extreme lengths in an attempt to achieve this, the imperative being reinforced by a knowledge that the organisations are vulnerable to equal-pay claims. Some go as far as to declare revealing pay information to be a disciplinary offence, punishable with a written warning. This seems to me to be an absurd approach to take, for two reasons:

□ because it is very difficult to track down the individual who is the source of a rumour, whatever it is about

□ because as a reason for dismissing someone, the fact that they told someone how much they were paid stands no chance of stacking up in an employment tribunal.

The alternative approach is to move some way down the road traditionally taken by public sector organisations. This has disadvantages as well as advantages, but should help to reduce staff turnover where it is being fuelled by perceptions of injustice about pay. The aim is to stop rumour-mills churning and to engineer a situation in which people are not 'shocked' when they find out what a colleague is being paid. The second requirement is to adopt pay determination methods that are both objective and seen to be objective. This requires the use of some kind of job evaluation system (where roles are properly graded according to an objective assessment of their worth to the organisation) together with a performance-based element which operates according to fair and objective criteria. Basing performance appraisals on the achievement/non-achievement of agreed objectives is a great deal more likely to fit the bill than evaluation based on supervisor ratings alone. Including an element of 360-degree appraisal also has a role to play.

Finally, there is a need, as far as practicable, to involve employees in the design and evolution of the payment systems that are used. This seems to me to be common sense, but is regarded as beyond the pale by many managers. Why not ask your employees how fairly they perceive your payment systems to operate, and what improvements could be made? Why not involve them in determining the criteria that are used to award pay rises or to set a basic pay rate for each major job group in the organisation? Not only will these approaches help to reduce turnover, they should also enhance morale and commitment more generally, and lead to better organisational performance.

Focusing on the market where it matters

On pages 99–100, six categories of employees were identified who, it was argued, were prepared to move jobs solely in search of a higher wage. The evidence suggests that these people form a minority of the workforce – but that does not mean that they can be ignored when drawing up a retention strategy. They include within their number some of the most able people (high-flyers) whose retention is particularly desirable because they have the capacity, as individuals, to make a real difference to the success of an organisation. In their case, individually negotiated packages that take account of their personal market-worth have to be created. More challenging are the other five categories identified, because they are frequently concentrated in particular professional groups and may well form a substantial block within the workforce. When turnover is too high among these groups, and where they have ready access to alternative employment, a distinct strategy must be developed which takes account of their sensitivity to market rates.

In theory, managing such situations is straightforward. The starting-point is to find out exactly what your organisation's major labour market competitors are paying and how the packages they are offering are made up. It is then a question of tracking developments over time and ensuring, as far as is affordable, that you match improvements so as to maintain your organisation's competitive position. Several alternative approaches are available to help you track competitor pay rates. The major tools are:

☐ published data (surveys published in *Labour Market Trends* and in IRS and IDS publications)

☐ participating in/purchasing commercial salary surveys

☐ commissioning a bespoke salary survey from a consultant

☐ setting up or joining a salary club

☐ informal approaches (eg looking at job ads, taking advice from recruitment agents, asking new employees who have joined from other organisations).

The next stages are harder and more involved. First, of course, there is a need to persuade the finance function that a pay rise is justified. This requires clear and unequivocal evidence that the pay package is uncompetitive, that people are leaving for this reason, and that matching the rates paid by competitors would substantially reduce turnover rates among the group/groups in question. The other requirement is, of course, a strong business case. You need to be able to show, beyond doubt, that the current costs absorbed as a result of staff turnover are greater than those associated with the proposed pay rise. The methods for costing turnover set out in Chapter 3 can be used to make this case.

If the business case can be sustained and a pay rise is decided upon, there are then implementation issues to handle. The major problem is the way that a pay rise awarded to a particular high-turnover group can affect or displace or even demolish established differentials in the organisation. Members of other staff groups which also suffer from high turnover but which are not as pay-sensitive are likely to object. Unless handled carefully it is all too easy to create the kind of dissatisfaction rooted in a sense of injustice that was noted above. The result is lower turnover in the group which is paid more, but higher turnover among other groups. At the end of the day there is no way round this issue. All that can be done is to explain the decision as honestly and openly as possible, and to phase in the pay increases at an appropriate time. It is also possible to use other (ie non-pay) human resource management interventions to reduce the extent that the unrewarded groups experience dissatisfaction. Examples of such approaches follow in Chapters 7 to 10.

The other implementation issue to consider is the possibility of equal-value claims being referred to an employment tribunal. In practice, cases of this kind are more often threatened than followed through to a hearing, but a professional manager will want to ensure that no basis is given for a case to succeed. It is really just a question of ensuring that any decision taken was based on an objective analysis of the labour market and the organisation's need to compete for staff. In other words, it is necessary to be able to satisfy a tribunal that the pay rise was clearly and unequivocally for reasons that had nothing to do with gender *and* that the changes were genuinely necessary for business reasons. The more that is written down in the form of reports to management and statistical data the better.

If alternatively it is decided that the required pay rise cannot be afforded, then it is necessary to take what other available steps can be adopted to reduce the turnover rate. This will involve working much harder at identifying and acting to dispel other major potential sources of dissatisfaction among the group concerned.

FOLLOWING THE MARKET

Where it becomes impossible to pay the market rate it remains possible for employers to attract and retain sufficient staff of the right calibre. This is achieved by paying below the market rate (following or lagging the market), while working a great deal harder in other areas to create a workplace which people are reluctant to leave. This is by no means an easy option, but it can be achieved with creative and effective managers who know how to motivate their staff and are given the opportunity to do so.

The approach involves taking a 'total reward perspective', which involves thinking about 'reward' in the widest sense rather than simply as money in the pocket. It recognises that people often value all kinds of things about their work in addition to the pay that they receive. It follows that many will happily 'trade in' a certain amount of potential pay in order to secure the other things that they value. The employers that retain people most effectively, according to this view, are not those who pay most but those who offer the highest level of 'total reward'. The following are some features of working life which people value and can thus aid retention where pay rises are not affordable:

☐ job security
☐ flexible working arrangements
☐ benefits such as free car-parking or staff discounts
☐ short commuter-journeys to work
☐ work that is satisfying or meaningful
☐ a pleasant working environment
☐ career development opportunities
☐ the opportunity to work for a respected 'big name' employer
☐ a respectful and considerate boss.

If you can *genuinely* offer several of these, you will probably find that you are able to retain people without the need to pay at or above the market rate.

Golden handcuffs

The third way in which pay is often believed to have a positive effect on employee retention is through the use of systems which, one way or another, reward people for remaining employed in the one organisation for a long time. There are four major approaches used:

☐ bonus systems that pay out after a set period of time (eg after five years' service)
☐ seniority payment systems which pay incremental increases after each year of service has been completed
☐ share option schemes of various kinds which restrict the purchase or sale of shares for a specific period
☐ final salary pension schemes (the design of which benefits those who remain employed for longest).

All of these systems are designed to meet several organisational objectives, but in each case the evidence suggests that employee retention is an important one.

Evidence on the actual (as opposed to the theoretical) link between pensions and staff retention is unclear (Taylor, 2000). On the one hand there is data which strongly suggests that pension scheme membership is associated with relatively low staff turnover, but on the other there is good reason to doubt the applicability of these findings (which are mainly US-based) to the contemporary UK environment. A major aim of regulatory reform in recent years has been to make it harder for employers to use their pension schemes as a staff-retention tool – an aim that appears to have met with considerable success. Current shifts away from final salary provision, despite tight labour market conditions, suggest strongly that employers no longer see their pension schemes as fulfilling a useful retentive function. In any case there has long been a question-mark over the extent to which the majority of UK employees understand, let alone appreciate, the true value of their final salary schemes. A prerequisite for their use as a tool of retention is thus an ongoing and effective communication exercise.

Share schemes have generally received a positive press from researchers working within a management frame of reference. They appear to be liked by employees and can encourage perceptions of participation where the allocation is sufficiently substantial (Pendleton *et al*, 1998). There is also evidence to suggest that a key objective of such schemes is staff retention (Pendleton, 2000, p348) and that an effect of their introduction is reduced turnover (Hyman, 2000, p188). However, as with pensions, it is difficult to isolate the effect of a share scheme which is intended to act as a long-term incentive. There is a plausible case for arguing that an employer who offers share options or shares to his or her employees is one who is unusually focused on human resources. The correlation that is observed could thus be between low turnover and good employment practices generally rather than being specifically related to a share scheme.

The theoretical case for a link between long-term incentives and retention is strong, making it easy to assume that most employees will delay departure from an employment in order to avoid missing out on a lump sum payment due at a specific future date. This is particularly true of senior managers (the major beneficiaries of such schemes) who tend to have both a good knowledge of their remuneration packages and a keen sense of their own worth.

It is also probable that there is a retentive effect in the case of some other people, particularly in the case of share options and other long-term incentives which are anticipated to yield a substantial return. Older people with substantial pensionable service are the only group who tend to remain employed simply so as to maximise their pension. In other cases where the likely reward is perceived to be relatively modest or uncertain, the effect will be marginal. People will not generally stay in jobs they find boring, unfulfilling or unpleasant just to secure a limited sum. The employer has more to gain by improving the working experience and by providing developmental opportunities than by seeking to buy long-term commitment with golden handcuff arrangements.

Moreover, as has been pointed out by Cappelli (2000) as well as others, pay is the element of an employment package that is most readily copied by labour market competitors. When market conditions are tight (ie when staff retention really matters) employers are both willing and able to 'unlock' any golden handcuffs by making commensurate financial offers to potential employees. The true extent to which such schemes actually serve to retain people *who would otherwise seek an alternative job* is thus open to question.

In terms of remuneration policy as a whole there is a good case for employers to focus on trying to develop a package that is hard for competitors to replicate (ie golden handcuffs which are genuinely hard to unlock). The key requirements are:

- to design a pay and benefits package that is distinct from those offered by other employers
- to ensure that the benefits offered are genuinely appreciated by employees
- to minimise the cost of the package.

There is most mileage in the kind of flexible cafeteria-style systems that have become common in the USA in the past decade. Their drawback is administrative complexity, which carries an associated cost, but in other respects they have a great deal to offer employers and employees. The principle underpinning flexible benefits is choice for individual employees over how their own pay packet is made up. There is usually a core package which everyone receives (eg base pay plus some pension plus some holiday), but beyond this, flexibility is permitted. Staff can thus trade base pay for other benefits such as more pension, health insurance, more holiday, company cars, staff discounts, or any other benefit that is offered and personally valued. User-friendly IT systems are now widely available to help with the costing and administration of flexible schemes, but it is actually very straightforward to design a simple scheme without the need for substantial investment. The simplest approach involves permitting employees a choice of half a dozen or so 'benefits menus' which are offered as tailored packages rather in the manner of banquets served in Chinese restaurants. Staff can be consulted about their preferences, and different menus drawn up accordingly. The following would be typical examples:

- the existing standard package for people who do not want to change
- a menu designed primarily for school-leavers and new graduates in their first years of full-time employment
- a menu designed mainly for people with young families
- a menu designed mainly for people in their late forties and fifties with long service
- a menu designed manly for people who enter the organisation for the first time late on in their careers.

Each menu will have the same overall value in financial terms, but the balance is made up differently. You would expect base pay to form the largest part in the package for people with young families, being replaced with development opportunities in the package for school-leavers and graduates, and a greater emphasis on the pension element in the package for the veterans in their forties and fifties. Employees can then be given the opportunity, perhaps every two years or so, to switch menus if they wish to.

The other great advantage of flexible benefits systems is their capacity to defuse potential harmonisation problems when organisations merge, take one another over or transfer staff across on different terms and conditions. Traditionally, organisations have been faced with two options in such circumstances:

- □ to continue employing staff doing the same work on different sets of terms and conditions
- □ to push everyone into accepting a standard package.

Both of these approaches are problematic, and both can readily lead to serious irritation on the part of employees who perceive that they have been treated unfairly. Flexible benefits systems provide a third option which is more complex, but is also more satisfactory from an employee perspective.

7 TRAINING, DEVELOPMENT AND CAREER MANAGEMENT

In this chapter we turn to a topic which is much studied but is rarely given the attention it deserves in work which focuses on employee retention. The urge to develop ourselves professionally and personally is very strong. When we get the opportunity to do so in our work our satisfaction is increased. By contrast, the experience of being denied such opportunities is highly frustrating and often leads to severe job dissatisfaction. Organisations which fail, over a period of time, to go some way in accommodating their employees' career aspirations will find that they lose people to others who are better able to do so. In the six case studies which are presented in Part 3, it is interesting to note that inadequate employee development opportunities is the one factor common to all of the professional groups when it comes to identifying major reasons for leaving.

Although the material discussed here is of general relevance to all employers, we focus primarily in this chapter on professionally qualified workers and on the more skilled types of jobs. This is because it is these people who are most concerned about their ongoing development and who tend to have the clearest vision of what they want to end up doing in the longer term. Three key topics are assessed and some conclusions reached about each:

□ debates about the link between formal training and staff retention
□ the significance of career structures within organisations
□ approaches to effective professional and personal development at work.

Many of the ideas I present here are derived from 'good practice' or 'best practice' thinking about the employment relationship. At base, like many of those assessed throughout the book, they have been minted by those who believe that good HR management involves seeking to become 'an employer of choice'. While it is true that employers who gain such a reputation are likely to retain people more effectively than their rivals, it does not follow that employers with more limited resources cannot also improve their retention rates by adopting employee-focused thinking. At the end of the day, all that is required to reduce the likelihood of voluntary departures is to provide a deal that is perceived by your employees as altogether better than any offered by your labour market competitors. Best practice is thus not necessarily a requirement. You just have to do things a bit better than other organisations who are competing in the same staff pool as you are. This is as true of training and development as it is of all the other types of initative outlined in this book.

Training issues

One of the most interesting debates in the field of employee retention relates to the impact of training on the propensity of staff to quit. Two entirely logical – but wholly contradictory – points of view are often put when this issue is discussed:

□ You can argue that investment in training for employees is essential if you want to encourage them to stay. A failure to train, or at least to offer training opportunities, will lead career-minded people to start looking for an alternative employer who will provide training.

□ You can argue that providing employees with training makes them more likely to leave because it provides them with skills that are sought by other employers. It opens up opportunities for departures which were not available to the employees concerned before they received the training.

The second point of view is one that is considered not 'politically correct' for forward-looking, modern managers to hold, but it cannot simply be dismissed for this reason. There is a genuine problem here. Training, especially training provided externally, can be very costly. The fees charged by colleges and consultants can be high, and there are also lost opportunity costs to be taken into account while employees are away from the coal-face receiving their training. This cannot represent a good investment from the employer's point of view if it makes staff more employable and more likely to be poached by rival employers. Why spend good money opening up opportunities for people to move?

Views like these are widely held and are not without foundation. I can think of numerous examples of students I have taught on MBA, CIPD, MA and MSc programmes over the past five years who have been sponsored by their employers, and who have subsequently used the qualification (or the fact that they are in the process of gaining it) as a means of securing another job.

For most this is not their intention when they start their studies, but it occurs nevertheless. In some cases they hear about alternative jobs from other course members or because opportunities are drawn to their attention by tutors. In others, the experience of undertaking the course opens up new horizons and makes them less satisfied with their more mundane current roles. A third group make it pretty obvious from their interviews onwards that their primary motivation in coming on the course is the opportunity it will give them to leave a job that they do not like. These people would in all likelihood leave their current employment anyway, but in the meantime they make use of their employer's willingness to pay for their studies as a means of helping them on their way.

We cannot therefore simply refuse to accept the validity of the argument against investment in training. But it is possible that an enhanced propensity to quit is a relatively uncommon response on the part of employees in receipt of employer-sponsored training. It happens, but in many more cases the investment is paid back by employees' staying for longer (and operating more effectively) than would have been the case had the training opportunity been denied. Fortunately, we have some robust research evidence on this question which suggests that much depends on the circumstances and the type of training that is provided.

Greenhalgh and Mavrotas (1996) make the following points in reporting UK-based research:

- A study by Wadsworth published in 1989 using Labour Force Survey data found no evidence of a link between training and job mobility.
- Dolton and Kidd's (1991) study of graduates found evidence to suggest that training reduces job mobility provided it does not result in the achievement of 'generally recognised' qualifications.
- Elias (1994) found that training reduced female job mobility somewhat, but had no significant impact on turnover among men.
- Greenhalgh and Mavrotas (1996), drawing on data from the 1980s, found that younger men had a higher propensity to quit after receiving training (more so than women). However, this effect was not observed in the public sector where mobility remained low despite a high level of training. They also found higher incidence of turnover in smaller firms than in larger ones.

More recently, Green *et al* (2000) in another large-scale study found that overall the effect of training on the propensity to leave was neutral, but that the type of training made a big difference. Their research was questionnaire-based and involved asking over 1,500 employees about their perceptions. Some 19 per cent of their respondents stated that receiving training was 'more likely to make them actively look for another job', while 18 per cent said that it was less likely to. The rest, comprising the substantial majority, saw training provision as making no difference to their interest in leaving. The key findings were:

- Training paid for by the employer appears to reduce the desire to quit.
- Training paid for by the government or the employees themselves tends to raise job mobility.
- Firm-specific training is associated with relatively low levels of turnover.
- Training that results in the acquisition of transferable skills is more likely to lead to turnover.

This body of research enables us to reach a number of conclusions. First, it seems clear that a distinction has to be made between training that relates to activity which is particular to the organisation and training that results in the employee's gaining skills or knowledge which are sought by competing organisations. The former, as far as it has any major effect, appears to increase the likelihood that an employee will stay rather than leave. We are talking here principally about training that is designed and delivered in-house or that is developed by consultants to meet specific organisational needs. Providing employees with the opportunity to undergo such courses will not – all things being equal – increase the chances that they will leave. Instead, it acts as an effective means of communicating to staff that they are valued and that the organisation wishes to invest in their development. Because it does not result in the award of any qualification that is 'generally recognised', such training does not hugely enhance employees' ability to secure work elsewhere.

A rather different picture emerges in the case of training that leads to the achievement of a qualification. National Vocational Qualifications (NVQs) clearly fit into this category, as do all the other qualifications employers look for when recruiting new employees. Here it does seem to be the case that one outcome is an increased propensity on the part of some employees to resign. However, resignation rates are a good deal lower when the employer pays for the training and actively encourages staff to gain the qualification concerned. This could be because of the widespread use of pay-back penalty arrangements (of which more later) but is more likely simply to reflect greater commitment being given to employers who are prepared to invest time and money in their people.

The opposite is the case when the employer refuses to pay and thus obliges employees either to stump up for their own course fees or to rely on state funding. Where this happens there is a far greater likelihood of a subsequent departure. The employee enhances his or her ability to find a better job and feels no obligation to the employer to hold back. It thus makes sense, where a valuable employee is determined to attain a recognised qualification, to sponsor him or her either wholly or in part. If you fail to do so in circumstances where employees are going to arrange it for themselves anyway, you are substantially increasing the chances that you will lose them.

Of course, we must acknowledge that employee retention is by no means the major purpose of staff training. In fact, it is often a second-order objective. First and foremost, training is given in order to enhance staff performance either directly or indirectly. It can also play an important role in attracting staff to the organisation in the first place. The fact that in some cases dysfunctional quitting may result should not necessarily deter employers from providing it for their people. Indeed, in some labour markets (eg graduates) it is a fundamental requirement if an employer is to attract and retain good performers. Moreover, as is rightly pointed out by Green *et al* (2000) in their article, it is quite possible for employers to deploy other retention tools (including organisation-specific training interventions) to counteract any negative effect of training provision on turnover levels.

Pay-back penalties

It is possible and common for employers to set up pay-back penalties as a means of enhancing the chances of employees' staying during and after receiving a programme of training paid for by the employer. Such arrangements are entirely lawful, provided they are set up in the right way. Essentially, it is a question of incorporating into the contract of employment a clause that says something like:

> The organisation will pay £X00 or £X,000 for you to undertake a specific course of training. If you leave voluntarily before completing the course or within X years of completing it, you accept that you will be liable to repay the cost of the training.

The courts have shown themselves very willing over the years to enforce contractual terms such as these, the current leading case being *Neil* v *Strathclyde Regional Council* (1984). However, pay-back agreements can only be valid provided they meet certain requirements. Employers have to ensure that these apply:

☐ The agreement must be clearly drafted and accepted in writing by the employee concerned.

☐ The training specified in the agreement must subsequently be delivered in practice.

☐ The agreement must be reasonable in terms of its length.

What employers cannot do – although they sometimes try – is to use such agreements as a means of entrapping trainees in their employment for many years. Although there is no clear legal guidance on this issue, it is likely that a court would say that a contractual clause was overly restrictive if it lasted for more than two or three years after the completion of the training programme. Moreover, of course, the training programme itself must be specifically identified. Employers cannot expect to be able to enforce a clause that requires repayments for unspecified on-the-job training which actually requires the employee to carry out the same basic duties as his or her colleagues do. Ultimately it is all a question of clarity and reasonableness. If the employee has signed up to a clear and reasonable contract that says he or she will pay back either all or a portion of the costs associated with a specific programme of training, then that agreement is enforceable in the county courts.

How effective pay-back arrangements are in practice as a retention device is a debatable point. On the one hand, because the sums involved are not normally very large as a proportion of earnings, they are readily paid by a new employer as a means of securing the services of the leaver. You may well thus find that your best employees are not deterred from leaving for this reason. If they are desirable enough in labour market terms, an alternative employer will happily compensate the former one, considering it a small price to pay. However, the same thinking is a good deal less likely to pertain in the case of the more average performers. There would also be limits on the extent to which many of the more bureaucratic public sector organisations would permit compensatory payments of this kind to be made to former employees.

In any case, there is probably an important psychological effect on employees who sign up to pay-back agreements.

Whatever the practical possibilities, they are likely to consider themselves bound to their employer for the duration of
the agreement and will thus not consider leaving in this time.
All thought of quitting is put off until the agreement reaches
its end-date.

Promotion opportunities

By no means everyone is interested in climbing up the greasy
pole or seeking promotion up a career ladder. Moreover, many
organisations have set out in recent years to reduce the
number of levels in their hierarchies, pushing towards harmonisation and a greater degree of teamworking. There are
good arguments for moving in this direction, but it remains
the case that some staff (often the better performers) are very
career-minded and will not stay for long in an organisation
which denies them the opportunity to advance upwards at
the speed they perceive to be their due.

Some professional groups, particularly those that are managerial in nature, tend to attract people who want to build a
career in this way. Failing to provide proper opportunities for
them to do so will lead to a continually high rate of attrition.
This may be a price you are prepared to pay for the removal
of layers of middle managers – but you must at least recognise
that where people's career trajectories are limited as a result,
a likely outcome is higher turnover. The consequence is a
need to work harder through the use of alternative retention
initiatives to keep these people.

Where a hierarchy is retained, the key is to ensure that
rungs are not missing from the career ladders that are provided. I have worked in several workplaces where individuals
left simply because there was no obvious internal 'next step'
for them to take if they were to continue developing their
careers. The organisations were structured very efficiently,
but not in ways that were conducive to regular promotion of
good people.

The problem and the solution are clearly, if rather crudely,
illustrated in Figure 3. Here we have two departmental structures, both containing 13 people. In the first, the gaps
between the three levels in the hierarchy are too large for

people to leap up. Were internal promotions to occur they would often end in failure because people would be being over-promoted too soon. Good performers would not be prepared to hang around long enough to gain the experience necessary to make the big leap necessary to be promoted. In the second, by contrast, there is more flexibility in terms of job title and salary. The structure provides every opportunity for all staff (except the Big Boss at the top) to move up the hierarchy should the opportunity arise. All the steps needed are in place.

These are clearly very simplistic examples, but they are

Figure 3

a) A department without sufficient career development opportunities

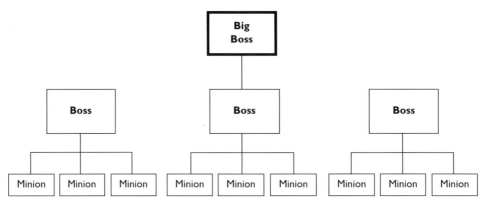

b) A department with reasonable career development opportunities

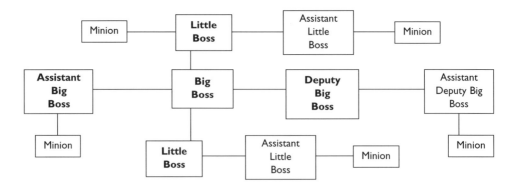

based on genuine organisations, and do serve to make an important point. As always in respect of employee retention (as with customer retention) all that matters at the end of the day is the perception of your staff. If they believe that they are unlikely to be promoted internally and they desire to move on in their jobs, they will leave. A structure that provides steps which they can reasonably aspire to climb will provide some incentive for them to remain. Structures matter because they affect the way that people think about their future careers from the first day that they start working for you. If insufficient promotion opportunities *appear* to be available, the employee will consider the relationship likely to last a relatively short time. The probability of a move in the foreseeable future is thus high, so the relationship is established on relatively weak foundations as of day 1. The opposite is the case where structures provide good grounds for anticipating that career aspirations can be satisfied internally.

For these reasons organisational restructuring exercises that bring greater efficiency can often be criticised for removing career development opportunities. Damage is done not just because people subsequently have to leave to achieve their ambitions but also because the nature of their psychological contract is changed. People who now think they may have to leave (when they previously thought in terms of a long stay) see their relationship with the organisation differently, and are likely to display less commitment as a result.

We must recognise, however, that there is more to the management of career expectations than the provision of suitable organisational structures. People also need to be given reason to believe that they have a good chance of being promoted should a vacancy arise. Managers thus have to be *seen* to be running things in a promotion-oriented manner. Examples of the types of activity that will encourage retention among people who aspire to be promoted include:

☐ ensuring that jobs are filled by internal promotion where it is practicable; trying to achieve a balance in recruitment between the employment of fresh blood from outside and the need to satisfy the legitimate aspirations of existing staff

☐ engaging in succession planning exercises, identifying individuals with the attributes required to be promoted and giving them the necessary experience when the opportunity arises

☐ encouraging first line managers and supervisors to discuss promotion possibilities with their staff during formal performance review or performance appraisal interviews

☐ providing an opportunity to attend formal training courses which set out to develop skills relevant to possible future (as well as current) roles

☐ allowing/encouraging staff who are candidates for future promotion to expand their current roles over time so as to enhance their chances of promotion.

This is all very straightforward and in many ways entirely commonsensical. But organisations very often fail to achieve some or all of these basic objectives. Inflexible management mindsets, rigid structures and task-focused (rather than people-focused) supervisors are the major causes. Others include managers' failing to develop subordinates because they fear for their own positions or, more often, because promotion means the loss of good people from within their ambits of responsibility. Organisations can best discourage such thinking by rewarding (and being seen to reward) supervisors who are particularly good at developing their own staff.

CAREER COUNSELLING AT SUN MICROSYSTEMS

In an article published in 1999, Ron Elsdon and Seemer Iyer describe the contribution to staff retention made by the Career Services Division that operates within the Sun Microsystems computer company.

The Division has evolved over a 10-year period to serve 26,000 staff employed in 55 different countries. Its main activity is the provision of confidential person-to-person career counselling sessions the aim of which is to help staff to draw up their own career development plans. Counsellors also run workshop and other training sessions to flag up the career development opportunities the company can offer. The purpose is summed up as follows:

> to help employees make well-informed career choices and to match their aspirations to opportunities within Sun Microsystems.

What makes this article particularly interesting is the work it reports linking the provision of career services with low employee turnover – particularly among women and staff establishing themselves during the first five years of their careers. Attrition across Sun Microsystems as a whole was kept below 10 per cent during the late 1990s, which is quite an achievement in the light of the fact that IT workers were leaving most firms at more than double this rate at that time. Research carried out in the company suggested that retention rates were highest in those units with staff who made most use of the career counselling services, and that turnover was rather lower among users than it was among non-users. Although the differential between the two groups was small (1 per cent), it was calculated to represent a very significant sum in cost terms (around $1 million), making it possible for the Career Services Division to claim that it provided an excellent return on investment for the company.

Indirectly, however, the presence of an accessible, well-advertised and professional career counselling service can be argued to have had a greater effect on retention rates in the organisation. While only 10 per cent of the company's employees make use of the service each year, the other 90 per cent know about its activities and understand that they may choose to make use of it in the future. Its presence thus makes a visible, general contribution to the perception that the organisation wants to retain people by developing them.

Personal development opportunities

As was recognised above, climbing hierarchies is only one way in which people seek to develop a career. Many people have no interest in taking on additional managerial responsibility and are not motivated (and may in fact be demotivated) by the sight of a greasy pole. Some are bored by the idea of managing other people, some just know that they are bad at it, and others are generally uneasy with the whole power-based orientation of the management role. Such people develop careers in other ways, most commonly through the acquisition and deployment of specialist knowledge or skills. Their overriding and underlying aims tend to be:

- to develop greater knowledge
- to achieve recognition as a specialist
- to exercise control over their own area of work
- to undertake interesting/high-quality work as far as is possible.

This is true of the majority of people who enter the professions – ie lawyers, chartered accountants, architects, engineers, teachers, academics, medics and members of the creative and design professions (see Chapters 15 and 16). What they primarily seek is the opportunity to use their skills and expertise and to develop these further. They are not generally motivated by a wish to make a great deal of money. Financial security, some year-on-year increases and a modest level of material comfort satisfy them on the pay front. Nor do they want to supervise others or play the political games that are often necessary to climb an organisation's management hierarchy. Failing to achieve promotion will not therefore lead them to leave voluntarily. Instead, they tend to quit for one or more of the following reasons:

- because they are not sufficiently challenged professionally
- because the work they are required to do is or becomes boring and unstimulating
- because they are required to spend too much time on managerial/bureaucratic/administrative tasks
- because they perceive that the more interesting or 'quality' work is being distributed unfairly
- because managers are believed to be intervening too much and denying them control over their own activities.

Members of these knowledge-based professional groups are generally content to remain in one employment for a substantial period of time, their job tenure rates being among the highest of all. This is just as well from a management perspective because these are the people whose resignations are most costly and are most likely to damage their organisations' competitive positions. Where turnover rates are high among these groups, it is thus reasonable to conclude that something is wrong with the way the staff are being managed. In many cases they leave because they are frustrated at being denied the opportunity to develop professionally and personally. Other major reasons are job insecurity and the perception that their managers are unfair in their actions, self-serving, or incompetent.

Retaining people who seek little more than basic professional fulfilment is straightforward. It involves leaving them to get on with their work with as little interference as possible, providing them with the opportunity to develop themselves in whatever direction they choose, making sure that they are managed in a professional manner and trying as far as possible to provide them with the resources they need. Unfortunately, these principles are often not followed in practice. The following are all examples of professionally qualified staff and the reasons they gave for leaving when interviewed by myself and other researchers at Manchester Metropolitan University over the past three years. Most of them worked at larger UK employers:

□ A highly paid graduate spent much of her first six months being required to undertake basic secretarial and clerical tasks.

□ A respondent discovered a manager promoting her own daughter to a senior position despite her having considerably less experience than other candidates.

□ Another respondent was exasperated to find her manager persistently giving the most interesting work to favoured subordinates.

□ A reorganisation led to a situation in which a respondent and other experienced staff were denied the opportunity to work on projects they had themselves set up and managed for some years.

□ An individual was refused permission to undertake basic training needed for her to keep up with professional developments.

Although the precise circumstances vary, we found several examples of each of these types of situation, leading us to conclude that a failure on the part of managers to grasp the significance of basic motivations and career objectives largely explained the resignations.

So what can be done to maximise the retention of people who, first and foremost, seek professional satisfaction and the opportunity to develop their skills and knowledge?

First of all it is necessary to deal with each individual separately. Organisations must avoid falling into the trap of assuming that everyone in a particular group wants to advance his or her career in the same way and at the same pace. Maximum flexibility is called for. It is really a question of speaking to each employee on a regular basis and trying to reach a joint understanding of his or her individual development needs. This can be done through a formal appraisal or development review system in which line managers meet with subordinates in a semi-formal setting.

The trouble here is that many such systems are designed to meet 'evaluative' as well as 'developmental' objectives. They are intended as a forum in which individual development needs are discussed, but fail to achieve this because they are also an occasion at which the employee's performance is judged – with a possible knock-on effect on promotion or pay or even on redundancy decisions. The result is a situation in which employees seek to blow their own trumpets, to flag up their achievements and to downplay their weaknesses. This is particularly true of average and weaker performers who have every reason to use their annual appraisal meeting to try to impress their managers. Evaluative forums are also a very poor occasion on which to raise grievances with managers or to complain, however reasonably, about the allocation of work or other ways in which personal development opportunities are being denied.

Career development needs are thus best dealt with through a separate organisational mechanism in which performance evaluation is not discussed. The focus can then be exclusively on career development issues and on how the organisation can facilitate what employees perceive to be their needs and desires. Alternatively, developmental discussions can take place with managers who do not have direct responsibility for the individuals concerned. They are thus well placed to take on some kind of mentoring role, give advice on career development matters and act as supporters. The third option involves making use of career counselling specialists such as those described in the boxed text above. Whatever the method used, the aim is to achieve:

□ an understanding, on the part of managers, of each employee's underlying and evolving developmental objectives

□ agreement on how and to what extent the organisation can satisfy them

□ an understanding, on the part of employees, that the organisation will try as far as is possible to help them achieve their developmental objectives.

In recent years it has been fashionable to give employees themselves responsibility for devising and setting up their own career development activities. There is much to recommend this kind of unstructured approach because it recognises the great diversity of career objectives that individuals have. However, the research evidence suggests that it can be taken too far, and that this leads to increased rather than decreased staff turnover.

Sturges and Guest (1999) found the absence of *some* structure provided by the organisation in the career management field to be a significant cause of early turnover among graduate recruits, but their findings probably hold true for more established professionals too. People often lack the self-confidence and understanding of what is in their own best interests to make a success out of these kinds of arrangement. Good people with a lot to offer lose out because they do not have the required political know-how. They thus fail to make progress and end up looking outside for opportunities that they are finding difficult to grasp internally. So a balance has to be struck between a highly structured approach that pushes everyone in the same organisation-led direction and one which leaves the lion's share of career development responsibility in the hands of employees. The organisation must give advice and guidance. It must also provide platforms in the guise of formal career development programmes from which employees can gain access to the experience and skills-enhancing opportunities that are available. This is a field in which managers need to avoid *prescribing*, but in which they must provide robust systems of support and encouragement.

Job sculpting

An idea that many employers will be uncomfortable with – but one that makes perfect sense in very tight labour market conditions – is the customisation of jobs to match people rather than expecting people to fit into the jobs that an organisation provides. This turns traditional thinking about a key aspect of the employment relationship on its head, reflecting the shift in the balance of power between employer and employee that we find is now occurring in some labour markets. Quite simply, advocates of job sculpting argue that in order to attract and retain the best people employers are increasingly having to find ways of providing jobs which satisfy the evolving preferences and developmental needs of their staff. Because employees vary so much in terms of their interests, circumstances and aspirations, it follows that jobs must be designed on a bespoke basis – each carefully tailored to meet the requirements of its occupant (see Chapter 15).

Total sculpting, whereby an employee designs his or her own job in consultation with the employer, is only practicable in certain types of situation. Moreover, it is only desirable from an employer's point of view to allow people to 'write their own job descriptions' where labour market conditions mean that there is no alternative in order to secure the services of particularly talented individuals. But this does not mean that some moves in this direction cannot be made for the majority of staff, a better record on staff retention being the outcome. Three approaches which can be described as 'partial job sculpting' are worth considering:

☐ giving employees assignments or project work to engage in which they are particularly interested in taking forward

☐ rejigging responsibilities between different individuals in a team or department so as to achieve a better alignment between organisational requirements and employees' developmental objectives

☐ when the opportunity arises, moving people around the organisation into new jobs which better meet their aspirations.

In each case the endeavour is, sometimes necessarily in quite a limited fashion, to find ways of better matching the organisation's developmental needs with those of its employees.

A most influential article on the subject of job sculpting was published in *Harvard Business Review* in 1999. Here Timothy Butler and James Waldroop outlined the findings of their 12-year research project looking into the career aspirations of professional employees working in different types of role. They interviewed 650 people in depth, and also asked them to complete a battery of psychometric tests. After analysing the results they advanced the view that it is possible to identify eight 'deeply embedded life interests' which account for the underlying work motivation of the vast majority of employees:

> Deeply embedded life interests are not hobbies or enthusiasms; they are innate passions that are intricately entwined with personality. Life interests don't determine what we're good at but what kinds of work we love.

It follows that managers interested in maximising retention levels in their organisations should find out which of these 'life interests' are most prevalent in individual employees and then try to 'sculpt' appropriate roles for them. Employees whose jobs do not give them sufficient opportunity to meet these aspirations are a great deal more likely to seek such opportunities elsewhere. Butler and Waldroop suggest that most of us are primarily motivated by two or three of the 'big eight' life interests. The eight can be briefly described as:

☐ the application of technology – people who are interested in how things work and want to find ways of making them work more effectively

☐ quantitative analysis – people who are interested in numbers and mathematics and who like using quantitative approaches to analyse issues

☐ theory development and conceptual thinking – people who tackle problems using theory and abstract thinking

- □ creative production – imaginative people who think original thoughts and enjoy innovating: they are particularly drawn to setting up new systems or projects
- □ counselling and mentoring – people who like to teach, coach and to guide others
- □ managing people and relationships – people who derive satisfaction from getting objectives achieved through others
- □ enterprise control – people who like leading, making decisions and taking responsibility for the completion of projects
- □ influence through language and ideas – people who gain satisfaction through writing and speaking: excellent communicators.

It is probably wise not to stake too much on the detail of these research findings. They are only based on one US study and will undoubtedly be refined and criticised by other researchers over time. But the underlying idea is worth considering and taking on board. It makes sense, if you want to retain people, to encourage them to develop their roles in directions that will bring them satisfaction while also meeting the organisation's objectives.

8   WORKING CONDITIONS

In this chapter a range of issues are discussed which relate in some shape or form to the conditions under which people work. These are working hours, the management of competing work and domestic pressures, physical working conditions, employment security, and the design of jobs. Dissatisfaction with one or more of these aspects of people's working lives is an important source of unwanted employee turnover. Yet for one reason or another managers are inclined to resist making changes to established approaches. This is partly because they fear the possible financial consequences and partly because the possibility of doing things differently does not occur to them.

The aim in this chapter is to argue the case for making substantial changes where labour markets are tight and skilled staff are in short supply. I believe that for organisations with a serious long-standing employee turnover problem there is a need for managers to start 'thinking outside the box' and to turn some established ways of managing people on their heads. In the end, if you want to retain your staff you have to accept the need to provide more attractive jobs than your competitors do. If you are unable to pay more or offer better career development opportunities, you must provide something different. Management systems conspicuously characterised by the following principles provide a good starting-point:

- □ flexibility
- □ autonomy
- □ variety
- □ responsiveness.

Hours of work

Working time issues, of one sort or another, are major causes of voluntary leaving. According to my research and that of colleagues at Manchester Metropolitan University, hours of work are far more frequently given as a primary reason for resignations than pay. However, there is no single, straightforward or easily identifiable link between hours and turnover. Different kinds of situation arise which affect different professions, different labour markets and different kinds of people in a variety of ways. For some it is a question of juggling the demands of job and family responsibilities, for others a more general matter of work–life balance, while for a third group it is a simple question of seeking to minimise the time spent carrying out a job that is not enjoyable or interesting. I find it useful, when thinking about working time from an employee-retention point of view, to divide the subject into two distinct topic areas. These are: resignations that occur because of long working hours, and those which occur because of dissatisfaction with the pattern of hours that are worked. These are reviewed separately below.

Long hours

It is generally accepted that employees in the UK work longer hours than their equivalents elsewhere in the European Union, and that the trend in the last two decades has been towards longer rather than shorter hours. This is despite the presence of Working Time Regulations since 1998 and of well-publicised concerns about the adverse effects working long hours has on our health. Although there is considerable evidence to back up the general trend, its exact extent is a matter of some controversy because the major source of data (the government's Labour Force Survey) is based on self-reporting by employees themselves or by people who live with them. Responses about the number of hours worked each week are not therefore objectively verifiable and may be somewhat exaggerated. By contrast, the other major source of data on working time (the New Earnings Survey) fails to record unpaid overtime, which is by common consent the category that has seen most growth in recent years (IDS,

2000b). Nonetheless, we can reasonably conclude that the following are credible claims:

- The average male full-time worker in the UK puts in around 47 hours a week.
- The average full-time female worker puts in around 43 hours a week.
- These figures represent an increase of two or three hours a week (about 120 hours a year) since the 1980s.
- More than 40 per cent of male full-timers and over 50 per cent of female full-timers claim to work unpaid overtime.
- Some 30 per cent of men and 10 per cent of women claim to work in excess of 50 hours each week.
- One in three women with children works for more than 40 hours a week.

We can thus state, beyond doubt, that UK workers perceive that their hours are getting longer, and that for a good proportion (either directly or indirectly) this is a factor which contributes to their decision to leave a job.

Drawing on evidence from the British Social Attitudes Survey and work carried out by the Institute of Employment Studies, Reeves (2000) shows that people who work long hours rarely conform to the stereotype of the 'exploited serf' that more radical writers tend to describe. In fact, 70 per cent of those who work for more than 60 hours a week say that they do it because they enjoy their jobs, and only 22 per cent say they do it because they have to in order to make ends meet. Far fewer people who work 'normal hours' like their jobs and many more see them as 'just a means of earning a living'. The reason is that most of the 'long-hours jobs' are stimulating, professional positions carried out by people who enjoy holding responsibility and who are heavily career-oriented. At first glance, when seen from an employee-retention perspective, this is welcome news. The majority of those working long hours are happy doing so, and are thus unlikely to leave in order to secure an easier life. However, on closer examination the evidence suggests that employers cannot be complacent.

Firstly, it remains the case that 30 per cent of people who work long hours are *not* doing so because they enjoy their jobs. Those who receive paid overtime have the consolation of money to reward them for their efforts, but many more do not get paid extra. They put the hours in either because it is expected of them (eg junior doctors) or because they feel the need to conform to the norms of a 'long-hours culture' (eg managers and providers of professional services). Most of these people are highly qualified, are expensive to hire and train, and are working in jobs which involve the development of long-term relationships with clients. They are thus among the groups for whom turnover is most damaging from the point of view of employers.

Secondly, among the 70 per cent who enjoy their jobs and are happy to put in the long hours, there are many who nonetheless end up resigning because they can no longer commit to the extent expected of them. In some cases illnesses result from excessive working that oblige people to leave. Others suffer some form of 'burn-out' in their thirties or forties and reach the stage where they can no longer keep going at the same pace. For a further group life outside work intervenes to put a halt to their long hours in the form of new relationships, the birth of children, or responsibility for the care of elderly relatives. Finally, of course, there are situations in which spouses and partners demand a fairer share of the employee's attention.

It is thus reasonable to conclude that long-hours cultures can often be the enemy of high rates of staff retention, and that unless other effective retention initiatives are introduced, employers who fail to address such issues will suffer from extensive unwanted employee turnover. Moreover, the resignees are in very many cases those whose departures are most costly and damaging from an organisational point of view.

Finding workable solutions to these problems is not easy. In many organisations where long hours are worked there is little alternative because employees are required to respond to customer needs. It is inevitable in such circumstances that individual commitment will, in large part, be judged on the basis of the hours that someone is prepared to put in. It follows that people will want to be seen to be committed in order to secure favourable performance ratings, pay rises, promotions and job security. However, there are ways forward which do not lead to a reduced level of customer service. The following suggestions are worth considering:

☐ Discourage presenteeism.

This occurs when people perceive that they are expected to be at work even when in truth there is insufficient work for them to do. Our research found numerous examples of 'macho' long-hours cultures existing and proliferating for wholly unnecessary reasons. In many professional services organisations junior staff seem to be convinced that they must be *seen* to be at their desks before the partners arrive in the morning and that they cannot leave until after the partners go home at night (see Chapter 16). The same attitude prevails in some public sector organisations as well as numerous companies. It is difficult to break such workplace assumptions down, especially when senior personnel had to work excessive hours themselves 'to get where they are today'. But it can be done with imagination on the part of managers, by making a strong business case and by actively encouraging people to work more efficiently but over fewer hours.

☐ Promote notions of 'time sovereignty'.

Reeves (2000) argues persuasively that the *number* of hours worked is often less the source of the problem than *where* they are worked and *when*. People find it far easier to cope with protracted hours of work when they exercise a degree of control (or sovereignty) over them. Where it is practical why not allow people to work from home for a portion of the time? Modern technologies have made teleworking a straightforward proposition for many roles, yet the evidence suggests that far fewer people work in this way than could. Instead, we continue to drag people in to city centre offices, requiring them to brace themselves for difficult commuter journeys to undertake work that could just as well be done from home. I am not advocating teleworking on a permanent basis (that brings many other problems with it), but there is no reason why many people, particularly in professional services roles, cannot work from home for one, one and a half or two days a week – or be encouraged to take work home to complete in the evening at their own pace, rather than have to sit in the office completing it until 10 at night. Another approach involves taking a much more relaxed view than is typical about people carrying out personal tasks during the working day. Where it can be arranged, let people take time out to go shopping in the afternoon, or to leave early to pick up children from school, or to go to the bank, etc. It is a question of employing people to do a job and not to work in a particular place for a set number of hours. Once the job is complete and there is no more to do, why require people to stay on until 6 o'clock purely to meet the requirements of a time-focused contract?

□ Make use of time-saving technologies.

The spread of the Internet and of e-commerce opens up lots of opportunities to reduce the amount of time people have to spend at work.

Encouraging customers and suppliers to communicate via e-mail and websites allows an organisation far greater flexibility in terms of when exactly it deals with most non-urgent matters. It takes away the necessity to have as many people manning telephone lines or just being on the premises in case a call is received. There are obviously limits as to how far you can go down this route, but it is often a great deal further than is currently the case. The key is to find ways of providing an Internet-based enquiry response service which is better than that provided by telephone or via face-to-face interaction. This requires investment in interactive websites which are easily navigated and which provide information that customers (and other callers) want in an effective and approachable way.

The human resource/personnel department is a very good example of an organisational function that stands to gain most from this kind of development. Building effective intranet systems and websites that cater for potential job applicants is an excellent route to the reduction of excessive working hours.

Patterns of hours

The development of a flexible management mindset is also important in tackling the problem of resignations that arise because of the pattern of hours that staff are expected to work. We often use the term 'flexible working' approvingly, but what we are describing is flexibility from the point of view of the employer and not the employee. The truth is that there remains, despite legislation on parental leave, family emergencies and atypical working, a strong tendency in UK industry to:

☐ see part-time or casual workers as a species inferior to their full-time colleagues

☐ view family responsibilities as something of an irritant and to expect employees to put their work ahead of these in their lists of priorities

☐ expect employees to alter their plans in order to meet the needs of the business at very short notice

☐ refuse, almost as a matter of principle, to allow people to change their hours to suit their needs even where it could be accommodated without any loss of organisational effectiveness

☐ insist that everyone is employed on the same identical, standard sets of terms and conditions as regards hours.

Many organisations, particularly in the services sectors (retailing, catering, cleaning, care work, call centres, etc) are guilty of one or more of the above. Managers may well argue that there are good operational reasons for it and that this is the approach that has always been taken in those industries. If employees don't like it, they say, then they shouldn't be looking for employment in these highly customer-focused roles.

The trouble with this argument, of course, is that this is exactly what employees do do. They find they don't like it and leave. These industries, as a result, have the highest rates of staff turnover in the economy. Yet it seems to me that they are the very industries that have the most scope for introducing highly flexible patterns of working. It should be possible for them, precisely because they operate well outside normal office hours, to offer employees and potential employees hours to suit their (ie the employees') needs, to a far greater extent than is currently the case. They do not do this, I sense, partly because it would challenge established work cultures which are often quite autocratic in nature, partly because managers think (wrongly) that it would necesarily lead to greater inefficiency, and partly simply because it means more work and hassle for hard-pressed managers. It is far easier just to impose a standard set of rules and require employees to fit their lives around them.

In my view this is short-sighted and based to a great extent on a failure to appreciate just how many people leave jobs in these industries for hours-oriented reasons.

Ironically, according to our research, it is the hours on offer that often attract people to these customer service roles in the first place. They are led to believe that they will be required to work certain predefined patterns, and they accept posts on this basis. They later find that these are frequently changed or extended at the behest of management or that they are regularly called in to cover for absences. The very factor that attracted them to the jobs is thus missing once they become established in the role. When it comes to changing hours to meet altered domestic circumstances, they might as well not bother to ask.

What is needed is an adjustment of focus among managers. They have to become less concerned about controlling their workforces and establishing their own authority, and more interested in resourcing their organisations effectively. This requires flexibility, an openness to new ideas about staffing patterns and a mindset which understands that staff retention involves thinking about work from an employee perspective.

In most locations there is a plentiful supply of people who are willing to work for short periods of time in the evenings, over lunchtime or at other busy periods. They can be used creatively to cover gaps in staffing. What they tend to want, however, is a predictable pattern of hours. They want to know when they are coming in (and for how long) ahead of time. Wherever this is possible it should therefore be provided. Why insist that all evening shiftworkers come in at 4 o'clock as many retailers do? This may be when the busiest period of the day starts, but it is also the time at which children come home from school and falls an hour or two before spouses return from their jobs. Yet there are other people, such as students and older schoolchildren, available to work from 4 to 6 who would be grateful for the opportunity to do so.

Why refuse to allow people to work on termtime contracts? There is a cost associated with the recruitment of replacements to work in the school holidays, but it is not difficult to find university students who are willing to do so – especially if the jobs on offer are part-time. Thinking creatively about patterns of working and tailoring them, where practicable, to meet individual needs means more work for managers and some hassle. But it distinguishes you from other employers and makes you more attractive to work for among those who want to work flexibly. People are much less likely to leave and join rival employers if you can offer them hours to suit.

MAKING IT DIFFICULT FOR STAFF TO STAY

Before becoming a university lecturer, I worked as an HR manager in the NHS and in the hotel industry for over five years. In this time I observed, and sometimes participated in, plans to force staff into working patterns of hours that did not suit their requirements. There were always good operational reasons for our actions, but in retrospect it seems as if our conduct was almost gratuitously stupid in situations where there was a staff retention problem.

I worked in a hospital in the mid-1990s when the current shortage of nursing staff was starting to kick in and cause major problems. This was the beginning of the boom era for the nurse banks, stepping in to provide staff to cover shifts at premium rates. Far from confronting this issue by allowing greater flexibility of hours, managers took the view that all nurses across the hospital should work the same pattern of rotating shifts. Everyone would be required to work a week of early shifts (7 am to 3 pm), followed by a week of late shifts (3 pm to 11 pm), followed by a week of nights. The decision was taken to issue all new contracts on this basis and to set about 'persuading' all existing staff on different terms and conditions to switch to the new standard shift pattern. Those who refused to change were put under quite serious pressure to yield. Good people were lost as a result of this absurd policy, while a great deal of goodwill was lost among those who remained.

> Before this I worked in a hotel at the peak of the late 1980s boom. There was a serious shortage of staff, necessitating regular trips overseas to recruit experienced people. The annual spend on recruitment advertising, employment agency fees and new uniforms ran into several hundred thousand pounds. This was a time when retaining people should have been the major focus of HR activity – but it wasn't. The 100 per cent-plus turnover rate was seen as something of an inevitable occupational hazard. Instead, our focus was on paring down the weekly wage bill. This exercise was undertaken not because the hotel was suffering economically. On the contrary, it was busier than ever in its history. We did it simply because we were short-sighted about staffing issues. We happily set about reducing our spend on wages, getting patted on the back by the general manager when we succeeded, while ignoring the knock-on consequences for the recruitment bill. I remember devising a system of split shifts for one group of staff which saved a few pounds a week but resulted in several resignations. We also had a policy of refusing requests from full-timers to work part-time on the grounds that they were occupying live-in accommodation on a full-time basis. The fact that we had no shortage of rooms for staff to live in didn't alter this view. People left, entirely avoidably, as a result.

Juggling work and family responsibilities

The Labour Force Survey consistently records that between 5 per cent and 10 per cent of people leave their employment for 'family or personal reasons' (IRS, 1999, p6). This suggests that hundreds of thousands of people quit their jobs each year not necessarily because they are unhappy with their working lives but because they find it impossible to juggle the demands of work with family life.

Studies carried out in the USA show beyond doubt that resignations for this reason overwhelmingly affect women. According to Hom and Griffeth (1995, p252), 33 per cent of American women have left jobs at some time in order to devote more time to their families, a response given by only 1 per cent of their male counterparts. UK job tenure figures also appear to give the same message. According to Gregg and Wadsworth (1999, p116), average job tenure among men in 1998 was 69 months. The figure for women *without* children was 59 months (not far short of that for men), while the figure for women *with* children was only 46 months.

These statistics carry very important messages for all employers, but particularly those whose workforces are largely female. For them there is a very compelling business case for investing in measures which serve to make it easier for staff to combine their work and family roles. Relatively little outlay should yield substantial returns as turnover rates fall substantially.

Although women with children of pre-school and school age are the prime target here, it is important not to ignore the contribution also made by many men in the domestic sphere. In our research we found several examples of men who had left jobs for such reasons – often in order to take up positions that were compatible with those of their wives. The wish to avoid or minimise childcare costs was the major motivation as well as a desire to spend more time with their children (see Chapter 17). As our population ages, elder-care is becoming a more important issue too, employees in middle age having to find ways of satisfying both the needs of their employers and those of elderly relatives for whom they have caring responsibilities. As is the case for parents of young children, when the two roles become incompatible it has to be the job that is dropped. You can change your job a great deal more easily than you can change your relatives!

In the section above we looked at flexible working arrangements that help employees to manage their time in such a way as to combine domestic and work reponsibilities effectively. Time management is the main issue here, and has the most potential for reducing turnover among the affected groups. However, other factors are just as important and can provide a means of improving staff retention at relatively little cost. As with all retention measures it is necessary to be as concerned with employee perception as with the practical realities. There is no point devoting a substantial amount of resources to initiatives in this field if your employees do not know about them or do not appreciate them. From an employee-retention angle the key is to get the message over that you are a more family-friendly employer than any of your competitors. The effect is not only to encourage existing staff with family responsibilities to stay – there is also an effect on those who think that they are likely to gain such responsibilities in the future. Promoting your practices effectively is thus as important as setting them up in the first place.

A most significant issue to consider in this context is the position of women who become pregnant while working for you. This is a particularly 'vulnerable' group in terms of retention because a good proportion choose not to return to their old full-time jobs following their maternity leave. Increasing the chances of a return is not difficult and requires no real expenditure, but it does mean that someone must keep in regular touch during the period of leave and take steps to show that the employees concerned are missed and that their return is keenly anticipated. The best way of helping to ensure that women fail to come back to their jobs after maternity leave is to do what many employers do and forget that they exist until the date of return looms.

The major areas to consider on the family-friendly front are:

☐ Offer a deal conspicuously better than you are strictly required to offer under relevant employment statutes (maternity pay, maternity leave, parental leave, paternity leave, adoptive leave, time off for family emergencies, right to request part-time work, etc).

☐ Consider providing childcare facilities, childcare vouchers or reserving places at a good-quality crèche close to your workplace.

☐ Develop a career-break scheme by which employees can take a period of time out on an unpaid basis with the right to return to their old jobs (or equivalent) after a few months.

☐ Encourage managers to show an interest in the juggling of domestic and work duties, and to raise the issue with employees formally from time to time with a view to providing assistance.

☐ Run a flexitime system, where it is appropriate, allowing staff to decide for themselves when they work beyond agreed 'core hours'.

☐ Provide sources of advice for staff with family responsibilities about how they can successfully combine these with the development of careers.

Ultimately, it is a question of making sure that you are genuinely a 'family-friendly employer' and that you are perceived as such by your staff. Many employers are strong on the first part of this equation but poor at actively promoting their practices on the shop floor. There is the world of difference, in terms of retention outcomes, between appearing grudgingly to provide family-friendly benefits and doing so with some pride and gusto.

The physical working environment

A relatively common factor contributing to dissatisfaction with a job is physical discomfort. In our research we recorded several instances of people leaving jobs in part because they were unhappy with some aspect of the environment in which they were required to work. Such factors are rarely the major cause of turnover. Instead, they take the form of an underlying and ongoing irritant which adds to a more general sense of unhappiness and hence to the decision to look for alternative employment. It is possible to categorise these as 'hidden' causes of turnover because they are rarely stated openly by employees at exit interviews. Employers may thus be unaware that there is a problem. Departing employees tend not to come clean about the true extent that their decision to leave was related to physical working conditions for fear that their managers will view the reason as trivial and (perhaps) think ill of them as a result. We recorded the following examples:

- someone who left a senior job because she was required to share an office with a smoker – nothing was done to move her, despite several requests, so when a similar job was advertised by a competitor, she applied
- a retail worker who resigned because she was required to stand all day – no chair was provided behind the counter for shop assistants to use
- two people who disliked working in large open-plan offices – they found the noise, lack of privacy and feeling of being 'constantly watched' very uncomfortable: other factors acted to bring about the resignations too, but in both cases

they might have been avoided or delayed with better office
design

☐ someone who was required to work in a noisy, over-
crowded office which became unbearably hot and smelly
in the summer months; insufficient numbers of fans were
provided, making each day an ordeal

☐ someone who worked in a job centre and feared for her
physical safety when security barriers were removed in a
bid to make the environment more comfortable from the
perspective of clients.

There is a substantial body of published research on 'optimal
workspace characteristics' which is interesting for our purposes. Much of it is concerned with maximising employee
performance through the provision of the best possible working environment, but it also has relevance to the field of
employee retention. The research suggests that superior work
performance derives in large part from job satisfaction, and
that this is enhanced in some environments. It follows that
job dissatisfaction is likely to result where the environment
is unsuitable or notably uncomfortable to work in. This leads
both to poor levels of performance and a higher level of avoidable staff turnover.

Hom and Griffeth (1995, pp203–205) cite the work of G. R.
Oldham and his colleagues in the USA who have focused particularly on office design issues. They have shown quite
clearly that large open-plan arrangements lead to serious dissatisfaction in the case of many employees. This occurs
because they act to reduce the sense of autonomy and significance that people enjoy in their work. More recently Leaman
and Bordass (2000) found that the optimum number of occu-
pants in an office was around four. A perception of loss of control kicks in quickly when the number becomes much greater
than this. However, they also found that people do vary considerably in their preferences. Some like to have their own
offices, while others prefer to share. Two sharing is fine, provided they get on well. But if they don't, serious levels of job
dissatisfaction occur. It is thus reasonable to conclude that
large partition-free open-plan arrangements are generally
more likely to increase than to decrease turnover, but that the

best situation is one in which people can exercise a degree of choice about where they work.

The main message to take from this research is that the environment in which people are obliged to spend their working hours is an issue that managers must take very seriously. It may seem a trivial issue in many cases, but it is clear that physical discomfort on the part of employees genuinely contributes to voluntary turnover. It thus makes sense to consult people regularly about these matters, particularly where health and safety is a possible consideration. Moreover, employees should always be involved in decision-making about refurbishment or redesign of their own workspaces. Where possible avoid standardisation for the sake of it. It may result in savings deriving from bulk ordering of furnishings and equipment, but potentially greater losses will be sustained if users find it so intolerably uncomfortable or inconvenient to use in practice that it pushes them into looking for an alternative job.

Job design

For as long as people have been employed in larger workplaces, managers have debated the best principles to adopt when deciding which tasks should be carried out by which employees. We can clearly distinguish two traditions of thinking in this area which lead to wholly different conclusions. First, there are cost-focused approaches of the kind pioneered by Frederick W. Taylor and his disciples in the early part of the twentieth century. Efficiency was their watchword as they sought to design organisations which maximised output and minimised cost. This led to the development in manufacturing industry of assembly-line approaches. Each worker was employed to carry out a narrow range of specialised tasks. This meant that minimal training was required, and that relatively low wages could be paid. Moreover, the number of more highly paid skilled staff needed could be kept to a minimum. Added to this was a requirement (driven by the moving assembly line) to work at a pace determined by management. This was challenging but readily achievable.

The same principles live on today in many industries. Aside from manufacturing plants producing large batches of standardised products, we see the same principles of job design employed in call centres, targets for the number of calls dealt with replacing a moving assembly line as the provider of 'pace'. In the public services, too, recent years have seen the vigorous application of 'Taylorist principles' through the use of skill-mix reviews. The aim is to cut costs generally, to reduce the extent to which services rely on qualified individuals in tight labour markets, and so to end up with a system of working in which qualified staff are required (and able) to spend 100 per cent of their time doing only what they are qualified to do. Other, less highly skilled tasks are carried out by support workers who are paid less and are easier to find.

The second tradition is that of the humanists such as Frederick Herzberg, who showed that Taylorist approaches to job design were not, in fact, the most efficient. This is because they involved de-skilling and de-humanising work, making employees fit around the needs of the technology and machinery rather than the other way round. The most efficiently designed workplaces were, in fact, less productive than others because many of the jobs they offered were extremely tedious to perform. Employees just did the same basic tasks repeatedly at a pace and in a manner that was beyond their control. The result was a tendency for employees to resist managers (who were perceived as distant, untrustworthy and unsympathetic characters) through the development of an adversarial employee relations environment. Rates of absence were higher in such dehumanised environments, while standards of discipline were poor. In addition, of course, retention rates were lower.

This led, in the post-war years particularly, to the development of different theories of job design. Instead of reducing the skill levels, employees were to be given every opportunity to build up their skills. Jobs should be made as interesting as possible through the techniques of job rotation, job enlargement and job enrichment. There had to be a move away from cost-focused approaches to job design towards those that were people-focused. Successful motivation of human beings was the true source of a commited workforce, and thus of competitive advantage. These ideas are now seen as mainstream and provide the core principles of 'human resource management' approaches to employment practices.

The truth, of course, is that a balance has to be found between the two approaches. Both are unsatisfactory in their extreme forms. Heavily cost-focused approaches fail because the jobs that they produce are unattractive, while approaches that are overly people-focused end up creating workplaces which exist for the benefit of staff rather than their customers. They also have an idealistic flavour – pleasing in principle but impossible to implement in practice.

What is called for is a blend of the two sets of guiding principles. Systems have to be designed which operate efficiently, but at the same time the jobs which make them up must be as interesting, attractive and motivating as possible. We need to pursue humanistic principles within the constraints of our competitive business environments. This means doing what we can to humanise jobs wherever the opportunity presents itself.

In practice, it would seem that many employers fail to achieve such a balance. In recent years, as labour markets have tightened, they have found themselves faced with critical shortages of staff. High staff turnover is now by far the most important personnel issue facing managers in call centres. It has risen over 30 per cent in many cases, making it increasingly difficult to operate effectively. Yet the companies concerned continue to offer jobs that are so tedious in nature that almost anyone qualified to do them is looking for a change after a few months. Instead of improving this situation, the response tends to be a drive to recruit more 'appropriate' people in the first place. This may help, but what is really needed is the adoption of more imaginative principles of job design.

In the public services, years of pressure to become more efficient has led to widespread skills shortages. Pay is a large part of the problem here, but job design and job content issues are very significant too. A major tool used by successive governments has been the introduction of league tables and performance indicators in a bid to encourage managers to extract from their workforces better value for money on the part of taxpayers. This is laudable in principle – but in practice it has led to a loss of autonomy on the part of key groups of staff and a far higher burden of administration.

We have also seen the systematic de-skilling of many jobs and up-skilling of others, creating a situation in which there is a far clearer distinction between different grades of staff. In this way senior, qualified nurses have gained more responsibility (though precious little extra pay), while the junior unqualified nurses have been reclassified as 'health-care assistants' and firmly placed in supporting and lower-paid roles. The same is true in teaching with the employment of classroom assistants, and will soon be true of the police with the creation of a new brand of sub-officer by the Home Office. In part these are a response to skills shortages, but they are also the source of such shortages in that they contribute to rising staff turnover rates. People are pushed, with little say in most cases, into more and more tightly defined roles. Flexibility is reduced, measures for accountability imposed, and there is increased control over what is done and how it is exercised from above. Little wonder that the result, in relatively poorly paid jobs, is increased staff turnover. It would probably be higher were the number of alternative jobs available to public sector workers not limited by the presence of relatively few private sector competitors. As with the management of call centres, the response of the government appears to be to avoid addressing fundamental issues such as job design. Instead, the focus is on tapping overseas labour markets while claiming publicly that the shortages of key workers are less severe than they really are.

Although it is possible to outline the principles of effective job design, clear prescription is impossible because these need to be applied differently in each case. Two streams of research carried out in recent years can, nonetheless, point us in the right direction. First there is the job characteristics theory that is associated with American academics Hackman and Oldham (see Fried, Cummings and Oldham, 1998, for a good summary of these ideas). They have found, using their Job Diagnosis Survey tool, that satisfaction with a job and motivation to perform it effectively derive from three 'critical psychological states'. If these are not present, it is reasonable to assume that the risk of voluntary turnover is higher. The three are:

□ experienced meaningfulness of the work
□ experienced responsibility for the outcomes of the work
□ knowledge of the actual results of the work activities.

The necessity for employers is therefore to design jobs that maximise the chances of employees' experiencing these states. Hackman and Oldham (1980) suggested five 'core job characteristics' that should be aimed for. Since then they have undertaken extensive research to support their original theory. The five are listed below. In my view the labels given in some cases could be improved, but the thinking behind each is entirely sound.

□ skill variety (the job draws on a number of different skills and talents that the job-holder is able to offer)
□ task identity (the job involves the completion of a whole piece of work – from start to completion)
□ task significance (the job has outcomes that have a substantial impact on the lives of others)
□ autonomy (job-holders are able to exercise substantial independence and discretion in carrying out their roles)
□ feedback (job-holders receive regular, direct and clear information about the effectiveness of their individual performance).

It therefore makes sense, when reviewing job content or establishing a new organisation, to adopt these key design principles and to maximise the extent to which each is present in every job. Of course, in many cases there will be operational and efficiency restraints which prevent their full adoption, but this does not mean that an attempt should not be made. A job that has some of these features, even if in small measure, is more likely to be occupied by its holder for a longer period. The other key message that flows from this research is to avoid removing any of these characteristics if at all possible once they are perceived by job-holders as being present. Because these are characteristics of jobs that can be shown to be valued by staff, getting rid of them is as damaging as cutting pay rates – it leads directly to job dissatisfaction and hence to voluntary resignations.

The second stream of recent research which points in a promising direction as regards the design of effective jobs relates to teamworking. While still very much in the minority, some employers have been increasingly experimenting with the development of 'self-managing teams' or 'autonomous work groups'. These are primarily associated with manufacturing, but are equally well suited to many service-sector organisations (see Parker and Wall, 1998, pp21–24 for a good summary and some examples). Essentially, the approach involves the creation of small teams of employees numbering around eight to 10, and handing over to them responsibility for carrying out a range of different but related tasks.

The most quoted examples focus on car manufacturing plants where assembly-lines have been replaced by teamworking of this kind. A system in which each employee undertakes one or two discrete jobs at a predefined stage of the manufacturing process is substituted for one in which small groups of employees work together to build the entire car. Each team is responsible for organising its own work and may even elect its own leader. Members are multi-skilled and responsible for their own quality control. Rewards are also team-based, bonuses being paid to the groups that achieve the highest level of productivity.

From a staff-retention point of view such systems have a great deal to offer. The daily work that people are employed to do is made more varied and interesting, people are able to exercise control over their own work, and there is opportunity for participation in decision-making and plenty of encouragement to innovate. Moreover, of course, strong team loyalty is developed which engenders fewer feelings of isolation and makes people less likely to consider leaving.

The more extreme forms of teamworking may not be plausible in many organisations or may be considered to constitute too great a financial risk to experiment with. But there remains a case, where it is practical, for delegating responsibility down the hierarchy to groups rather than to individual supervisors, giving them a budget and the necessary equipment, and leaving them to meet their targets in their own way. The upshot is an organisation in which people are able, to a substantial extent, to design their own jobs to suit their own preferences and abilities. This is a sure way of reducing staff turnover. It might even work well in call centres and public services which have retention problems.

Employment security

In recent years a great deal has been written about the virtues of flexibility from the point of view of employers. We should, it is argued, be prepared to employ people on a variety of different types of contract in order to secure competitive advantage. Some types of flexible arrangement – notably part-time working and flexitime systems – are as attactive to potential employees as they are to employers. As shown above, these have an important contribution to make to the retention of staff. However, other forms of flexible working are inherently unattractive to most people because they create insecurity. The result is a situation in which those employed on these contracts are continually seeking greater security both inside and outside the organisation.

No more is this true than of temporary and fixed-term contracts, whose use has increased somewhat in the UK over the past 20 years. They are extensively used in higher education, and I myself was once employed on a succession of fixed-term contracts in a university. It is not a pleasant experience. However reassuring your colleagues are about the likelihood of renewal, you are continually worried about what you would do and how you would survive financially were your contract to come to an end. In addition, of course, there are other very real practical difficulties – such as problems getting access to a mortgage. As a result, you never settle, never feel able to give your employers 100 per cent loyalty, suffer considerable stress as the renewal date comes near, and have to think about applying elsewhere for permanent positions.

Employing people on fixed-term contracts has the same effect in employee-retention terms as keeping them under permanent notice of redundancy. They act as a massive statement of limited confidence in the individual concerned. The consequence is an entirely understandable willingness on such individuals' part to seek jobs elsewhere. Moreover, it often occurs even when they are otherwise very happy in the job and would stay if given a chance to do so.

This chapter therefore concludes by offering sharp words of criticism to human resource management theorists and consultants who preach the virtues of 'employability'. The 'employment society' is on the wane, they argue. Instead, we must all get used to the idea that we are going to become self-employed and will have to work on a series of short-term contracts for different employers in the future.

This is simply incorrect.

Employers who embrace such thinking are likely to end up with poorer-performing uncommitted staff who are unable to find permanent jobs elsewhere. It is essential if you want both to recruit and to retain the best people to offer them as much job security as you are able to. It is very much the minority of people (the more well-paid, as a rule) who are genuinely comfortable with insecurity and prefer the world of 'employability' to that of 'employment'. Most people will opt for security where they can get it – and this often means leaving a temporary job for one that is less attractive but offers longer-term prospects.

9 RECRUITMENT, SELECTION AND INDUCTION

You may find it surprising to find an extensive chapter on recruitment and selection in a book about employee turnover and retention, but there are very good reasons for including one. At base it is because much of staff turnover – of both the voluntary and involuntary kinds – can be avoided by paying greater attention to the recruitment, selection and induction processes. Getting things right at the start of the employment relationship helps to ensure that it remains in place for as long as possible.

In this chapter we focus particularly on the problem of early leaving, which accounts for a sizeable percentage of the total number of separations in many organisations. It is turnover in the first months of employment which offers the most scope for reduction as a result of improved job-entry processes. Better employee selection helps ensure that the right person for the job and for the organisation is appointed in the first place. Ideally, the intention is to appoint people who are both willing and able to fill your job, who fit in well with the organisation's culture and who are content to work on the terms and conditions you offer. Getting such decisions wrong, by applying invalid selection criteria, rushing appointments, and thus hiring unsuitable people, greatly enhances the likelihood of early resignations.

Of course, there is also a responsibility on the employee to make the right decision. Many jobs come to a swift end because people take up posts they are not suited to or able to perform satisfactorily. The basic need to find a job often accounts for this. Applicants oversell themselves to prospective employers because they want to be given the chance to try a job they think they might enjoy and which they know will bring them an income. They only find out that the job is not for them once they have been doing it for a month or two. In other cases, pressure is placed on people by family, friends and job centre advisers to go for interviews and take up job opportunities which, in truth, the applicant does not want. For employers, such situations are not altogether unavoidable, but can be substantially minimised through the use of recruitment processes which give applicants every opportunity to self-select themselves into an appropriate job or out of the running for an inappropriate one.

Honesty is important here. Employers who want to avoid early turnover have to restrain themselves from building up false expectations about jobs, or more commonly, take action to ensure that false expectations are not built up by job applicants off their own bats. Careful handling of the first weeks of employment is as important in this context as the way you interact with potential employees before offering them the job.

Early leaving

A large proportion of employee turnover in the UK is accounted for by people either quitting or being fired in their first few months of employment in a new job. At any one time around one and a half million people (5 per cent of the total working population) are in their first three months of employment in a new job (*Labour Market Trends*, 2001c), but the percentage is a good deal higher among some occupational groups. Up to 10 per cent of employees in retailing, catering and cleaning jobs can be classed as new starters. The chances of these people still being in the same job in a year's time is only just over fifty-fifty, large numbers moving on for one reason or another during their first year.

In a fascinating article, Gregg and Wadsworth (1999) report the results of their study of job tenure based on the government's Labour Force Survey data for the five years between 1992 and 1997. Their starting-point was a 'cohort' of people who took up new jobs in the spring of 1992 – a time, it should be remembered, at which UK job turnover rates were at historically low levels due to high unemployment. They calculated that of the 870,000 workers starting jobs at that time, some 147,000 left within three months (ie 17 per cent). After six months only 68.4 per cent (595,000) were still in the job. And after nine months, the figure was 62.1 per cent (540,000). After a year, over 42 per cent of the original cohort had left. Once two years had passed only around 33 per cent of the workers were still in their original jobs.

Employment turnover rates tend to fall considerably after two years' employment, indicating that people do tend to stay in jobs and with employers they like once they have found them. Labour Force Survey data published in 2001 showed job tenure for the total workforce to break down as depicted in Table 8 below.

The evidence thus reveals a clear pattern of a diminishing rate of employee turnover over time. People seem to make up their minds fairly quickly about whether or not they are going to remain in a job, large numbers deciding that it is not for them within a few months. Once people find a job they are happy doing and which meets their needs, their preference is to stay for some years.

According to Gregg and Wadsworth (1999, p114), around 22 per cent of turnover in the first year of employment is accounted for by short-term contracts' coming to an end, a further 12 per cent occurring as a result of redundancy. The rest occurs either because employees leave of their own accord or because they are asked to at leave by the organisation. The cost to organisations is vast, irrespective of the lost opportunities. Every year hundreds of thousands of people are recruited, selected, inducted, trained, paid and given valuable experience – only for it all to be wasted when they leave within a few months of starting. It is impossible to avoid concluding that something is going very wrong here. Managers

Table 8

Job tenure until departure	Percentage of the workforce
up to two years	32
two to five years	21
five to 10 years	15
10 to 20 years	20
more than 20 years	12

Source: Labour Market Trends, 2001a

are making poor decisions about who to hire, while employees are deciding to enter jobs which do not suit their needs or which they quickly find to be unsatisfactory. It is also probable that employers are not paying sufficient attention to the needs of new employees in their first weeks or months of employment.

Realistic job previews

The second body of research evidence which forms the foundation of my arguments in this chapter is that which has been carried out in the USA on the subject of realistic job previews. The evidence produced is compelling and should be taken on board by all managers who want to reduce the amount of early leaving in their organisations. The idea is simple and commonsensical but, it would appear, relatively rarely adopted in practice.

Giving prospective employees a 'realistic job preview' (RJP) means telling them, or better still showing them, exactly what they will be doing in the role, pointing out *both* its good *and* its bad features. The purpose is to help ensure that new starters enter your organisation with no false preconceptions about what you are offering, and no inflated hopes about the job they will be filling. If achieved successfully, the RJP should ensure that new employees do not have unrealistic expectations which are subsequently dashed when they understand the true nature of the role they are being employed to carry out.

Whereas RJPs have a role to play in most recruitment and selection situations, they are particularly important when the job applicants are not in a position to know a great deal about what the job they are applying for really involves. The major examples are:

□ the appointment of school-leavers and graduate recruits into their first career-related jobs

□ their lack of prior work experience means that they often suffer from a form of 'reality shock' when confronted with the actuality of their new workplace

□ the appointment of people to jobs which are not usually observed by the general public (ie principally carried out behind closed doors)

If recruiting people from outside the industry, it is foolish to expect applicants to have any real perception of the jobs in question. A good example of an industry which suffers from serious early leaving of this kind is funeral-directing.

☐ appointing people to jobs which tend to be portrayed inaccurately in the media, thus giving applicants something of a false impression

Some jobs are glamorised, while others are depicted as being more interesting or 'action-packed' than they are in real life. Examples are hospital roles, some media jobs, and posts in the police and criminal justice systems.

In all of these cases costly early leaving can occur. However, even where people do not leave in the first months, dashed expectations mean that the decision to leave is made early on. A graduate trainee or junior doctor, for example, will choose to complete his or her training before resigning. But she or he will have reached a judgement fairly early on that this is unlikely to be a job to remain in for the long haul. A temporary, semi-committed mindset is thus created from the start.

Realistic job previews seek to prevent this type of situation from developing by giving people every opportunity to gain a full understanding of the job (warts and all) before they enter it. Two possible outcomes result:

☐ Those who are not going to enjoy success in the job or who are not going to fit in well with the organisation are given the opportunity to select themselves out of the picture before agreeing to take the job on.

☐ People enter the job and the organisation with an accurate idea of what they will be doing – of both the good and the bad aspects. The development of inflated expectations and subsequent feelings of disappointment are thus avoided.

The research evidence in favour of RJPs as a method of turnover reduction is robust. Several major studies have been carried out in the USA over the past 20 years which appear to establish beyond doubt that RJPs effectively serve to improve staff retention. The major pioneer of this research has been John Parcher Wanous (1992), further notable work being carried out by Hom and Griffeth (1995) and Phillips (1998). These researchers, in slightly different ways, have shown quite comprehensively that RJPs reduce the propensity of staff to resign voluntarily from new jobs. Several industries have been studied, the same outcome occurring in each case.

The approach involves dividing substantial numbers of new starters into two groups. One is given a standard recruitment and induction programme, the other is given one that is designed as a RJP. Over time, departure rates are then recorded and compared between the two groups. They are invariably substantially higher among the control group than they are among those who have experienced the realistic job preview. In some studies the differences have been very marked, turnover rates being three or four times higher among those who did not get the RJP compared to those who did.

It is difficult to avoid concluding that realism in recruitment, selection and induction processes is thus important where early leaving is a problem. An added attraction of the approach, of course, is its relative cheapness. This is not an employee-retention tool that is going to require major expenditure. The gains to an organisation clearly outweigh the costs in financial terms.

However, there are arguments against some forms of RJP which have to be taken on board and acknowledged to have validity.

The major drawback is the probability that an organisation which gives prospective employees realistic job previews will be less successful at attracting talented recruits than its rivals who do not.

There is evidence to suggest that this is the case, particularly in competitive employment markets in which companies are obliged to 'sell' their jobs with some assertiveness. Graduate recruitment is an example, particularly where larger companies are looking for 'top talent' to fill places on their fast-track management training programmes. But the same can be true of less glamorous positions as well. Wherever a labour market is tight there will always be a strong temptation on the part of managers to talk up the job in order to attract sufficiently high-quality people. The alternative, in some cases, is to come up with no applicants of the right calibre at all. A balance has thus to be struck. How to strike it effectively is a major theme of the rest of this chapter.

RECRUITMENT IN NURSING HOMES

In 1998, together with colleagues at UMIST, I carried out research into recruitment practices in private sector nursing homes in the north-west of England (see Carroll *et al*, 1999). We found that early turnover was a particular problem among care assistants, a good proportion of whom were hired without prior experience in a similar role. Managers had little choice but to take inexperienced staff on for several reasons:

☐ There were not anything like enough experienced staff looking for work.

☐ Pay rates were low because, in most cases, the fees paid by residents were capped by local authorities.

☐ Required staffing levels were set out in health authority guidelines and enforced by health authority inspectorates.

In many cases, we were told, only a very few people would apply for jobs when they were advertised. The managers of the homes, however, had to make swift appointments simply so that they could cover their shifts in the coming weeks.

Given the selection procedures and the speed with which vacancies had to be filled, it was unsurprising to find that many staff resigned within a few weeks of starting their jobs. Many were wholly unprepared for the realities of working with elderly people and found themselves unable to cope pretty soon after their first day.

This is a classic situation in which realistic job previews can play an important role in reducing early turnover. What was needed was for potential recruits to be invited to work alongside an existing employee for a shift so that they could observe exactly what the job would entail and what a nursing home is like as a workplace. One of the homes in our sample had introduced such an approach and had found it useful as a means of filtering out applicants who, while keen on the idea of caring for the elderly, were unprepared for the realities.

The recruitment stage

Research carried out in the USA and reviewed by Wanous (1992) reveals the following:

☐ People entering new jobs tend to have inflated expectations about them.

☐ Some sense of disillusionment or of 'dashed expectations' is thus very common in the first months of employment. Far fewer people end up being positively surprised by their experience in a new job.

☐ A major cause of inflated expectations is impressions gained during the recruitment process.

☐ This is a major cause of early turnover.

However, while the research message is unequivocal, the practical implications are not quite as clear. Every move that is made to make recruitment processes more 'realistic' brings with it some other downside aspect. It is therefore necessary to strike a balance and to handle these matters in a careful, considered way.

Informal recruitment

When seen purely as a means of minimising early turnover, there is a lot to recommend the use of some informal recruitment mechanisms. The major categories are referrals from existing employees, the rehiring of former employees, 'poaching' individuals you or your colleagues know from other employers, the recruitment of 'walk-ins' (people who drop in asking for a job) and forms of 'word of mouth' recruitment. Such approaches are typically denigrated by those who advocate 'good practice' in the HR field – but they are very widely used in practice. *Labour Market Trends* (2001d) reported the results of a UK-based survey in which a very large sample of people were asked how they had found their current jobs. The results were as shown in Table 9 opposite.

These figures suggest that at least half of us find our jobs via informal rather than formal channels. What is more, it would seem that those who are hired informally tend to end up performing rather more effectively in their jobs and staying for longer than those recruited through formal

Table 9

Recruitment method	Percentage of respondents	
	Men	Women
Hearing from someone who worked there	33	28
Replying to an advertisement	21	30
Direct application (ie walk-in/on spec)	16	16
Private employment agency	10	10
Job centre	8	7
Other	12	9

Source: *Labour Market Trends*, 2001d

mechanisms such as newspaper ads or job centres. Research carried out in the USA (see Barber 1998 for a summary) demonstrates clear effects of this kind, although the size of the differences observed between the two groups is not especially marked in every case. What is less clear is why there is this link between longer tenure and informality in recruitment.

Both of the most common explanations relate to realistic job previews.

First, it is probable that people who are recruited via some types of informal channels enter the organisation with their eyes wide open, with few inflated expectations and with a pretty clear idea of what their working lives will entail. This is evidently true of rehires returning to a former employer, but it is also often the case with friends and family of existing employees. They will come in with some ideas of the upsides and downsides of the job, of the pressures and of what will be expected of them. They are thus less likely than colleagues recruited formally to suffer from 'reality-shock'. Moreover, where their expectations are dashed, there are people around who they know to help them through the period of disappointment.

The second major explanation is based on the idea that informal recruits are better placed to self-select than formal recruits. The nature of the two applicant pools is thus different. Informal recruits, because of their 'inside knowledge', are unlikely mistakenly to apply for a job for which they are unsuited. Possession of a fair degree of knowledge about the real nature of the job in question means that applicants who come forward on an informal basis are genuinely interested and honestly believe themselves to be suitable. Otherwise, they would not apply in the first place. This is less true of applicants who come forward through formal channels. However much research they do about the employing organisation, they are less well placed to know whether or not they are suitable for the job vacancy. Their applications are thus more speculative in nature. They may turn out to love the job, once appointed, and to stay for a long time – but there will be more who mistakenly accept a job to which they are not well suited than is the case with informal recruits. Other things being equal, therefore, informal recruits represent a better bet than formal recruits, from the employers' point of view.

On the face of it there is thus a good case, where it is practicable, for abandoning the more expensive forms of recruitment (advertising, agencies, education liaison, etc) and replacing them with cheaper informal approaches. The problem, of course, is that informal approaches can be (and indeed have been) rightly criticised on other grounds. Their major drawback is their tendency to produce rather small applicant pools. The people who come forward are more likely to be long-stayers, but there are only a very few of them to choose from. By contrast, a recruitment advertising campaign will normally yield several times more applicants, giving the employer a far wider choice. Additionally, there are major fairness issues at stake here. Informal recruitment builds barriers between an organisation and its potential labour markets. It means that the employer fails to consider employing people from the wider community, focusing instead on those known to it and to its existing employees. The workforce thus tend to suffer from a lack of diversity, similar types of people from similar backgrounds mostly being recruited. The result may be a harmonious group of staff at ease in one another's company, but new recruits are less likely to bring with them fresh perspectives or new ideas. There is thus some danger of stagnation and of a reduced capacity for creativity and innovation. Moreover, where an organisation aims to serve the needs of a wide range of consumers, a competitive edge may be lost if its staff are not properly representative of the whole community.

The ideal situation, therefore, is one in which a large and diverse applicant pool is assembled and the best person or persons subsequently selected. This will normally require the use of formal (and expensive) recruitment channels. However, it is not going to happen without the use of accurate selection methods. Because these tend to be the most sophisticated and expensive, the 'ideal' is not always a feasible option. I would therefore argue for the use of informal approaches *where there is an early turnover problem and where the more sophisticated recruitment and selection procedures are not affordable.*

You are usually going to be better off recruiting 'the devil you know' (or one of those your employees know) where a key criterion is the wish to employ someone over a relatively long period of time. Stagnation and lack of diversity may become a problem if the strategy is too successful – but where people are leaving in large numbers in their first weeks or months, the dangers associated with a stagnant workforce are the least of your worries.

There is an outside chance of discrimination claims arising when informal recruitment is used. People have brought cases to tribunals in the past in situations where they have been denied the opportunity to apply for a job because informal channels were used. However, such cases are rare and are usually extremely difficult to prove in practice.

Selling the job

Where formal recruitment mechanisms are used, much can be done to minimise the chances of early quitting, as well as early dismissals, by providing applicants with every opportunity to select themselves out of the running for a job they are likely to have difficulty settling into. However, this must be done in such a way as to avoid encouraging those who are genuinely appropriate to select themselves out of the running too. This is often a difficult balance to strike, but it can be achieved by adopting a few basic 'golden rules' and thinking carefully about the recruitment messages you are putting out.

At root it is about being honest about the job you are

offering, and providing as much relevant information as possible up front from the start. If all employers were to take the same approach, it would be a very straightforward task. You would simply describe the job and the organisation, pointing out the good and the bad points. If the job was pretty tedious or stressful, then you would say so. Alas, things are not so simple in a world in which there are plenty of labour market competitors taking a different approach. If you are totally honest and open about the negative aspects of your job while they are emphatically selling theirs with some aggression, you are likely to lose out when it comes to attracting decent applicants. So more subtlety is called for.

Central is the need to make a distinction between a recruitment message which presents the job in an honest but positive manner and one which actively misleads. Achieving the former should ensure, as far as possible, that the right people apply and that the wrong people (ie those who are most likely to leave early) choose not to. It is not necessary to give an inventory of all the unpleasant aspects of the job, or even to mention some of them at all. But you do need to 'come clean', from the outset, about any major features of the job or the organisation that might be considered negative by many people. Failing to do so is at best a waste of time and money, because people will apply for jobs they have no intention of taking. At worst it will lead to early turnover as new starters react to the discovery that they have been misled. So if you are not in a position to offer job security, do not give the appearance that you are. If hours are variable or if the jobholder will be required to travel away from home frequently, say so, up front in your advertisements.

A good, systematic approach entails the following:

☐ Start by focusing on the major reasons that people leave jobs of the type you are recruiting for – particularly in the first few months of employment. This will give you a clear view of the major drawbacks of the job when seen from a labour market perspective. It may be pay, it may be hours, it may be stressors in the job, or the work environment, the organisational culture, or the fact that the job is boring in some shape or form.

◻ Then start thinking about examples of people who have stayed for a long time in the job in question. Go and ask those who are still employed what their view is of the drawbacks as well as what they think are the positive features. It is particularly important to take note of the language the 'satisfied' staff use to describe the less attractive aspects of the job.

◻ Try to work out which attributes tend to be shared by the 'stayers' and which are shared by the early leavers. Then think about forms of words that can be used to convey the importance of the stayers' attributes in your recruitment messages.

This kind of straightforward but systematic and considered thought-process should provide the raw material for a successful recruitment campaign. You should come out of it with a clear view of the positive aspects of the job, of the negative aspects and of ways of expressing the negative aspects in terms that are not off-putting to people who would genuinely succeed in the job. Importantly, these positives and negatives are just as likely to be about the organisation (in terms of its culture, structure and market position) as about the jobs on offer.

Furthermore, you will have a view about the type of attributes that are associated with those who tend to stay longest in the job. It may be people who are conscientious, or competitive, or sociable, or hard-working. Alternatively, it may be people who have certain skills, interests or experiences in common. The aim is then to convey in recruitment literature and in any associated presentations that these are the types of attribute you are seeking.

The approach is best illustrated with an example, starting with a straightforward analysis of the negative and positive aspects of a junior management job in a customer service organisation:

Major sources of reasons for early leaving:

◻ long hours
◻ inability to cope with the responsibility
◻ failure to fit in comfortably with the 'work hard, play hard' organisational culture

- □ reluctance to implement/carry out management instructions
- □ dislike of dealing with difficult customers/customer complaints
- □ administrative aspects of the job tedious.

Major reasons for job satisfaction among longer-serving staff:

- □ varied and sociable work
- □ early responsibility
- □ competitive rates of pay
- □ challenges associated with satisfying customers
- □ possibility of promotion
- □ enjoying the company of colleagues.

Attributes shared by longer-serving job-holders:

- □ genuine enjoyment of the work
- □ keenness to advance in their careers
- □ possessing a strong work ethic
- □ enjoying holding responsibility
- □ sociable disposition
- □ thick skin.

It is clear from this kind of analysis that this is a varied job which is reasonably well paid and offers reasonable career prospects. However, it is also very demanding in terms of time and effort, and involves dealing with difficult situations. There is a good deal of responsibility to be carried, but little influence over policy and practice. The wrong person is going to hate working in this kind of role very quickly; the right person will thrive in it and will happily allow it to take over a major part of their lives.

It is always tempting, when faced with such a vacancy, to write a recruitment advertisement which focuses entirely on the positive aspects. This, it is thought, will bring in a good number of applicants who can be sifted down during the selection process. Managers will spot the people who are unsuitable and reject their applications. The following type of advertisement is thus placed in a relevant publication:

STORE MANAGER

Excellent salary and career prospects

We are looking for keen and ambitious managers looking to start a career in retail management

If you enjoy taking responsibility and like working with a wide range of people, we would like to hear from you.

Previous experience in a customer service role is desirable, but not essential.

Telephone **Paula Smith** on XXXX XXXXXX to discuss this exciting opportunity!

The problem with this kind of positive approach is that it does very little to encourage unsuitable people to select themselves out. Relying on managers to spot these applicants at the selection stage is risky, because most of us are practised at making a good impression at interview and will want to be offered the job if we can secure it. Once we have been short-listed and are invited in for interview, we become competitive. As a result we are not going to come clean about our weaknesses or our doubts. Doing so, we believe, will scupper our chances. We may reject the job later if offered it, but we certainly want to be offered it if we can.

It is far better for the organisation to publish an advertisement which is 'realistic' to start with. This should help to ensure that people who will not be happy in the job, and are likely to leave sooner rather than later, fail to apply in the first place. On the following page is a revised version of the above job advertisement which aims to be realistic rather than negative. It signals the less desirable aspects of the job, but should not put off the more appropriate candidates from applying.

The same principles should apply when you are undertaking more sophisticated recruitment activities – the only difference is that with these there is more space available to set out the realistic picture. Underlying it all – presentations to university students, recruitment brochures, longer advertisements, web-based information – is the need to put

---

ASSISTANT STORE MANAGER

Are you prepared to work long hours and to take on responsibility?

Do you welcome the opportunity of managing in a busy
customer service environment?

Can you work well with all kinds of different people?

Do you relish the chance to prove yourself in a tough and
competitive management role?

If you're the right person, we can offer a competitive salary
and good career prospects.

Telephone **Paula Smith** on XXXX XXXXXX to discuss this
challenging role.

---

across a core message which does not mislead people and
which conveys clearly the major features of 'life in the job'.

Although it is harder to remain in control, you should
endeavour to ensure that any recruitment agent acting on
your behalf puts out the recruitment messages that you consider are appropriate. Agents have good reason to adopt 'hard-
sell' tactics when seeking to attract possible applicants. It is
in their economic interest to place people in jobs quickly.
Unfortunately, in the process they can end up giving potential
candidates misleading information and are often guilty of
'overselling' jobs. To minimise this kind of effect, in labour
markets where you have no choice but to use the services of
agents, you are recommended:

☐ to choose an agent with whom to work closely, giving
them a measure of exclusivity in return for a measure of
control over the approaches they use

☐ where you have reason to believe jobs are being oversold
by agents, to brief them about the job in more detail and
require them to put out a more realistic recruitment message

☐ to correct any misleading information or misleading
impressions given to candidates by agents at the earliest
possible opportunity.

The selection stage

When it comes to employee selection, there are two things to bear in mind in order to enhance the chances of employing long-stayers rather than early leavers. Firstly, there is a need to exercise good judgement yourself when looking at the candidates presented to you. You want to be in a position, as far as is possible, to assess how long each is likely to stay if offered the job. You may choose not to offer the job to the person you consider the best bet in retention terms because other criteria may be more or equally significant. But you want to be in a position to allow 'likely length of service' to be a factor in the decision should it be considered relevant. Secondly, there is a self-selection aspect. As with the recruitment processes we noted above, one aim of the selection stage is to provide an opportunity for candidates to make their own balanced decision about whether to take the job if it was to be offered to them. Selection, and particularly job interviews, thus act as a further opportunity to give candidates a 'realistic job preview'.

In this section we briefly explore ways of achieving these two objectives.

Selecting to retain

On one level this can simply be seen as a matter of employing robust selection techniques. People who represent the best 'match' in terms of their personality attributes, skills and experience are those who are likely to perform best in the job against a range of criteria. They are also the people who are most likely to remain employed for some time and the least likely to take the first available opportunity to leave. For managers the need is thus to employ sound approaches to selection which involve considered decision-making on the basis of good, hard evidence about the candidates who present themselves. In an ideal world this is best achieved using the more sophisticated (and expensive) selection tools such as assessment centres, tests of mental ability and well-designed personality inventories to supplement impressions gained in selection interviews. The more cogent and relevant information you have at your disposal, and the more carefully you use this information, the more likely you are to reach a good decision about who is best suited to fill the post.

It is beyond the scope of this book to discuss the various types of selection methods in detail. Other CIPD books cover this ground very effectively from a variety of perspectives (Roberts, 2000; Taylor, 2002; Toplis *et al*, 1997). However, it is useful to point out those ways in which there is a direct link between action taken at the selection stage and subsequent employee retention.

First, we must acknowledge research evidence which shows that individuals' past turnover records are reasonably accurate predictors of later turnover behaviour. In other words, some people seem to be more prone *generally* to moving jobs than others. The chances are that if a candidate has a history of short spells of employment in the past, he or she will also remain in your employ for a short time too. There is now a considerable volume of US-based research which backs up this perception (see Griffeth and Hom, 2001, pp110–112) with its finding that some people are more 'affectively disposed' than others. Whether this results from life experience, beliefs or inherited traits is a matter of debate, but it would appear to be the case that some of us are naturally inclined to be more negative about the contemporary world of work than others. This translates into the workplace, people who exhibit 'negative affectivity' being more likely to go absent and subsequently to quit than those who do not.

However, this does not mean that employers are wise to take a knee-jerk approach and reject at the shortlisting stage anyone who has been in their present job for a relatively short period of time. People may well have good reasons for quitting jobs early. Making assumptions about likely future job tenure without first examining the causes behind past resignations could mean that you are actually eliminating the best person for the job. On the other hand, you are probably safe to assume that someone who has averaged more than one job a year over a prolonged period of time (five years or more) is predisposed to quit and can safely be rejected at the shortlisting stage.

Ultimately, you must take a pragmatic, balanced view on these matters. It helps a great deal to include on application forms a space for people to state their reasons for leaving previous jobs. This will enable you to decide how reasonable a justification they put forward for a career punctuated by frequent job moves. If the reasons appear to be both sound and believable, and the candidate concerned is qualified for your job, it makes sense to interview him or her. You can then take the opportunity of a face-to-face encounter to question him or her in greater depth about the reasons for leaving former jobs.

Indeed, asking about former job moves is in itself a useful type of question to include in a selection interview. It is potentially very revealing about people's motivation, ambitions, likes and dislikes, as well as the type of experiences that are likely to bring about an early resignation in the future. The problem is getting interviewees to give full and honest answers to such questions. Many will prefer to give a rehearsed answer (which may or may not contain an element of truth) because they fear that giving a true answer may damage their chances of securing the job. They may be concerned that interviewers will regard the true reason as trivial, unjustified or unreasonable in some other way. 'I had a personality clash with a colleague,' or 'I couldn't stand my new boss' are given as answers as infrequently as 'I was fired' when questions about departures from former jobs are asked. People prefer to give a solid, professional and inoffensive reason which has some credibility, but which is not necessarily true. If the answer can be made to sound impressive, all the better. This is why candidates tend to state that they left in order to gain broader experience, to develop their careers, to take on a more challenging role, or to travel the world.

The only way to get somewhere near the truth is to refuse to take a simple two- or three-sentence answer and to ask follow-up questions which probe more deeply. This makes it harder for the candidate to get away with giving you only the rehearsed answer. In my view the best approach involves asking candidates to tell you the story in some detail of their decision to leave a former (or their current) employer. When did they first think about leaving? What were the major triggers? At what stage did they actively start looking for another job? Did they have second thoughts?

Self-selection

Employment interviews are, in one respect, a poor forum in which to persuade unsuited candidates to select themselves out of the running for a job. As I argued above, most of us go into an interview with a view to securing the job. The mindset is positive, we think competitively, and set out to give a good impression. If asked if we have doubts about the job or about our ability to handle its pressures, we confidently affirm our self-belief and state that we would relish the challenge. We typically do not thank the interviewer for questioning our ability to perform the job well before agreeing to withdraw.

However, this should not mean that interviewers should refrain from taking the opportunity given by an interview (especially a second interview) to explain in some detail the good and bad points of the job and the organisation. On hearing the 'realistic' account candidates may react as if the negative aspects do not bother them or state that they see them positively – but they may think differently later on after the interview is completed and they are reflecting on its content. On occasions it will lead to the withdrawal of plausible candidates who impress you, but who themselves know that the job is not for them. Moreover, of course, the experienced interviewer will be able to make inferences from the true reaction of candidates to RJPs from their body language and facial expressions.

There is no need to give undue prominence to the negative aspects of the job (or to those aspects many people would view negatively). It is not a question of trying to put people off. Instead, the aim must be to ensure that the candidate, if offered the job, accepts knowing full well what will be expected of him or her by managers, customers, fellow-employees and others who he or she will interact with. He or she should also be aware of what the day-to-day experience of working in the job and for the organisation in question is going to be like. In other words, there should be no nasty surprises in the first weeks of employment. It also makes sense to show candidates exactly where they will be working and to introduce them to possible future colleagues. You should also give them every opportunity, both during and after the interview, to ask their own questions about the job to which you give full and frank answers.

The induction stage

The link between effective induction and the successful retention of employees in the first months of their employment is obvious. We should not need the large amount of solid research evidence that has been published on the link to acknowledge its existence. Yet it is still common to find examples of organisations which handle induction very badly. It almost seems, in some cases, that there exists an ambition to make life as difficult as possible for newcomers. They are left alone and expected to find their own feet, they receive training only when colleagues find the time to spend with them, jargon is not explained properly, nor are the rules and customs of the organisation.

I can recall several cases from my own career of extraordinarily poor experiences given to employees on their first days. In one instance a colleague of mine spent his first day ordering a desk and chair for himself. In another someone spent his first morning sitting in his car before a manager returned after lunch to greet him and set about finding him an office. On other occasions new starters were simply put to work on day 1 without any proper training or orientation, and expected either to sink or to swim. Some people, particularly those with some experience of similar types of workplace, are able to sail through such experiences and to establish themselves quickly in the job. For those who are inexperienced in the industry concerned, and for young people entering their first few jobs, the results are very different. An already difficult type of situation is made far worse. Confusion, discomfort and depression are experienced, and in many cases this leads to early turnover. So common is this type of situation that it has been given a title that is widely used in management circles – 'the induction crisis'.

A second common approach, which is better but by no means perfect, is to see induction as an event rather than as a process by which a new employee is helped to acclimatise. Here a day or two are set aside for some kind of formal induction training. In high-turnover organisations these are held weekly and are normally attended by employees on their first days of work. In most larger organisations they are held monthly or bi-monthly and are thus attended by all new starters within their first few weeks of employment. The programmes vary considerably, but typically involve presentations and the showing of videos about different aspects of the organisation. Senior personnel introduce themselves, fire regulations are explained and the corporate mission statement is explained.

Such events can play a useful role, provided they are held soon after the employee starts and provided they include the opportunity to meet and establish relationships with other new starters. It also helps if a relatively small group of people are inducted at the same time. As soon as more than a dozen or so participants are involved, there is a tendency for those who are suffering from a lack confidence to retreat into their shells and say very little. This is a problem because it is these individuals (ie those suffering some kind of induction crisis) who are most likely to leave at an early stage if the opportunity is not taken at induction events to instill greater confidence in them.

In practice, however, many induction events play only a marginal role in assisting in acclimatisation and in preventing early turnover. There are two major reasons for this:

☐ Management (including the HR function) have a tendency to see them as something of a tedious necessity rather than as occasions of some significance. They are thus typically led by a junior member of the management (or training) team and are delivered in a lacklustre fashion. The fact that the same type of event has to be held repeatedly makes it unglamorous from a management perspective and low down the list of HR priorities.

☐ The content is determined by what managers think is necessary and not by what employees actually need. The practice of 'inducting' all kinds of different newcomers from all over the organisation at the same time leads to generalised content of limited relevance to each individual participant.

The result is an induction programme that meets some management objectives (fire regulations, health and safety, communicating details of the pension scheme, etc) but which does very little to ameliorate the symptoms of an induction crisis, or indeed to assist people to become comfortable (and hence productive) in their new jobs. The socialisation aspects are then left to individual supervisors to arrange, with hardly anything by way of intervention at the organisational level. Some appreciate the importance of effective induction and set aside sufficient time to meet each new employee's needs. Others do not, and it is often their lack of effort in this area that results in excessive early turnover.

So what form should a really effective induction programme take?

First and foremost it should be seen as a process that begins before the employee joins the organisation and that continues for a number of weeks (or even months) until he or she is settled and working at full capacity in the new job. The pre-employment phase is crucial in helping to manage expectations and thus in avoiding subsequent disillusionment. It involves keeping in regular touch with those who have accepted jobs with you but are working out their notice. Ideally, they should be given the opportunity to meet with their future colleagues before starting and should, if it is considered appropriate, be sent copies of documents and/or e-mails that are relevant to their coming role. All these steps help reduce the sense of strangeness that people experience in a new job and assist them in adjusting quickly.

At the other end of the process it is important that regular and semi-formal meetings are held between supervisor and new starter for two or three months after the start date. These provide the opportunity for the newcomer to ask questions and to express any concerns. Early resignations are far less likely to occur where people are able to voice their difficulties and have them dealt with sympathetically.

The second feature of an effective induction is that it genuinely acts as a learning experience. The aim is to make people comfortable in their new jobs, confident in their ability to reach the required level of performance and crystal clear about what the organisation expects of them. This involves thinking about induction from the employees' point of view and including within the programme all the information they need to know in order to become effective. Employees will learn all this at some stage, but including it in the induction helps ensure that they do so sooner rather than later. Griffeth and Hom (2001) quote the work of Chao *et al* (1994) to illustrate the different categories of information that new employees must assimilate fully. Their checklist includes topics that are rarely covered formally in induction programmes:

☐ performance proficiency (job requirements and the skills/knowledge required to perform effectively)
☐ people (how to establish effective and satisfying work relationships)
☐ politics (who are the influential people and how organisational politics work)
☐ language (acronyms, slang and jargon unique to the organisation)
☐ goals and values (the organisation's purpose and current direction)
☐ history (the origin of organisational structures, customs, myths, rituals, etc).

Third, there is a good case (especially in organisations with a real early turnover problem) to address directly and deliberately the common causes of resignations in the first months of employment. There is no need to sweep these issues under the carpet. The only way to reduce early turnover is to address its causes, and induction has an important part to play here. The best approach to use when developing this kind of programme is set out by Wanous (1992). He suggests that the way to start is by asking recent starters about their experiences. Find out from them what caused them the greatest stress in their first weeks. What made them most tired? What did they find confusing? What came as an unpleasant surprise? What would they have liked to know up front from the start? You then make use of this information to design a programme which:

- warns newcomers about the difficulties they are likely to face in their first weeks
- makes it clear that the organisation understands, sympathises and will help new starters to overcome these difficulties
- provides practical advice as to how the stressors can best be managed.

Here too, what we are seeing is a further attempt to give new employees some form of realistic job preview. The aim is to manage expectations in such a way as to reduce the likelihood of a 'hard landing' or of people's experiencing 'reality shock'. Instead, they know what to expect ahead of time, are equipped to deal with problems, and know to whom they should turn for help should they need it.

THE TEXAS INSTRUMENTS STUDIES

A classic research exercise designed to investigate the benefits of induction was carried out in the USA in the 1960s by two occupational psychologists called Gomersall and Myers. Working among employees at an electrical assembly plant, they started by ascertaining from existing employees what aspects of the work they had found to be most stressful when they first took up their jobs. Acting on this information, they designed a six-hour orientation programme designed to reduce stress among new starters. The course covered four areas:

- New recruits were assured that failure rates were very low and that the vast majority of starters quickly learned to perform to a satisfactory level.
- They were told to expect some baiting from established employees, but to ignore it because the same treatment tended to be given to all new starters.
- It was suggested that they took the initiative in terms of communication with others, including their new supervisors.
- They were each given some specific advice about how to build up a good working relationship with their particular supervisors.

A hundred new starters, selected at random, were then put through the new orientation programme, and a further hundred given the standard two-hour course offered by the company. The result was a substantial divergence between the performance of the two groups, those who had attended the six-hour session achieving higher productivity rates. They also had better attendance records and required less training time than those who had been given the standard two-hour introduction.

Source: Wanous (1992, pp178–179)

10 EFFECTIVE SUPERVISION

The final chapter in this section focuses on the day-to-day management of people in the workplace. I use the terms 'supervisor' and 'supervision' throughout, but these should be taken to relate to any situation in which one person has direct line management responsibilities for others. The supervisor–subordinate relationship is the most important in the organisation when seen from the point of view of employees. To a very great extent it determines how happy they are in their jobs, how good their prospects are within the organisation, and the quality of their day-to-day experience in the job. Where such relationships are characterised by trust and loyalty they are healthy. Not only does this enhance the level of performance produced by employees, it also substantially reduces the likelihood that they will consider looking for alternative employment. On the other hand, where the relationship is poor, weak or non-existent, voluntary resignations are a good deal more likely to occur.

I start here by setting out the evidence, such as it is, for a link between staff turnover and ineffective supervision before trying to explain why poor supervision appears to be – is – so common in UK workplaces. The rest of the chapter goes on to suggest various ways in which improvements can be made. The key principles of effective supervision are set out, before a final section argues for organisation-level interventions that serve to improve the supervisor–subordinate relationship. Much of what I have to say here is really just common sense. But my experience as an employee in several workplaces and as a researcher in the field of staff turnover tells me that many organisations are weak in this area and are suffering poor retention-rates in consequence.

The significance of effective supervision

In our research we have found that poor or ineffective supervision is the most common reason given by people when asked about why they left their last job. We have recorded dozens of instances in which people resigned as a direct result of being treated badly by their line managers, and many others where there was a clear, if indirect, link between the quality of supervision and the decision to leave. Unless those we have surveyed and interviewed are misleading us on a significant scale, it is fair to assert that the major cause of voluntary turnover in the UK today is incompetent supervision. Organisations which focus on improving this aspect of their operations thus stand to gain greatly from reduced staff turnover.

What also seems clear is that employers are often unaware of the extent to which their line managers are contributing directly to their turnover. This often occurs because it is the line managers themselves who are responsible for recording and reporting the reasons people leave. In most cases it is they who undertake exit interviews (where it happens at all) and they who state on 'leavers' forms' or on computerised personal records why someone has decided to quit. I am not claiming that they actively mislead when undertaking these activities, although some do seek to downplay their own role. In most cases I think the under-recording occurs for other reasons:

☐ Leavers are reluctant to tell their bosses that they are leaving because of the bosses' own actions or inactions. They may hint that this is the reason, but understandably prefer not to tell the whole truth.

☐ Like all employees, supervisors often have little conception that they are carrying out an aspect of their job poorly. They like to think that they are good managers of people. They thus choose not to register mentally any evidence that contradicts this belief.

☐ There appears to be a tendency in organisations – deriving in the main from the propagation of a positive, 'self-believing' culture – to blame employees for their own decision to leave. Quitting is seen as being a mistaken act in many cases. No consideration is given to the possibility that it might even be the right thing for the employee to do, and that the organisation and its management are themselves largely to blame.

Some American studies have come up with similar findings (Griffeth and Hom, 2001, pp85–93), yet questions about supervisor relationships do not seem to be asked in most questionnaire-based surveys of reasons for leaving. It is not, for example, included in the UK government's Labour Force Survey questionnaires that ask people why they are looking for another job. However, in those in which dissatisfaction with the quality of supervision is included it is invariably found to be a prominent cause. Zarandona and Camuso (1985), for example, found that it was the principal reason given by 24 per cent of their respondents.

The term 'poor supervision' can of course cover a wide variety of different types of situation. Below, distilled from stories told to us, are several of the more common examples:

□ supervisors who fail to respond to grievances

   We have been told of many resignations that have come about because managers avoided confronting issues that were important to employees. They often prefer to sweep problems under their office carpets.

□ supervisors who act autocratically

   These are situations in which, for no apparently good reason, managers impose their views on their subordinates without discussion, irrespective of the effect such decisions have on their working lives.

□ supervisors who abuse their positions

   There is a tendency for supervisors to treat subordinates rudely, to make jokes at their expense or to criticise them unfairly (often when they are under pressure) without subsequently issuing any kind of apology.

□ supervisors who show undue favouritism to some staff

   Those who see their colleagues being given more responsibility, praise, interesting tasks or pay than they are getting – *when it is not justified* – develop very negative feelings and often quit.

□ supervisors who fail to appreciate their subordinates' efforts

Another common cause of dissatisfaction, and hence of voluntary leaving, is situations in which people put in extra effort, complete a project or make a special contribution in other ways – and get insufficient recognition or feedback.

□ supervisors who are very self-centred

Another common situation is one in which career-minded supervisors give the appearance of running their domain in their own interests rather than for the good of their teams or, in some cases, their customers.

□ supervisors who fail to deliver on their promises

This covers situations where indications are given that things will improve in the near future or that other commitments will be met. If in practice the promises are not subsequently delivered, the result is greater resentment than was felt at the start. This can push people over the edge into looking for a new job.

It is not my intention to lambast all supervisors here. They have a difficult job and frequently commit one or more of the above 'errors' despite managing their staff with the best of intentions. It is also true that employees sometimes gain an unfair perception of their own supervisors and claim that they have done things or are responsible for actions which are actually the consequence of circumstances or done at the behest of more senior managers. Nonetheless, it remains the case that many avoidable departures occur, either wholly or in part, because of supervisors' actions or inactions.

As always when seeking to reduce staff turnover, it is the perceptions of staff that are important and not the reality. If employees are given reason to believe that they are being treated poorly or unfairly, and this subsequently leads to resignations, the organisation must count this as a failure. So although bettering the quality of supervision is important as a basis for improving staff retention, being seen to do so is just as necessary.

Before we go on to discuss how these issues can be

addressed, two further points should be made by way of qualification.

Firstly, it is important to recognise that industries vary considerably in terms of the quality of supervision. The biggest problems occur where people are promoted into supervisory roles at a young age before they have had the opportunity to observe and experience other supervisors at work. Promotion of inexperienced people occurs mainly in high-turnover low-paying service industries such as catering and retailing. Many of the real horror stories that we recorded originated in these sectors. However, there are also major problems in the professional services sector and others in which supervisors are put under very considerable pressure to produce results without being given sufficient resources. We recorded fewer problems of this kind in the public services and in larger manufacturing companies where line managers seem to be promoted at a later stage in their careers. Nonetheless, it remains the case that there is room for considerable improvement in all sectors.

Secondly, we must acknowledge that the extent of the link between poor supervision and voluntary departures varies depending on labour market conditions. Except where supervisors behave wholly inappropriately or incompetently, people will only leave their jobs for these reasons when they have found suitable alternative employment. In loose labour market conditions or where people have few satisfactory career options, they are inclined to stay and put up with their supervisors in the short term. They grin and bear it in the expectation that their supervisor will soon move on or that a reorganisation will relieve them in due course. So organisations must focus mainly on deficiencies in the quality of supervision when their labour markets are tight and when their employees have few difficulties finding themselves other jobs in the locality.

SOME EXAMPLES OF REASONS FOR LEAVING GIVEN BY OUR INTERVIEWEES WORKING IN THE PROFESSIONAL SERVICES AND RETAILING INDUSTRIES

I felt as though I didn't get the support from my superiors. I have always considered myself a loyal employee – but when I didn't get the support I needed from my superiors, I began to become increasingly dissatisfied.

I had constantly spoken to people who supposedly had some sort of power to do something about the lack of support and training I was receiving, and it was as though only lip-service was paid to my complaints. So much that I decided I had had enough. I gave them the opportunity to make a difference, and they did nothing.

I continually expressed the urgent need for more employees at different levels, but was continually ignored at management meetings. When nothing ever happens and nothing is done about it, that's it ... There's no point any more.

Managers and partners have their favourites and work is delegated by them. If you are not a favourite, you don't get the good work.

Because I didn't fit into a clique I got the boring, monotonous work and felt I was never being tested or able to push myself. Consequently, I saw colleagues who had joined at the same time progress and gain broader experience when in comparison my career appeared to have stagnated.

I wasn't one of the manager's favourites, so I wasn't getting good work. The more I raised this issue and stood up to her and made it clear I wasn't happy, the more she disliked me.

I felt that I didn't get the recognition I deserved. This led me to feel very frustrated and undervalued in what I was doing.

I was never given praise or recognition for a job well done, and compliments on the quality of my work – which were made by clients – were never passed on to me. I often felt that good work went unrewarded or unrecognised. All I wanted was respect and recognition for my efforts.

My immediate boss was under immense pressure from work and was bidding to win promotion – but never did she get support or recognition from her superiors. I saw how unhappy she had become, and she was working as hard as she possibly could.

The supervisors simply did not care. They didn't know if they were coming or going, and were totally unprofessional. But then, what do you expect from a 19-year-old on £4.50 an hour?

We would be a couple of staff down, and customers would be getting frustrated at the queue on the counter. A manager would walk past, see the commotion and look away, so you couldn't get his attention to ask for help.

He always shouted at me across the shop floor, referring to me as 'Oi, you!' So I said to him, 'If you don't mind, my name is *xxxx*, not Oi.' He turned to me and said in front of my colleagues, 'I don't care what your name is – you are a bakery manager. There's lots of bakery managers out there. I can get another one.' At that point I decided to let him find himself another bakery manager.

It was dreadful. She upset everyone who worked for her. No one worked there for long – they just couldn't stand it for long. So you never made many friends at work as people just came and went. Even if you were friends, you wouldn't dare talk to each other. It was like a prison camp.

Why is the standard of supervision so poor?

It is not difficult to answer this question. In many ways it is a good deal harder to establish why we persist in allowing the standard of supervision to remain so poor.

The main reason is simply because good supervision is difficult, and good supervisors are therefore a rarity. Like good parenting, good supervision is not something that comes naturally to everyone. It is a skill that is gained over time through experience and by learning from one's own and others' mistakes. Yet despite this evident truth, organisations rarely offer people formal training in supervisory skills either before or after they take up their first posts which carry responsibility for the management of others. It should therefore come as no surprise that so many supervisors are ineffective.

The problem is compounded by our tendency to appoint people into supervisory positions for the wrong reasons. It is relatively rare that someone is appointed because of their supervisory skills. Instead, we promote people who are good at doing their present jobs, assuming maybe quite wrongly that this will make them good supervisors of others doing that job. Such people are often respected for their technical abilities, which helps, but many turn out to be poor managers of others.

Another common situation involves the promotion of the longest-serving member of a team into a supervisory role, or the most highly paid. Sometimes we simply choose the person who wants the supervisor's role most, or worse still, allow the former occupant of the post to select his or her 'favourite' as successor.

The same is true in the case of many external appointments. Proficiency in the current role is used as the yardstick as much as or more than someone's supervisory potential. The result is an inexperienced and ineffective supervisory cadre in the organisation, often more concerned with establishing their own authority over disrespectful subordinates than motivating a team of individuals to achieve organisational objectives.

Finally, having appointed someone for poor reasons, we have a tendency to judge their subsequent performance without reference to their achievements as supervisors. Provided organisational goals are accomplished, we see no need to question how effectively someone manages his or her team. Because managers who lose their staff as a result of their incompetence as supervisors pay no penalty, they do not concern themselves too much when their people quit.

Six golden rules of effective supervision

It is my belief that a great deal of unwanted staff turnover could be avoided if people in supervisory roles were helped by their organisations to be more effective supervisors. As pointed out above, supervisory skills do not necessarily come naturally. They have to be learned. This means formally training people in the principles of effective supervision both before and after they take up posts which carry responsibility for the management of others. The six most important lessons that must be learned seem to me to be:

1 Give praise where praise is due

Supervisors often forget to praise staff when they do their jobs well. It's almost as if we expect our employees to perform at the highest level consistently and anticipate no less. Why praise someone just for doing their job? The same principle, of course, does not apply when people slip up or perform badly. Then the supervisor steps in and is quick to criticise.

This is a tendency which all supervisors must guard against. They must remember that most staff, especially the average performers, see themselves as being more effective employees than their bosses do. The majority of people, when asked, rate their own performance as 'above average'. They therefore expect this to be recognised and are disappointed when it is not. If they then receive criticism on the occasions when they do perform poorly, it is seriously unappreciated. As a general rule, except in the case of genuinely poor performers, supervisors should try to praise twice as often as they criticise. Giving people a 'kick up the arse' at one point, and failing to give them the requisite 'pat on the back' at another, is a sure way of storing up resentment and precipitating a voluntary resignation.

2 Avoid the perception of favouritism

Treating people fairly is a fundamental principle of effective supervision. Again it is a question of looking at what goes on, as far as possible, through the eyes of your subordinates. Whatever your views about the relative merits of your team members, and however much you personally like and trust some more than others, it is essential that you are seen not to be acting unfairly. Once the perception of favouritism is established it is difficult to regain the trust and support of those who believe they are being denied opportunities that are their due. You may succeed in motivating your apparent favourites, but you will demotivate everyone else. Some will be more likely to leave as a result. More often than not, it will be the more able whom you lose first because they are best placed to secure an alternative job.

3 *Talk to every team member regularly*

Another common reason that supervisor–subordinate relationships deteriorate is simply a lack of contact between the parties. Irrespective of whether you want to praise or criticise, it is above all necessary to *notice* your staff, to show an interest in what they are doing, and to give them feedback. Even when you have nothing significant to say to your staff, you should make the effort to talk to them, ask them what they are doing, and provide some kind of support. This goes equally for work-based and non-work-based activities.

The alternative is the fostering of a distant relationship that works against the development of trust and loyalty. People are more likely to quit when they think that their absence will not be noticed or where they see themselves as being undervalued as human beings. It is not necessary to be over-friendly or gushing in any way. It is just a question of ensuring that some kind of genuine relationship of mutual respect is established and continues over time.

4 *Act when you suspect there are problems*

It is very easy for busy supervisors who have important work of their own to do to act deaf or turn a blind eye when they believe their subordinates to be unhappy with some aspect of their work. Sometimes this means that small problems grow into very much bigger ones, making them far harder to deal with later on. The aim should always be to sort out difficulties at an early stage. Once you know people well, you can tell something is wrong from their body language and the tone of their voice. You should also be able to spot that there is some problem even if the individual concerned is doing a reasonable job trying to cover it up. It may, nonetheless, be an issue that will ultimately lead to a resignation. We know that people leave as a result of personality clashes with colleagues, of an inability to cope with a workload or of strain caused by problems originating outside the workplace. In many cases judicious and early intervention by a well-meaning supervisor can defuse such problems and serve to retain individuals for longer.

5 *Give people as much autonomy as you possibly can*

A view that is pretty well unanimously shared by management researchers across all disciplines is the damaging effect
of overly close supervision. The good supervisor should therefore minimise the extent to which his or her subordinates
perceive themselves to be supervised at all. Wherever possible
you should find ways of allowing your staff freedom to carry
out their own work in the way that they want to. They should
be encouraged to use their own judgement and to develop systems of working with which they are comfortable. Where
standardisation across an organisation or part of an organisation is genuinely necessary, then rules should be drawn up
and agreed with the consent of the supervisees. The more
highly qualified and experienced your staff are, the more
advantage is to be gained from allowing them the greatest
possible measure of autonomy. A sure way to demotivate and
to precipitate voluntary resignations is to give the impression
that you are standing over people and watching them unnecessarily. Some management control usually has to be exercised to ensure that the organisation achieves its objectives
effectively, efficiently and fairly. But control for the sake
of control is unhealthy and simply serves to make an
organisation less effective.

6 *Involve people in decision-making*

As well as allowing people – and, indeed, encouraging them –
to take responsibility for their own areas of work, good supervisors also involve staff in the decisions that they have to
take themselves. This need not be done in a formal way. All
that is usually required is to ask employees their views ahead
of time. Doing so shows in a very direct way that each individual's contribution is valued, and that management is
carried out by consensus rather than by *diktat*. Involving
people in decision-making serves to boost their self-esteem –
whereas failing to do so serves to depress and demotivate. It
is particularly important, in my view, to involve new staff as
far as is possible. Asking someone who has just joined your
team to contribute his or her views helps to build trust in the
early weeks when, as we have seen, a lot of voluntary resignations occur. What better way is there to demonstrate that a

new person is welcome, valued, and needed than to ask him or her for an opinion on significant issues?

However, involvement on an informal scale only works if it is genuine. Visibly going through the motions for the sake of appearances may well actually make matters worse than if decisions are simply imposed from above. Pseudo-consultation builds mistrust and makes voluntary resignations more, rather than less, likely.

EXPLORING REASONS FOR TURNOVER AMONG NURSES

In 1996, a large NHS Trust hospital in the north of England undertook a detailed investigation of the high turnover rates among junior qualified nurses, which was running at 23 per cent. An independent researcher was brought in to conduct a questionnaire survey of 193 nurses who had left voluntarily over the previous two years, and to undertake interviews with nursing managers about the causes of turnover in their departments. Over 70 per cent of the nurses who had left were still employed in the NHS, and all but 5 per cent had remained in nursing or nursing-related careers.

The questionnaire results showed that 63 per cent had left for reasons that could be categorised as 'controllable'. Although a number of reasons for turnover were established, three were particularly significant. These were: a poor working relationship with the supervisor; failure to secure promotion; and general dissatisfaction with aspects of the working environment (including low staffing levels). Of particular interest was the identification of departments in which there was a pattern of poor supervisor–subordinate relationships. It became very clear from the questionnaire that some nursing managers were far more effective motivators than others, and that developing their supervisory skills would lead to improved retention of nurses in their departments.

Source: Burton, 1996

Organisation-level policy

So far in this chapter we have focused on approaches that can help reduce turnover through action at the level of the individual supervisor. This is where the greatest impact can be made. But the chances of good supervision becoming a reality are greatly aided when 'helpful' policies and practices are in operation across whole organisations. The most important, as noted above, are:

☐ selecting supervisors, to a greater degree, on the basis of an assessment of their supervisory skills

☐ providing supervisors (new, established or potential) with training in the skills of effective supervision.

Yet a great deal more can be done. It is mainly a question of putting in place a policy that conspicuously backs up the principles of good supervision set out above, and that helps to make them part and parcel of an organisation's people management culture. The following approaches should help to inspire confidence and trust on the part of employees, and hence serve to reduce unwanted turnover.

A commitment to equality and diversity

One of the great paradoxes of modern management is the apparent mismatch between the rhetoric on the subject of diversity and the reality in our organisations. The more we commit ourselves to the principle of equal opportunities, the less actual impact seems to be made on the ground. It is over 25 years since the passing of the Race Relations Act, and over 30 since the Equal Pay Act came onto the statute books, yet ethnic minorities and female employees still appear to suffer from substantial discrimination at work. Women's pay is still only around 80 per cent of men's and seems set to remain at this level for some time to come. Differences between the sizes of male and female pay packets begin to open up very early in our respective careers, there being a substantial differential observable in the case of graduates within a year or two of leaving university. Members of certain ethnic minorities also continue to be discriminated against to a severe degree. Unemployment among graduates from these groups is more than double that of white graduates, even where their qualifications and awarding institutions are identical (Elliot-Major, 2001). Inequality of treatment is thus alive and well in British industry, and members of the groups who are discriminated against are right to be on their guard against it.

This has important implications for organisations seeking to reduce staff turnover, because one of the significant reasons that people resign from jobs appears to be the belief that they have been unfairly discriminated against on grounds of their race or gender. This is certainly a message that comes over loud and clear from the extensive American studies carried out on the subject (Hom and Griffeth, 1995, pp239–252) and is one that anecdotal evidence supports as far as the UK is concerned. It is reasonable to believe that the same is true in relation to discrimination against people suffering from a disability or to discrimination on any other unfair grounds. For these groups there is often therefore an additional bitterness felt when one or more of the following occurs, simply because they think that it might well have something to do with who they are and not what they contribute:

- supervisor bias towards others
- a disappointing or non-existent pay rise
- lack of support from colleagues
- failure to be promoted
- failure to be given the more interesting job tasks.

The extent to which supervisors actively and knowingly discriminate in these ways is a moot point, as is the whole question of how far organisations in the UK can accurately be described as 'institutionally racist'. It is true that other explanations can be advanced to explain the differences in pay and career prospects between different groups, and it is also true that some women and members of some ethnic minorities compete very effectively with white men. But it is my belief that a great deal of active discrimination continues to occur, as well as much that is subconscious.

You do not have to look very hard to find examples. I observed quite serious cases in every personnel management job I held prior to becoming a lecturer, and have recorded several more in interviews with managers while carrying out research. In the end, when seen from an employee-retention perspective, the reality is not important. What matters is the perception. However much managers in an organisation believe they do not discriminate unfairly, they will lose staff unnecessarily if the perception is otherwise.

Assurances are therefore insufficient. What organisations have to ensure is that they are quite clearly *seen* to act fairly and that they are *seen* to be intolerant of unjust discrimination. It is a question of going the extra mile and bending over backwards to guarantee that you are perceived by your staff as genuinely committed to the principles of equal opportunities and diversity. This requires the ongoing and conspicuous development of policies in this area, and their effective communication and enforcement. Sometimes these kinds of initiative are resisted by managers because, from their perspective, they are unnecessary and therefore a waste of time and money. They are also often regarded as incidental to the real priorities in the human resource management field. This is not so where employee turnover is a problem and where managers are serious about improving their retention rates.

Appraising supervisors

Another way in which organisation-level policy can contribute to more effective supervision is through the development of appraisal systems that focus specifically on supervisory matters. Essentially this means refraining, when formally appraising people with supervisory responsibilities, from focusing exclusively on the delivery of organisational objectives. There is also a need to appraise them on their performance as managers of people. In my experience this happens relatively rarely, the result being that poor supervisors who nonetheless manage to deliver financially are not tackled. They thus continue to lead demotivated teams which under-perform and which could achieve a great deal more. They also continue to lose valuable staff unnecessarily. In many cases they remain blissfully unaware that their supervisory skills could be substantially improved.

Various approaches can be used here. Some organisations have experimented with 360-degree appraisal systems which require supervisors (along with everyone else) to be formally appraised in terms of their performance by subordinates and peers as well as by their own line managers. These systems are attractive in principle but can be difficult to make work effectively in practice. It is, for example, difficult to ensure the total confidentiality that is necessary if staff are to give honest appraisals of their own managers' performance. 360-degree appraisal is also ill-suited to some more traditional workplace cultures. Here, its introduction can lead directly to the resignation of good supervisors who are uncomfortable with the idea of being appraised 'from below'.

There is really no need to go this far. All that is necessary is the inclusion in formal appraisal reviews of discussion about supervisory achievements. How many staff have left voluntarily during the review period? What were the reasons? Could the resignations have been avoided? What has the supervisor been doing to boost the commitment and motivation of each team member, and the group as a whole? What are the main performance problems? What has been done to tackle these? What else could be done? And so on. Including such issues prominently in appraisal interviews helps to flag them up as major organisational concerns. At the end of the day your supervisors will not treat the problem of employee turnover seriously, or give proper attention to their possible role in reducing it, unless it is very clearly demonstrated to them that it is a matter of priority. Including it in formal performance appraisals helps ensure that this is achieved.

Voice v exit

Above, employee participation in decision-making was described as a key principle of effective supervision. More generally, however, there is a role for institutional arrangements which operate at the organisational or business-unit level and which serve to provide employees with an opportunity to influence policy and express their discontent to managers.

Freeman and Medoff (1984) were the first to link this issue very directly with that of staff retention in their work on the value of trade unions from an employer's point of view. They identified two broad types of organisational response to legitimate employee grievances. The first category is characterised by an acceptance that unhappy employees leave – a policy of 'exit'. In such organisations there are no channels available for dissatisfied employees, either individually or collectively, to express their views, or for managers to hear them. They therefore either have to suffer in silence or opt to resign. The second category, by contrast, is characterised by a policy of 'voice'. Opportunities are actively created for employees to utilise as a means of sorting out their problems by bringing them to the attention of management. The wish to leave is thus averted in a proportion of cases because an accommodation between employee and employer is reached.

However, it is important to recognise that organisations cannot just be defined as falling into the 'voice' or 'exit' categories on account of their institutional arrangements. Culture matters too. Many organisations have formal grievance policies, for example, which are never used in practice because employees fear the consequences of doing so. Others recognise trade unions but minimise contact with their officials and maintain an adversarial type of relationship. A third group hold regular consultation exercises but take little real account of what their employees say in response to management proposals. Such employers have in place formal communication channels but are not genuinely encouraging their staff to come forward with their grievances or participate in decision-making. As a result they are likely to suffer from more voluntary turnover than is necessary.

Developing a genuine dialogue with employees or their representatives at organisational level can lead to the reduction of employee turnover in other significant ways too. Aside from providing a channel for grievances to be expressed, it helps keep managers better informed more generally about 'feeling on the shop floor'. As a result it permits problems to be anticipated ahead of time and acted on before they become formal grievances and lead to resignations. Moreover, such approaches help embed a culture of employee involvement in the organisation generally, so that employees are consulted as a matter of course by all managers ahead of important changes, and are able to get used to the idea. This is especially valuable in employee-retention terms in industries in which employees' voices are rarely heard in practice. There is a great deal to be gained if your employees perceive alternative employers to operate more autocratically.

Frog-marching and related practices

The final set of points to be made in this chapter involve setting out the case against certain ill-advised practices that are carried out, as a matter of policy, in many UK organisations. One is the preference for 'escorting' employees off the premises with little ceremony as soon as they offer their resignations (frog-marching). In return for this rather humiliating treatment, the employees concerned are not required to work their notices. The main purpose, presumably, is to protect the organisation's interests by preventing leavers from taking with them confidential or commercially sensitive information – but employers may also be seeking to deter other people from quitting by making the process conspicuously unpleasant.

This practice seems to me to be wholly futile and utterly counterproductive. It is just about justifiable in some cases of dismissal where there is a real danger that a disgruntled dismissee will wreak physical revenge on the organisation, given half a chance. But where people resign voluntarily it serves no purpose at all.

For a start, the fact that people know they will be frog-marched out as soon as they resign means that they prepare for it. If they want to take commercially sensitive data with them, they take care to photocopy it surreptitiously and to take it home in the days or weeks before they resign. However, the practice is actually damaging for organisations in that it means people keep totally silent about their impending resignations and earlier job searches until the last moment. Colleagues sometimes have their suspicions, but no one can be sure that a resignation is going to occur until the moment it happens. Aside from the fact that this encourages a persistence of low-trust relationships at work, it also helps to ensure that the organisation is unable to respond until it is too late. Managers are unable to nip discontent in the bud at an early stage, and are instead left making rather desperate counter-offers to valued individuals on Friday afternoons just after they have announced their intention to quit. Frog-marching thus makes unwanted turnover more, rather than less, likely.

The same is true of less dramatic types of practice which operate in a similar way. There are, for example, some organisations which encourage or allow managers to down-grade people (in a virtual rather than contractual sense) as soon as it becomes known that they are looking for another job. They are cut out of decision-making, taken off project-teams, given tedious tasks to do, or simply excluded from corporate social activities. Sometimes these kinds of practices operate very subtly. On other occasions there is a more obvious withdrawal of support. In either case the result is the same. Such approaches to management make people more secretive about their thought-processes while they are considering leaving and during the time that they are job-hunting. As with frog-marching, the result is less opportunity for the organisation to respond in good time, and a greater, rather than lesser, chance that valued people will leave rather than stay. They serve no useful purpose at all. Far from deterring leaving, they reinforce a culture of artificial (as opposed to genuine) workplace relationships and make the prospect of remaining employed somewhere for a long period unattractive for many.

It is much better to be straightforward and open on the question of voluntary quitting. Accept that you are going to lose people from time to time, and accept that they will leave when they are unhappy or believe that they can get a better deal elsewhere. Stop treating such people as pariahs who dare to be disloyal, avoid playing fatuous corporate games with them, and instead deal with them as the rational adults they are. It is far far more fruitful to encourage open discussion about their choices, to seek to understand the underlying causes of their decision to quit, and then to address these where you can. You may not prevent them from leaving, but you will gain a better insight into their reasons for doing so. You can then make use of this understanding to reduce the incidence of unwanted turnover in the future.

PART 3

CASES

11 INTRODUCING THE CASES

In this final part of the book six case studies are presented. Each has been written by a different author about a different professional or occupational group. All the findings are based on research carried out prior to the submission of a Master's dissertation or a Doctoral thesis. In most cases the authors have also drawn on their own experience as managers in organisations which employ the professional groups concerned.

Each author has addressed two basic questions in writing her chapter:

□ Why do people in the particular occupational group leave their jobs?
□ What human resource management interventions could be successfully employed to improve retention rates among members of the occupational group concerned?

Our major aim in writing these case studies is to illustrate how the various approaches to the management of employee retention assessed in the book can be applied in practice. In particular, we have sought to show how it is possible to analyse the main labour market dynamics that operate in the case of diverse professional groups. Prevailing economic circumstances have a different impact on the recruitment and retention actions of each group. They also differ substantially, one from the other, in terms of established custom and practice in the profession and in expectations of management.

In short, this means that managers stand most chance of success in improving rates of retention when they focus on the particular forces that drive staff turnover in each of the separate labour markets in which their organisations compete. Broad-brush organisation-wide initiatives are often too 'hit and miss' in character. There is a need to avoid assuming that all staff, of whatever occupational group, will respond in the same way when management action is taken. Instead there should be careful diagnosis of what causes unwanted turnover among each separate staff group, followed by the development of appropriate, tailor-made prescriptions to suit. This approach has been advocated throughout the book and is illustrated here more directly through the presentation of these cases.

In Chapter 12 Shirley Jenner draws on her Doctoral research to write about retention issues for employers of new graduates. Her research, conducted at the Manchester School of Management (UMIST), has focused on the different approaches companies take to the early development of graduates and the consequences for their retention. Using data provided by managers and employees in 11 large UK companies from diverse sectors, she shows how some are a good deal more successful at retaining their new graduate recruits than others. She explores the likely reasons, and makes recommendations derived from her research.

The remaining chapters have been written by research students based at the Manchester Metropolitan University Business School. In Chapter 13 Claire Barnes looks at the particular drivers of turnover among employees in call centres, one of the fastest-growing occupational groups in the UK. Claire draws on her extensive experience as an HR manager in call centres to identify the major reasons that employees in these jobs have for resigning. She goes on to outline, in a very pragmatic fashion, the types of HR intervention that stand the best chance of improving retention rates. Many of the approaches described earlier in the book are put into context by this chapter. Claire has also studied different approaches to call centre management in the UK and in the Netherlands (where turnover levels are a good deal lower). Her recommendations are informed by these research findings.

In Chapter 14 our attention is turned to major issues facing managers of key public services. Lynn Cross, herself a serving police officer, reports initial findings from her Master's research looking at the reasons for increasing staff turnover in UK police forces. Drawing on data from Home Office studies, on figures provided by her own force and on her own interviews with former police officers, she identifies several key drivers of employee turnover. Importantly, these include organisational policies which serve to encourage rather than discourage early retirement. She goes on to argue the case for the reform of long-established practices such as these and for some cultural change too as the basis for reducing turnover rates. Changes in developmental and promotion systems are also highlighted, illustrating how much could be achieved in more bureaucratic organisations if a greater degree of flexibility was to be permitted.

The final chapters by Mary Veitch, Claire Repath and Claire Sweeney (all practising HR managers) also draw on research carried out prior to the submission of Master's dissertations. All three authors used a similar methodology but studied employee-retention issues among very different professional groups – automotive engineers, employees in professional services (ie accountants and solicitors) and retail workers respectively.

In each case between 20 and 30 employees working in these industries were interviewed in depth about their last job moves. These subjects had all switched jobs during the previous two years and were asked, stage by stage, to talk about their own resignation processes from the first consideration of quitting to their actual departure. Probing questions were asked for clarification purposes, but the interviewees were not prompted to think about any particular factors. As a result it was possible for each author to identify the chief causes of voluntary turnover among each group, and to recommend courses of management action that stand the best chance of improving retention rates.

The studies are especially interesting in the way they show how very different factors seem to drive staff turnover in these professional groups. In the case of the engineers, leaving was a more considered and drawn-out process than for the others, push-and-pull factors playing equal roles in most cases. For the retail workers, accountants and solicitors, it was clear that the push factors (ie dissatisfaction with their existing jobs) were far more significant causes of turnover than the pull factors (ie positive attraction to another employer). In both cases poor standards of supervision were notable turnover drivers, but other factors were found to be major contributors too. Hours, shift patterns and problems associated with combining careers with domestic responsibilities are central in the case of retail workers. Among professional services employees more concern was expressed about developmental opportunities and the distribution of quality work, but long hours were very much an issue here too.

Readers with responsibility for the employment of professional groups not covered in these six cases should still find them useful. Many of the factors identified are common across different sectors, while all should serve to provoke useful and constructive thinking about the successful management of employee retention.

12 NEW GRADUATES

by Shirley Jenner

This chapter provides a framework for designing a turnover-resistant graduate employment system. It is based on a study I carried out in 2001 examining the early career experiences and organisational commitment of 205 graduates who had been employed for two years.

The study shows how graduates interpret their lives through the images and messages embedded in graduate recruitment activity. These narratives provide a framework within which graduates establish goals and values and form a career identity. The chapter closes with a summary of best-practice guidelines that can improve retention drawn from this research.

Features of graduate recruitment, selection and retention

The recruitment, selection and retention of new graduates differs from that of most other employees in several important ways:

☐ The rationale for recruiting graduates tends to be complex, balancing the requirement for individuals who can make an early contribution to a specific job in the workplace with the requirement also to identify future leadership and senior management potential. As a consequence, recruitment and selection procedures are often resource-hungry in terms of management time and direct costs.

☐ There is intense competition between employers for graduates. Many employers face skill shortages annually, especially in engineering, IT/computing, science, research and development, finance, accountancy and sales. It is important to retain these staff for basic operational reasons and to ensure longer-term competitiveness. The majority of organisations that employ graduates still recruit their intake at one or two fixed entry-points per year, which makes replacement difficult (AGR, 2001).

☐ A large proportion of graduates leave university with uncertainty about the sort of career they are suited to. These graduates are at risk of early resignation due to an unsuitable or misconceived choice of career or organisation.

☐ Although the age/prior-work-experience profile of graduates is changing, many still have little experience of the realities of work. Generally, graduates leave university with high expectations of finding a stimulating job with good career prospects. Campus recruitment materials directly influence graduates' expectations. Moves towards 'employer branding' and participation in a 'war for talent' mean that the dominant messages in recruitment are often overly positive and aspirational.

☐ New graduates usually receive a large proportion of training in the early weeks and months of their employment, and as such represent a 'front-loaded' investment.

Facts about graduate turnover

Although retention rates are a topic of frequent discussion among HR professionals, there is little published data on them in relation to new graduate employees. The most extensive surveys are those conducted annually among members of the Association of Graduate Recruiters (AGR) by the Institute of Employment Studies (IES) and EP-First (formerly EP-Saratoga). The IES figures show significant differences in retention patterns between sectors. Generally, the manufacturing/industrial sector retains more graduates during their first two years of employment than the financial and legal or the service sectors. The median rate for manufacturers is 86 per cent, compared to 83 per cent in services. However, the service sector has the best retention rate for the graduates who have been employed for three to four years (68 per cent) and five to six years (53 per cent). The retention rates for financial and legal services and manufacturing are 8 per cent to 11 per cent lower than the service sector for the graduates in the three- and five-year tenure cohorts (AGR, 2001).

Although these median figures are useful for broad benchmarking purposes, they do not reveal the extent of the spread of respective retention rates at the organisational level. Evidence from the latest EP-First Annual Graduate Recruitment benchmarking survey demonstrates that organisations vary significantly in terms of their ability to retain graduate employees (see Table 10)

This study shows that whereas some organisations keep 100 per cent of their graduates during the first year, others lose as many as 9 per cent in the same period. The average turnover among graduates in their first years across the UK, however, is only 4 per cent. A more subsantial variation in turnover rates emerges in the second year of employment, when the best performers achieve retention levels of 98 per cent and the worst performers keep only 64 per cent of their graduates (UK average: 84 per cent). In the third year of employment the best retention rates are 96 per cent, while the worst drop to to 54 per cent (UK average: 71 per cent). According to EP-First (2002), this represents a slight increase in turnover rates as compared with previous years.

The fact that organisations can vary so much in terms of their graduate turnover rates requires explanation. Most managers will be interested to know exactly who is leaving, from which departments, and why. High turnover among a specific group of employees can damage productivity, morale and customer service, and delay the completion of important contracts and projects.

Table 10
GRADUATE TURNOVER: BEST AND WORST PERFORMERS

	Percentage of graduate employees retained		
	Best (90th percentile value)	Average (mean)	Worst (10th percentile value)
Up to 1 year	100	96	91
1 to 2 years	98	84	64
2 to 3 years	96	71	54
3 to 4 years	92	67	41

Source: EP-First, 2002

The graduate recruitment/development/retention process

The stages of recruitment, selection, induction, training and career development each need careful design and planning. Each part of the system must contribute to the system's overall effectiveness and integrity. Although the nature of the 'recruitment/development/retention chain' varies according to each organisation's needs and according to the different types of graduate vacancy to be filled, all comprise an intricate array of interrelated organisational practices.

I suggest that there are five main stages in the retention process (see Table 11). The organisational responsibilities shown in the table will be familiar, but this model emphasises the parallel choices and experiences of graduates and

Table 11

THE KEY STAGES OF THE GRADUATE RETENTION PROCESS

Stage	Organisational issues	Individual/graduate issues
Pre-recruitment	defining the graduate role organisational image on campus employer branding	acquisition of knowledge, skills and aptitudes forming expectations of self and work choice of occupation/career direction/employer

Recruitment	job specifications
	choice of graduate labour market
	attracting the right number of the
	    right candidates
		gathering accurate information about jobs
		    and employers
		choice of employer/occupation

Selection	choice of assessment methods within
	    resource constraints
	balancing quality and cost
	logistics: design and implementation
	    of selection methods
		coping with selection procedures
		developing impressions of jobs and
		    employers
		realistic job/organisation previews

Joining	joining induction early orientation	role transition from student to employee coping with disorientation and 'entry shock' decoding employer culture
Adjustment to work	socialisation work effectiveness training and development provide support relationships career planning job design promote loyalty and retention	re-evaluating choice of employer matching expectations to perceived reality adjusting to work re-evaluating self and future career potential thoughts of leaving psychological withdrawal

Source: adapted from Jenner and Taylor, 2000.

employers. The HR practitioner with a detailed understanding of the complex nature of this employment relationship will be better prepared to design and deliver a turnover-resistant graduate employment system. In my study I examined HR policy and practice in case study companies using this framework.

The research took place in 2000/2001 in 11 private sector UK-based organisations. The participating companies were all well-established graduate recruiters drawn from a wide range of sectors (see Table 12). Data collection involved interviewing business managers, HR professionals, supervisors and graduate employees. I also sent a comprehensive questionnaire out to the graduate employees in the companies who had been employed for approximately two years. The professional and functional group profile of over 200 graduates who responded is shown in Table 13 overleaf. These responses, together with the interview data and other published research, give a good insight into the causes of graduate turnover.

Table 12

GRADUATE QUESTIONNAIRE RESPONDENT PROFILE, BY COMPANY AND GENDER

Company		A Business services	B IT support	C Aerospace	D Transport engin.	E Food manufacturing	F IT and mobile technology	G Bank	H Electrical engineering	All cases per cent
Male	n	18	27	22	12	10	19	6	12	126
	%	52.9	81.8	75.9	85.7	47.6	73.1	42.9	70.6	67.0
Female	n	16	6	7	2	11	7	8	5	62
	%	47.1	18.2	24.1	14.3	52.4	26.9	57.1	29.4	33.0
Total										
	n	34	33	29	14	21	26	14	17	188
	%	100	100	100	100	100	100	100	100	100

Table 13

GRADUATE QUESTIONNAIRE RESPONSE, BY PROFESSIONAL/FUNCTIONAL GROUP

Professional or functional group		Research and development	Finance	Accountancy/ audit	Tax consultancy	Sales, marketing and commercial	Engineering	Information technology	Supply/ purchasing	HR/other	Total
Total	n	19	10	23	9	10	46	45	12	9	183
	%	10.4	5.5	12.6	4.9	5.5	25.1	24.6	6.6	4.9	100

The main causes of graduate turnover

My research, as well as that of others (Arnold and Mackenzie Davey, 1992; Sturges and Guest, 1999), shows that graduate employees have a complex range of reasons for resigning from their first career-related jobs. In line with well-established theories of motivation we know that job satisfaction and sustained commitment are vital if low turnover rates are to be maintained.

My questionnaire asked graduates about their experiences of career decision-making, recruitment, induction, work and training. Graduate employees were also asked about their intentions to stay, and whether they were actively seeking work with another employer. Using these responses it was possible to conclude that the following are the main factors that combine to affect turnover:

Influences on graduate job satisfaction

- □ unrealistic expectations (due to lack of experience and general campus recruitment activity)
- □ unmet expectations (the extent to which the actual job compares with the one specifically promised during selection)
- □ career maturity (the graduate's own clear sense of career identity and direction)
- □ graduate role (interesting, challenging work; clear status)
- □ supervision (the quality of support, feedback and associated identification of training needs)

- colleagues (convivial relationships with peers and other employees)
- recognition (acknowledgement and reward for contribution).

Influences on commitment

- organisational image (the culture of the organisation, the size and status of the employer)
- training and employability (the quality and relevance of training and development programmes)
- job security (long-term tenure options or sequences of short-term contracts)
- career prospects (future career possibilities, clarity of career pathways, fairness)
- work–life balance (long-hours culture, flexibility, opportunity for additional leave to follow non-work interests)
- reward (appraisal systems, pay progression, allocation of stretch assignments and high-profile projects).

The HR system: policies, problems and pitfalls

My case studies showed how each of the participating companies had strengths and weaknesses in their HR systems. Although space does not allow in-depth analysis, important information drawn from my data is provided in the following sections. The variation in the intentions of graduates to stay or to seek alternative employment enables us to identify best-practice guidelines.

Defining the graduate role

The graduate labour market is extremely complex and highly segmented in terms of both demand and supply. There have been a number of attempts to classify graduate work, described in detail elsewhere (Jenner and Taylor, 2000; Purcell *et al*, 1999). Some organisations still hold to the notion of recruiting high-potential graduates who may become the technical experts, senior managers and company executives of the future, but many organisations now have a wider and more varied range of reasons for recruiting graduates.

In my study the following reasons for recruiting staff were expressed:

- as a source of future senior managers
- for their technical skills and knowledge
- as a source of professional staff
- to maintain or improve research capability
- to establish a particular 'employer brand'
- to enhance competitiveness
- to assist in a culture-change programme
- to complete specific projects.

Many human resource management staff responsible for recruiting graduates agreed that their rationale for recruiting graduates was confused and, in some cases, contradictory. In a good number of cases the graduate was expected to 'add immediate value' to the business as well as to enter a future-oriented 'talent pipeline'.

Achieving this delicate balance between objectives is proving to be difficult. HR personnel accept that there are problematic ambiguities at the heart of their graduate strategies and that these lead to problems downstream. Over 41 per cent of the graduates who responded to my questionnaire felt unclear about their status, and for many, role confusion was a source of stress.

Career indecision and turnover

The most common tools used in graduate recruitment derive from the 'matching model' established by differential psychologists. These approaches emphasise psychometrics and scientific methods of selection. However, they often do not take sufficient account of the fact that many graduates are unclear about their careers.

Only half of all graduate questionnaire respondents felt that they had a clear idea of the type of career and job they wanted on leaving university. Those entering business services (in roles such as accountancy, audit and tax consultancy) were the least decided, only 35 per cent feeling a clear sense of direction on leaving university. By contrast, at the other end of the scale, 62 per cent of engineers stated that they had been clear about careers at graduation:

> Choosing a career is the hardest thing to do and when I find what I'm looking for I'll be happier.
>
> (male, engineering)

> I will be more careful in choosing my next place of work – in particular to find out about the company culture ...
>
> (female, purchasing)

The study suggested a strong correlation between those who expressed career uncertainty at the recruitment stage and those who stated they were now 'actively seeking a new employer'. In the light of the fact that many graduates leave university with little idea of their future career direction it is therefore important to carry out the following activities:

☐ Review the extent to which recruitment activity reaches graduates after university. Recent reviews of the HE Careers Service indicated that this is an area that requires improvement.

☐ Consider raising the importance of career-decidedness as a selection criterion, especially where the graduate work available offers little scope for substantial changes in direction.

☐ Recognise that targeting graduates into specific or narrow functional streams may not take sufficient account of their underlying career indecision. Where possible, providing some scope for moves between functions may help to reduce turnover out of the organisation altogether.

It is also important to understand the complex way in which career identity forms. Many graduates were still uncertain about their career direction after two years. Those unable to change direction while remaining with their first employer were the most likely to leave in order to find a new direction.

Graduate experiences of recruitment

My questionnaire asked graduate employees how well the recruitment process had informed them about their work. As is indicated by the following comments, many of those who responded regarded their recruitment process as a period of organisational hard-selling and impression management:

> Expectations set by the organisation have not been met.
>
> (female, finance)

> I was bullsh–tted into my job, and I regret it now.
>
> (male, software engineer)

On the other hand, well-designed and -delivered recruitment and selection can have a positive effect:

> The main interview was conducted by a person in the unit I was to join. He provided very helpful, useful information and persuaded me to take this job, rather than another one I was seriously considering.
>
> (male, accountant)

Results for eight of the case study companies are given in Table 14. The sample sizes for three further respondents would not permit statistically valid comparisons. The answers reveal a substantial variation between employers in the level of accuracy about graduate work and career prospects communicated during recruitment.

Table 14

GRADUATE PERCEPTIONS OF RECRUITMENT

Percentage of graduate employees in agreement with questionnaire statement *Rank out of 8 shown in ( )*	A Business services	B IT support	C Aerospace	D Transport engin.	E Food manufacturing	F IT and mobile technology	G Bank	H Electrical engineering	All cases per cent
'The recruitment process provided an accurate picture of the work I would be doing'	23.5 (8)	45.5 (4)	32.1 (7)	57.1 (1)	47.6 (3)	34.6 (6)	50 (2)	35.3 (5)	38.5
'Career prospects had been accurately described to me'	85.3 (1)	51.5 (6)	35.7 (7)	57.1 (3)	52.4 (5)	53.8 (4)	64.3 (2)	11.8 (8)	53.5

Importantly, I found evidence of a strong correlation between those who felt the recruitment messages they received had been inaccurate and those who were now seeking an alternative employer. These results provide compelling evidence that there is scope for organisations to improve the accuracy with which graduate work is portrayed.

Starting work: a shock to the system?

The study also supports the notion that many graduates find starting work very difficult, stressful and challenging. I have been able to demonstrate that organisations are not always successful in managing this early period effectively. A good number of graduates felt that they struggled to survive in their early months at work, while some experienced 'entry shock'. This is shown below by the numbers of employees who agreed that during the first three months they felt:

- surprised by the job or organisation (67.6 per cent)
- exhausted at the end of each day (46.3 per cent)
- difficulty in admitting that they had a problem (21.8 per cent)
- initial regret that they joined the company (16.7 per cent).

Almost one in ten graduates was *not* welcomed by other staff at their level, a significant number reporting considerable hostility from non-graduate staff.

> The bitterness of non-graduates to those on the fast-track programmes has been astonishing and disappointing.
>
> (male, research and development)

Graduates who experienced a good induction programme and support in the early days felt this gave them a favourable impression of the organisation as a whole and helped them through difficult times at work. Anecdotal evidence from graduates suggests that a significant number of fellow-graduates left during the early months due to 'entry shock'.

Graduate work and job security

Graduates desire challenging work but need support as they adjust to additional responsibilities. They are motivated by interesting work and are frustrated when given too great a volume of boring tasks, especially if this was not highlighted at the recruitment stage. A third of graduate respondents agreed that they had been given too much boring work. However, the proportion was much higher (63.3 per cent) among those actively trying to leave. Clearly, graduates do not tolerate boredom.

They also drew attention to the frustrations and stress caused by confusion and ambiguity concerning their status at work. Some felt that their status as a graduate 'trainee' was undermined by line managers' refusing to release them to attend their training programme courses or by being given dull, repetitive work. Others felt thrown into unexpectedly demanding work with responsibilities that caused stress.

Although graduates are aware of competitive and turbulent operational conditions, the survey revealed that over 71 per cent of respondents expect and desire job security, a finding supported by other research (Universum, 2002). My data indicates that a quarter of graduates felt that they could not be optimistic about their future career with the organisation, and this was a reason that they were seeking a new employer.

Training and development

The offer of substantial ongoing training and development is known to be a key factor in a graduate's choice of organisation. They join with high expectations that the promises made during recruitment will be delivered. Graduate comments show that it is essential to take detailed account of the graduate role for which training is being designed. This involves careful consideration of the locus of control (ie the perception of where ultimate authority over one's life lies), especially in the way that training needs are identified.

> The graduate programme that I undertook has very little relevance when you seek your first appointment in the organisation. I feel as though I have wasted two years ...
>
> (female, marketing)

Line managers, reward and performance

Over 82 per cent of graduate employees said that they had good relationships with line managers at a surface level. However, 15.3 per cent felt that they did not receive adequate feedback about their work or guidance in how to improve performance. Again, those graduates who were actively seeking a new employer were those who reported poor relationships with line managers and who complained especially about a lack of performance review.

An average of 45.5 per cent of respondents agreed that they were satisfied with pay. At the organisational level, figures ranged from a low of 18.2 per cent (Organisation B – IT support) to a high of 88.2 per cent (Organisation A – Business services). However, the proportion of graduates actively seeking to leave who were dissatisfied with pay was only about 10 per cent above survey average, which indicates that pay is a factor in turnover but for most graduates is not the main cause of the decision to leave.

The graduate's intentions to stay or go

As was stated above, the case study questionnaire asked graduates two separate but related questions about the possibility of quitting. The first focused on the level of *current* job-seeking activity, while the second asked respondents to state whether or not they intended to stay with their present employer *for the foreseeable future*. This information provided a means of comparing the likely turnover profiles of participating organisations. *Overall, the number of graduates searching for a new employer was 15 per cent, but there were significant variations between different companies (see Figure 4 overleaf).*

Case study organisations E and H had the largest proportion of graduates who were actively seeking a new employer, whereas in organisation B there were no respondents at all who indicated that they were presently seeking work. Insights provided in my interviews suggested that this may be due to the fact that individuals in this sector are often the focus of vigorous head-hunting activity and have no need to seek alternative work. Organisations A and D can anticipate

Figure 4

IMMEDIATE AND FUTURE RETENTION TRENDS

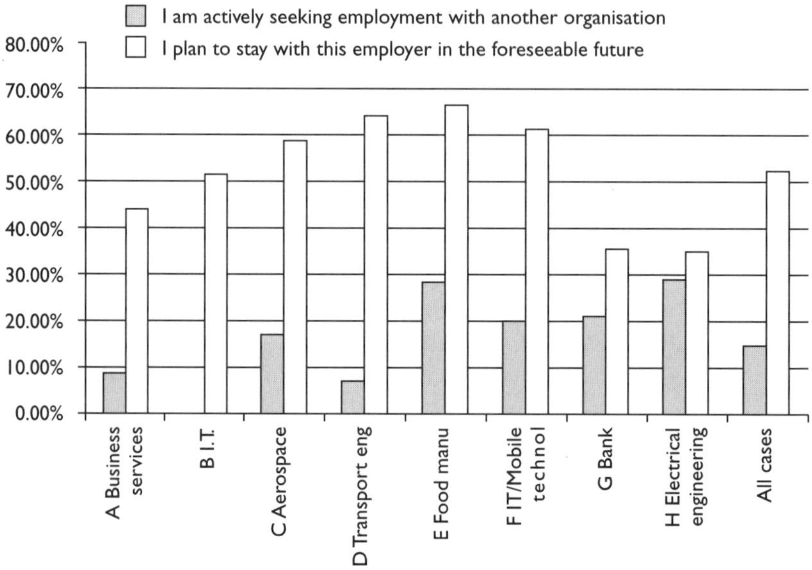

low levels of short-term voluntary turnover. Figure 4 also shows the wide variation in graduate employees' intentions to stay in the longer term.

The questionnaire also gave respondents an option of saying that they were undecided whether to stay or to go. Responses to this question revealed that, on average, over a quarter of graduate employees are unclear about whether they will be remaining with their employers. Clearly, there are a substantial number of graduate employees in each organisation who have not yet decided to move on and could be encouraged to stay if the right employment conditions are provided.

Conclusions

In conclusion, I would like to identify a range of human resource management practices that my study suggests can enhance retention among graduate recruits. These are summarised in the checklist below.

Job rationale

- ☐ The rationale for employing graduates should be clearly expressed then translated into recruitment materials and selection criteria.

Recruitment and selection

- ☐ A recruitment campaign should provide accurate information about company culture, graduate work, training and career prospects.
- ☐ Employer branding must be based on reality.
- ☐ Selection methods must include realistic job previews that correspond to the target role.

Induction

- ☐ The induction programme must be timely and appropriate.
- ☐ It must be evident that the graduate supervisor recognises the challenges and demands of transition and understands the needs of newcomers.
- ☐ In a first job a graduate should have a supportive supervisor in a dynamic, friendly work setting.

Graduate work

- ☐ A graduate requires a challenging work role that limits the extent of mundane work while recognising business needs.
- ☐ Early jobs should involve real work and lead to constructive feedback and learning. There should be an opportunity for stretch assignments and scope for testing alternative career directions.
- ☐ There should also be scope for individual discretion concerning the hours worked and respect for work–life balance.

Training and development

- ☐ A graduate requires a high-quality training programme that is tailored to the needs of the individual's work role and future career plans.
- ☐ There should be careful management of the period after the formal graduate training programme ends in order to avoid a training vacuum.

Career development

☐ Career development should be regarded as shared between the graduate and the organisation.

☐ Job moves must be planned to meet both business needs and emerging or changing career aspirations.

Reward and performance

☐ Success at work must be recognised and rewarded.

☐ There must be regular, fair and effective appraisals – likewise, supportive and trusting relationships with line management.

13 CALL CENTRE EMPLOYEES

by Claire Barnes

The face of customer service has changed dramatically during the last 20 years. In the past, employees in the service sector were encouraged to build face-to-face relationships with their customers. An emphasis was put on getting to know the customer and their personal preferences so that a long-term relationship between the customer and the business could be built. The network of banks, building societies, post offices, retail outlets and other service industries was vast, most customers having the opportunity to visit an establishment which was local to them. Similarly, employees tended to reside in the area in which they worked. There was a 'job for life' mentality and culture within such organisations, and many employees stayed with their employer for most of their working lives.

The recession of the 1980s hit the service sector hard. Companies could no longer afford the overheads associated with running branches in small towns and villages across the UK. These branches were closed down and customers were encouraged to visit larger regional outlets. This move marked the first stage of organisational centralisation in the service sector. Then in the 1990s the growth of technology, and in particular the Internet, meant that once again the service sector had to make changes in order to survive. Customers were now able to order products, transfer money and even have their weekly shopping delivered to their front door without leaving the comfort of their own homes.

More and more organisations began to favour the use of a centralised approach to customer service. The creation of 'call centres' or 'contact centres' gave businesses the opportunity to offer a variety of services to their customers all under one roof, leading to more efficient and easily manageable business processes. Together, these factors have meant that over the past decade the contact centre industry has experienced massive growth. The industry in the UK now employs people more than the car, steel and coal industries combined (Grayson and Hodges, 2001, p19).

Despite the benefits associated with contact centres, the industry in general has seen much bad press over the past few years: comparisons have been made with sweat shops and 'dark satanic mills' by journalists and academic writers alike. Descriptions such as these have done nothing but add to the ongoing battle experienced by HR managers faced with the task of recruiting and retaining contact centre staff. In fact, research has shown that most contact centres do not deserve the bad press they have often received. Many employers have made impressive efforts to make their workplaces both comfortable and flexible for employees. Nonetheless, overall staff wastage in the industry remains troublingly high.

What are the main reasons for turnover in contact centres?

In a joint study carried out by the IRS and the Call Centre Association Research Institute in 2001 (Pearson, 2001), 331 call centre managers responded to a series of questions about their reward policy and staff turnover levels. The results of this survey revealed that the median turnover was 18 per cent per annum. However, one in ten call centres reported that its turnover was 49 per cent or higher. Employers whose turnover was more than 32 per cent stated that turnover was a problem to them, whereas those whose turnover was less than 10 per cent did not feel that their attrition rates were problematic.

High levels of staff turnover bring significant costs to employers. Contact centres usually employ at least 200 staff, and often more. Substantial numbers of new hires thus have to be found and trained up to the required standard each year simply to replace leavers. Financially, this has a major impact on recruitment and training budgets – but perhaps more significantly, high levels of wastage affect both morale and the potential efficiency of organisations. Talented and effective employees are walking out of call centres every day despite the presence of measures introduced specifically to encourage them to stay. The major reasons are as assessed below.

Job content

Contact centres are designed to offer a swift service to their customers to ensure that service standards are met and call volumes are handled effectively. This means that customer service staff are often encouraged to keep customers on the line for as short a time as possible. The introduction of 'call trees' means that customers have the ability to direct their call before it is even answered. In some cases customers can even answer their own queries before they get through to a representative. Most call centres train their staff to take calls within a specific 'call time' so that the business can handle the maximum number of calls every day.

In an attempt to keep call times down, staff are normally trained to deal with matters linked to specific areas of business activity. For example, when calling to book a holiday the customer may be given the opportunity to choose from a tour operator's summer or winter holidays brochure using their telephone keypad. The holiday company then needs only to train the portion of its employees who take summer holiday bookings on their 'summer sun brochure' and the 'winter' employees on the winter brochure. On the plus side, this can make the employees more efficient because they have better product knowledge. However, it can also mean that there is little variety within the representative's role.

Management style

The management style used within contact centres has come under considerable critical scrutiny in the past. Although many of the more lurid horror stories are often unfounded, it is true that the call centre environment is usually governed by strict guidelines. There is close supervision of individual performance and a specific premium placed on employee punctuality. In an office administration role it may not be an issue when employees arrive five minutes late for work. In a contact centre this is a problem not because management are authoritarian but because if every representative were to be five minutes late the business would lose a lot of custom.

Such guidelines have to be handled correctly. If employees feel that they are being managed too dictatorially, they are unlikely to stay in their job. It is a fact that employees often leave contact centres because they do not like the way rules and regulations are enforced.

Communication

As in any business, poor communication is the source of many human resource problems in contact centres. Because of extended opening hours and the varied shift patterns associated with call centre work, it is essential that communication across the business is both consistent and frequent. Ineffective communication of change within the working environment can cause distrust and demotivation among the workforce. Poor communication breeds insecurity. Employees who feel unsure about the security of their own position are more likely to look to move to another company which offers a safer option.

Upward communication channels must also be in place. Employees often leave call centres because they feel they are not being given the opportunity to share their opinions with management. It is essential that there is a forum whereby employees can share their thoughts and ideas. If no such forum is in place, frustration and disappointment result. Moreover, this is often most keenly felt among those employees whom the business would benefit most from retaining.

Reward

In 2001 the Call Centre Association reported that over 400,000 people were employed in call centres in the UK. Competition to attract staff is becoming fierce, particularly in those areas of the country which have a high density of centres. Employees are sometimes willing to move from one contact centre to the next for as little as 50 pence extra per hour. Pay is not usually the only factor that encourages employees to change jobs, but they tend to know if their pay rates are uncompetitive, and this in turn breeds disdain.

Progression and development

Managers of contact centres should not dismiss the importance of succession planning or formal employee development schemes. One of the most common reasons that representatives leave contact centres is a belief that there is no opportunity for progression. There is often a large skills gap between representative roles and the next level up the hierarchy – the team leader role. This makes it difficult for employees to develop and grow their careers within a single organisation, and reduces the average period of time ambitious employees remain with a contact centre.

Poor performance

Dismissals usually account for a fair proportion of staff turnover within contact centres. Strict guidelines and service standards mean that breaches of conduct occur far more frequently than in most industries. The major issues concern 'misconduct' in the form of unauthorised lateness or absenteeism. Management of under-performance is necessary, given the nature of the work, and although this type of turnover can be reduced through HR interventions, there will always be employees who have to be 'managed out' of their roles because their performance is unsatisfactory.

What human resource interventions can positively affect turnover?

Several tools and techniques can be introduced to reduce high staff turnover levels. All of the issues raised above can be positively affected using HR interventions. Managers must accept, however, that some negative features of call centre work are 'necessary evils', so the best approach is to ensure that the more positive areas are promoted and fully utilised.

Setting expectations

A good retention policy starts at the pre-recruitment stage. Contact centres offer employees a different work experience from that of other industries, and for this reason clear expectations must be set from the start. When selecting candidates managers should make them aware of the environment and the details of the role. This may seem like common sense, but roles can often be inappropriately 'glamorised' when managers are desperate to recruit. This is not the answer. If an employee starts work expecting the role to be far more varied and interesting than it is, he or she will leave very quickly.

Employers should regard the interview as the first opportunity to induct the candidates into the business. They should show them the call centre where the job is going to be based, and let them listen into a call and see exactly what they will be doing. In addition, the recruiter should run through performance expectations with each candidate, and look at the reward package and training dates. If a realistic expectation is set, the employee is far less likely to leave within the first few months of employment.

Job design

According to call centre analysts, the most effective way of coping with high volumes is to keep call times short and direct calls to staff with the specific skills to deal with the particular query. By contrast, the fundamental principles of human resource management and occupational psychology stress the need to keep job roles varied. Effective job design is seen as a vital retention tool because it should prevent employees from becoming bored. In relation to contact centre representatives, a degree of compromise between these two positions is essential.

A good way to ensure that staff experience variety in their work is to rotate the teams within a call centre every so often – for example, every three to six months. Managers must be prepared to invest in training for this method to work, but it has two positive outcomes – variety, and skill development. Development of employees' skills gives them more opportunity to progress within an organisation through internal promotion.

Succession planning and employee development

Spending time on a realistic and achievable succession plan is always time well spent. Internal progression is an excellent way of retaining talented and hard-working individuals. In a contact centre succession plans should be structured to allow representatives to reach the team leader level. This is best done by creating a role which falls in between the two (eg a senior representative role).

Employees should also be involved in creating their own development plans with their line managers. Management should encourage the use of SMART objective-setting so that performance can be clearly measured. Development and performance plans should be reviewed on a regular basis, the most important aspect being the 'buy-in' (wholehearted commitment) of the employee. Performance reviews give managers the opportunity to build a level trust and confidence with people who report directly to them. They also give employees a forum in which they can articulate their future aspirations.

Management style

Management within contact centres does generally have to be strict. However, it does not need to be unpleasant. Managers and team leaders must educate their employees about why the centre has to operate with certain policies and procedures. It is important to ensure that employees understand the reasons for adherence to guidelines. Induction programmes should include background material on the nature of the industry, together with full explanations about how business would be adversely affected were business standards not to be met.

Emphasis should also be placed upon the importance of each individual employee. Without high-quality staff the business would suffer – and it is beneficial to tell employees that they are important to the company. All too often in call centres employees are left feeling as if they make little difference.

The relationship between the team leader and the team member is also key. The team leader has the opportunity to build a level of trust and respect with his or her team which will go a long way towards ensuring that representatives feel valued at work. Simple points like greeting each employee as they arrive in the morning may seem obvious, but when a team is made up of over 20 employees, that can become easy to forget. Similarly, it is important to ensure that return-to-work interviews are carried out by team leaders after any period of sickness. Apart from contributing to the management of individual performance, this also allows the line manager to check that the employee is really well enough to return to work. Moreover, it gives employees the opportunity to talk to their line manager about any personal or medical issues that may be affecting their performance or attendance.

Team leaders should be encouraged to promote a team-oriented environment in which representatives are encouraged to work together. 'Fringe techniques' can be used to promote such an environment – for example, company-funded team nights out, team bonuses, and so forth. This increases the opportunity for team members to befriend their colleagues, and makes them more likely to remain with the company.

Communication

Communication is one of the biggest challenges in contact centres. It is essential that top-level managers indicate their commitment to communication within the business, and that this should be detailed in a policy document. Managers should look at introducing communication tools which are available to all, no matter what time of day employees start their shift. During the induction programme employees should be made aware of where they can find different types of information. Using e-mail and intranet systems allows all employees to be reached, but face-to-face communication should never be discarded.

Employee forums are an excellent way of giving employees the opportunity to raise their concerns and issues with management. These should always include representation from each group of employees within the contact centre. Such forums help to ensure that managers are kept in touch with operational issues that may be affecting morale.

Flexible working

Attracting candidates to work in a call centre can prove challenging, not only because of competition from other contact centres but also because of the different shifts that have to be filled. Many contact centres are open from dawn until midnight, and shift patterns are not always particularly appealing. Quite a few centres struggle to recruit and retain staff because they do not want to work until midnight one week and then from 7 o'clock in the morning the following week.

Flexibility in terms of hours worked is one of the most powerful tools available to contact centre managers. Recruiting a diverse workforce is not only positive for company culture and values but it also adds a new dimension to retention. Diversity means employing people with many different backgrounds and personal circumstances. Contact centres with extended opening hours give employees with personal commitments the opportunity to work the hours they are able to commit to. Contact centre managers should thus look at being far more flexible in the organisation of shift patterns than is usually the case. Many centres opt for structured shift rotas. These may seem the most straightforward to manage – but the drawback is the way they provide little flexibility for employees. By offering a wide variety of shift patterns and being as flexible as possible with existing staff, a business recognises the importance of its employees' personal lives. This is something that employees always appreciate. If work is convenient for them, they are less likely to resign.

Conclusions

Managing employee retention in a contact centre environment is challenging because turnover in the industry is always likely to be higher there than in others. While it is necessary to accept this, it is also important not to stop trying to retain employees. As in any industry, one of the most effective tools is empowerment. If employees can feel empowered in their jobs and truly valued by the company they work for, they are far more likely to stay. Contact centre positions may not always be the most varied roles, but employers should remember that it is not just the role that makes an employee feel valued. The actions of the employer and the prevailing workplace culture are just as important.

14 POLICE OFFICERS

by Lynn Cross

Traditionally, people have embarked on careers in the police as a vocation. Pay levels allow officers to live comfortably, but money is not (and never was) a prime factor in attracting recruits. Once established, people have tended to stay because of the prospect of excellent pensions, and have really only left when declared unfit or following some form of disciplinary action. As a result, wastage levels have always been low in comparison to other occupations. The CIPD's annual surveys have typically recorded turnover levels in the police as being well below 10 per cent, but since 2000 the figure has been creeping up to between 12 per cent and 13 per cent each year. This is a cause for concern because of the high costs associated with training a police officer (over £50,000 in the first year alone) and the importance of ongoing familiarity with activity in distinct communities.

One reason is the general shift in career aspirations over recent years. Fewer people now expect to enter a job and remain employed in it for 30 years or more. There is less loyalty on the part of both the employer and employees, the typical psychological contract having changed as a consequence of high unemployment in the 1980s and early 1990s. The employment market has also changed. Gifted prospective employees now look for high earnings, and this makes a policing career less attractive than used to be the case. Moreover, personal lives are more disjointed than they used to be. Graduates have different expectations from the ones they had years ago, with an apparent hunger for a reasonable work–life balance, better training and development, and the chance to travel around the world. In addition, change and volatility in career terms is more accepted, leading us all to develop different expectations of our work.

There have also been major changes in the job of a police officer in the last 10 or 20 years. In particular, the Police and Criminal Evidence Act (PACE) has changed the way police officers work on a day-to-day basis, requiring them to be more accountable and to take much more personal responsibility for their actions. The 1980s brought an upward spiral in anti-social behaviour and general crime, together with a miners' strike in which the police played a controversial role. A different style of policing was adopted which, in some quarters at least, led to a loss of respect for the police. The revival of a 'Dixon of Dock Green' approach in the 1990s has attempted to re-establish relationships between the police and public, but there remains a good distance further to go. Police recruitment has certainly been affected by these trends.

Years ago, cadet schemes were available for 17-/18-year-olds and were a major source of police recruits. Many cadets had a low educational attainment but had relatives who were already in the job. They were almost bred into the police service, and saw entering it as a natural progression. Now, more mature recruits (mid to late twenties) with broader work and life experience and a higher educational attainment are looking to join the service. For them it is one possible career among many, so they are better placed than their older colleagues to enter different employment should they subsequently become dissatisfied with police work.

Why do people leave the police service?

In the force I studied, over 300 hundred officers are now leaving each year. This is considerably more than was the case a few years ago. The reasons cited on the exit interview forms submitted in 2001/2002 were:

- ill-health retirement
- service/age retirement
- being transferred to another force
- being unsuited to the work
- finding a better job
- domestic reasons
- dislike of the shifts
- other

In comparison with previous years we can observe an increase in the proportions citing reasons other than retirement as explanations for their decision to leave. Ill-health retirements have actually declined in recent years. However, it must be noted that fewer than a third of those leaving returned their exit forms, so we cannot be sure that these figures are an accurate reflection of the real reasons people have for leaving the force.

Other factors, as well as those listed above, have been cited in internally circulated Home Office papers. The major ones, judging from these and my own research, are:

☐ poor management of probationers

A particular problem is that people are resigning within their two-year probationary period. This appears, in part, to be caused by the large number of direct line managers probationer constables can end up reporting to during this period. Inconsistency arises because supervisors are promoted or moved internally to work with special squads or other groups. The result is confusion, lack of continuity and instability during the most pivotal time in a police officer's career.

☐ patterns of work

Although this is primarily an issue for female police officers, the shift patterns, numbers of hours worked and the lack of flexible working is a significant cause of voluntary resignations. Such concerns are particularly important in explaining why female officers tend not to rejoin after a break has been taken to have a family. They act as an important barrier to returning to work.

☐ career progression and development

Comparative studies looking at the experience of graduate recruits across several occupations have found that employers in other sectors are nine times more likely to have a career plan for their graduates than is the case in police forces. Furthermore, these plans were more likely to have met the graduates' expectations of career development than those provided in the police service (James, 1992).

Home Office research (Bland *et al*, 1999) found that officers from non-Caucasian ethnic minorities were twice as likely to resign voluntarily from the force than their white counter-parts. Differences between the respective career structures and advancement of ethnic-minority and white officers in terms of recruitment and promotion 'for specialist posts' were specifically identified in this research.

Fundamental to career progression and development is access to training. Traditionally, training within the police service is undertaken at residential training centres. These can be inaccessible to those police officers who have domes-tic responsibilities, increasing the chances that they will leave.

□ job dissatisfaction/low morale

A recent survey carried out among employees of the police force I studied received a 29 per cent response rate. As many as 77 per cent of those officers who responded said that the organisation did not value its staff, while 87 per cent perceived morale within the force to be 'low'. Increased pressure and the evolving nature of the work officers are required to carry out are the major reasons for these results. Only 11 per cent of the respondents, for example, said that they had access to the right information to allow them to do their job effectively *all* of the time. It would be surprising if there was not some knock-on effect as far as employee retention is concerned.

□ workplace culture

Police work is characterised by the presence of a strong, informal, collective culture operating at the 'shop-floor' level. Colleagues are expected to work closely together and to support one another in all circumstances. Conforming with this prevailing culture is necessary in order to gain and retain the respect of colleagues on whom all officers rely on a day-to-day basis. As a result, maverick figures are unwelcome, there is great pressure to 'fit in', and an infor-mal penalty is imposed when people 'swim against the tide'. Complaining about the conduct or poor performance of colleagues can cause a person to be ostracised to an extent, and this makes the work harder. There is therefore a tendency for people who are unhappy to leave rather than to stay and use the formal processes that are available to sort out their difficulties.

What HR interventions would have a positive effect?

Having studied the reasons that people leave the police, I believe a great deal could be done at the organisational and public-policy level that would have a positive effect on employee turnover levels. Some of the issues are complex and difficult for managers to address. There are at least nine issues, however, that might well repay consideration.

Pension and age issues

The police pension scheme makes it almost impossible to stay on after the completion of 30 years' service without losing out financially. This means that physically fit and knowledgeable officers may find themselves obliged to retire at ages as low as 47 due to the absence of a system which provides proper incentives to carry on working. The only way they can currently stay on without suffering a loss of income is to take a lump sum together with a pension, and to carry on working while no longer being members of the scheme. However, the danger here is that they are not financially protected if they suffer serious injury or death in service. This is an area where relatively straightforward changes could be introduced to encourage more police officers to stay on.

Government restrictions mean that most officers are currently required to retire at the age of 50 years. There is some flexibility in that police officers and sergeants can stay five years beyond the age limit if they are fit for duty, while senior ranks beneath that of Chief Superintendent can stay up to the age of 60. Chief Constables and Assistant Chief Constables need not retire until 65 – a choice denied to their lower-ranking colleagues.

Many police officers would stay if it was financially beneficial but, as noted above, the pension does not make allowance for this. Research should could be carried out to establish what can be done to raise the age of compulsory retirement and to make later retirement more attractive.

There may be a cost associated with the provision of insurance beyond the current age limit, but then the costs of replacing these officers' accumulated knowledge is also high.

Medical retirements

A possible solution for officers who are declared medically unfit by the Force Medical Officer might be to redeploy them in other areas of police work. There are plenty of important tasks that do not require a great level of fitness but where police knowledge and experience could be utilised in a way beneficial to the force. However, it would be necessary to ensure that support jobs were not taken over to accommodate medically unfit police officers in a manner that would cause ill-feeling or low morale among the existing support staff sector. That would be anything but beneficial to the organisation.

Transfers to other forces

Officers who transfer out of the force to join others do so for a variety of reasons. Many believe that there is 'less stress in smaller forces', while others perceive that there are either better promotion prospects elsewhere or easier promotion routes. There is some truth in these perceptions because promotion routes and arrangements do vary considerably across the country.

The force I studied is one of only a few which operate an assessment centre for promotion from the rank of police constable to police sergeant. The pass rate is not favourable. Officers who fail the assessment centre are required to 'go acting' (ie to act as a temporary sergeant to gain the necessary practical experience to enable them to improve upon their performance at the assessment centre the next time). An alternative approach would involve awarding 'conditional passes' and to devise formal action plans to aid development and to help individuals reach the promotion standard more quickly. However, more fundamental change may be needed because the force I studied was also unusual in requiring attendance at an assessment centre as a prerequisite for promotion. Other forces simply allow their officers to pass their law and practical exams before being rewarded with their promotion. Given these differences, it is unsurprising that good people are being lost to other forces.

The point about stress also has some validity. The force I surveyed is one of the very busiest in the country, dealing with 17,500 incidents per 100 officers every year. The sheer size of the workload is daunting to some, while others are genuinely unable to give the required level of commitment at the same time as undertaking domestic responsibilities. There is thus a case for seeking an accommodation with such people. They should be able to reduce their hours, and to transfer to less busy divisions or to police districts that are closer to their homes.

'Better job' cases

In tight labour markets with lots of opportunities for people with strong interpersonal skills, it is inevitable that people will be lost to the force because of alternative job offers from other public services or from industry. There are few HR interventions that can have much effect here, because in truth there *are* 'better jobs' available. However, a great deal more could be done at the recruitment and selection stage to improve the chances of a good person–job fit, and thus to help make sure that the 'right' people are taken on as officers in the first place. Pre-recruitment induction procedures have a great deal to offer in this regard. Very often prospective new recruits are unaware of the amount of paperwork and bureaucracy involved in a police officer's job. Many are thus unpleasantly surprised, not to say horrified, when they start work. Recruitment and selection procedures and processes should highlight all aspects of the job to ensure that each candidate is fully aware of what is involved.

Domestic reasons

Domestic reasons can encompass many different factors. The case has already been made for more flexible working to help people cope with the stresses associated with juggling domestic and stressful working lives. Career-break schemes have particular potential here, in that they would allow people an opportunity to sort out domestic issues before returning full-time to their jobs. There is also a case for the better training of senior officers to help them identify domestic difficulties before such problems grow so large as to precipitate a resignation. Difficulties of this kind could then be discussed and appropriate support given before the services of a valuable officer are lost to the force.

There are many ways in which patterns of work could be adjusted in such a way as to have a positive effect on retention. Job share and part-time working have a far greater role to play than is generally accepted in the force. Above all it is necessary to change the mindset so that there is greater acceptance of flexible working arrangements on the part of officers and greater respect for those (predominantly female) who wish to take up such opportunities. Too many currently hold the view that flexible workers cannot do the job as effectively and efficiently as their full-time (mostly male) counterparts. That said, it has to be accepted that for some senior ranks (eg superintendents) the nature of the job seriously limits the possibilities of flexible working.

'Unsuited to the work' cases

The term 'unsuited to the work' can encompass many different factors. Pre-recruitment induction courses (ie realistic job previews) would help here, because they would provide more of an opportunity for those who are not suited to police work to screen themselves out of the selection process. More generally, however, it is necessary to sit down with these people well ahead of their resignations to ask the question, 'Why do you think you are unsuited?' The organisation can often help. Many different career preferences can be accommodated in a large force which has all manner of specialist roles available. The best approach would involve holding regular one-to-one career development interviews, and to use them to guide officers who are either unsure or just unaware of what may be available to them within the force.

Probationer resignations

The key here is to find ways of structuring the probation period more effectively and to provide greater continuity in terms of reporting relationships. It is really a question of introducing more effective core HR practices of a formal kind.

There must be greater attention paid to succession planning, to mentoring and to performance appraisal for officers starting out on police careers.

Progression and development issues

There is an argument in favour of decentralising a good deal of career management and development activity so that local managers are empowered to act when they spot potential among their subordinates. The system is too regimented and rather slow at present, promotion from rank to rank occurring through formal, centralised assessment centres and on-the-job training. The whole process typically takes two or three years, which is not fast enough for the more ambitious and high-achieving officers.

Some graduate recruits and other officers who are fortunate enough to be picked are currently placed on the force's Accelerated Promotion Scheme (APS). This provides them with a set career plan, including pro-active management assistance to help them achieve their objectives. There is no equivalent career planning activity carried out for the benefit of other officers. Instead, they are left to organise promotion opportunities for themselves, and tend to advance at a slower pace. There is a good case for extending the career planning techniques used for APS members to a wider proportion of officers. This would, at least, give everyone a sense that the organisation *expected* them to advance and wished to encourage their development. Such actions would serve to motivate people who are currently demotivated – and would play a part in reducing turnover.

There is also a case for providing a greater level of access to courses run by local colleges and universities. There is a cost, of course, but it is a great deal less than the costs associated with voluntary leaving. For some people, whether they are enrolled on a course of study or expecting to be enrolled soon, there will be a greater incentive to remain in the force for longer than otherwise would have been the case.

Resignations resulting from the informal police culture

The main action required here involves a tightening up of procedures. Rather greater attention should also be paid to

training managers in their effective use. As in many organisations, newly promoted police officers (eg acting sergeants)
are often insufficiently aware of grievance procedures, correct
disciplinary procedures and established equal opportunities
policies. Moreover, even where they have received some
training, there remains a degree of suspicion about such procedures and a lack of faith in their effectiveness. Some fear a
negative reaction from their subordinates if they were to take
a formal approach to management by using all the available
procedures. The result is too informal a management style,
leading to inconsistencies and other examples of unfairness.
This naturally breeds resentment and results either directly
or indirectly in resignations. The provision of fuller and more
effective training in these matters (both in terms of substance
and effective application) would go a long way towards
improving the quality of staff management. It might also lead
to greater use of grievance procedures by dissatisfied staff, and
consequently to the resolution of problems before the staff
decide to quit.

Exit interviews and attitude surveys

One of the main conclusions of my research is the need for
the police force I studied to develop more effective exit interviewing processes. These are unsatisfactory at the moment.
Too many officers fail to complete forms when they leave,
and many more are not properly questioned about their
reasons. The result is a situation in which managers are genuinely unaware of the full causes of voluntary resignations.
The extent to which departures could be prevented through
the adoption of better welfare facilities, a greater commitment to equal opportunities or cultural adjustments, is thus
unclear.

At present, although exit surveys are carried out, there is
little evidence that action is being taken in response to the
messages that the results contain. Retention policy is not currently shaped by the data collected through the exit survey
system. Not only, therefore, is there a case for more effective
exit interviewing (carried out by someone other than the
resignee's line manager), there must also be far greater

attention paid to the outcomes than is the case today. There is a better record of action stemming from the workforce surveys that are periodically carried out, but here, as with the exit documentation, there is a poor participation rate. Getting more officers to communicate their views in an honest and frank manner must therefore be a priority. The data collected could then provide a platform for effective management action on the reduction of turnover rates.

15 ENGINEERS

by Mary Veitch

The engineering labour market has been very tight for several years. The excess demand for engineers with the required qualifications and experience has led to a situation in which:

☐ skills shortages exist throughout the industry

☐ companies are forced to compete fiercely with one another to attact candidates

☐ candidates can be selective about which job they choose and are more demanding of their employer

☐ engineering salaries have escalated substantially.

Moreover, this situation is likely to worsen (from the employer's point of view) as a result of the year-on-year decreases in the number of students electing to study engineering at university. In a 'candidate-driven market' such as this, recruitment is very difficult. Finding effective ways of retaining existing staff has thus become a crucial objective for human resource managers.

Why do engineers choose to leave their jobs?

My research, conducted in the summer of 2001, involved interviewing 25 automotive engineers in depth about their most recent job moves. All were currently employed by the same well-known motor manufacturing company, but each had moved there from a different former employer. I found that in most cases a range of different factors had contributed to the decision to leave. Some were essentially 'push factors' (ie resulting from dissatisfaction with their contemporary jobs), but there was also clear evidence that 'pull factors' (ie positive attraction to the new employer) had had an effect too. The major causes of resignations are described below.

There were three significant push factors at work – job inse-curity, boredom, and lack of career progression – and four key pull factors – the desire to work for a large company, effective brand marketing, development opportunities, and new prod-uct development.

Job insecurity

Job insecurity is an extremely strong push factor. It is the most significant single underlying reason that engineers resign from jobs, arising directly from the current unstable nature of the UK car industry. Even the slightest suggestion of job losses in a particular firm causes a 'jump-ship mental-ity' as people seek greater security in organisations which they perceive to be better placed to weather the storm. The effects of redundancy warnings in one or two companies can extend to the whole industry. Even those engineers formerly employed in stable jobs attribute their resignation decisions, in part, to job insecurity in other companies and the desire to look for a job which offers the best chance of a secure and long-term future.

Boredom

Lack of challenge and role development are also significant push factors. Engineers are motivated by challenges in their day-to-day work. Their job satisfaction is hugely reduced if their work becomes routine. Coupled with the desire for new challenges, engineers want regular changes in their role to help maintain their interest and to allow them the oppor-tunity to further develop their skills.

Career progression

Younger engineers, in particular, perceive regular job changes as important for their effective career progression. They fear being pigeonholed in a certain role because they believe this will cause their careers to stagnate. If promotion or a change in role is unlikely in their current employment, they will seek it elsewhere.

Large company backing

In a labour market where there is so much uncertainty, any investment made by the larger automotive companies creates a feeling of security. In comparison to their competitors, such organisations are seen as having a more positive and long-term future. This is especially important for the older engineers, because a decision to take a new job often means relocating their familes to new areas of the country. Aside from this, being part of a larger automotive manufacturing group means there are possibilities of secondment overseas. Such opportunities are viewed as very attractive, especially by the younger engineers.

Brand marketing

Engineers often want to work for well-known and respected corporations with international reputations. Having the name of a well-known and prestigious marque on their CVs is perceived as providing a substantial boost to their chances of securing desirable jobs in the future. The larger, successful companies thus have a considerable advantage when it comes to labour market competition.

A reputation for manufacturing a high-quality product also often extends to the reputation of the organisation as an employer. Engineers are therefore attracted to the manufacturers of well-known high-quality brands because they perceive that they will be managed professionally and well looked after by their new employers.

Development opportunities

For engineers, development opportunities are the most important feature of a job. When looking for new jobs, the technical content of the job is therefore a central factor. Smaller employers can be more attractive in this respect because they can offer jobs that are distinct in terms of their content. Here, engineers are often not required to specialise to the same extent because there are fewer of them. This gives them the chance to gain new skills and to explore areas in which they they may wish to specialise later. It also serves to prevent boredom and provides more material for their CVs. In the case of younger engineers, time served in a varied role helps them to avoid being pigeonholed too early in their career. For the same reasons, in larger organisations engineers want chances to transfer to other teams and to other companies within the group wherever possible.

If the engineers are given the opportunity to influence the content of their roles and to determine for themselves their responsibilities, they will take the opportunity to enhance their careers by gaining new skills and further developing others. Companies that offer such opportunities and establish such a reputation in the industry attract applicants from rivals who require everyone to fit into a particular mould.

New product development

The nature of the product they will be working on is a central motivating factor for engineers. Any new product development activity provides both a challenge and an exciting and rewarding time spent as part of a development team. The chance to be associated with the design and manufacture of a high-profile new product, as well as to be given an opportunity to gain new skills, is seen as too good to miss. Engineers are also attracted by a product's market image, especially if it is glamorous and prestigious. They want to contribute to a high-quality product and to be seen to have done so. Companies that cannot offer such experiences lose staff to those that can.

Pay

Pay acts as both a push and a pull factor, but weakly in each case. Only one of the engineers I interviewed had left his previous company primarily because of his salary level. His real complaint was with internal relativities. He was not happy with the fact that he had worked in his previous job for eight years and that new recruits had been hired to do the same kind of work but were being paid more. He felt he deserved more – so he left. However, apart from this one example, pay had not been a push factor affecting leaving decisions among those I interviewed.

In attracting engineers, pay is generally not an important factor. It is a small industry in which information circulates quickly by word of mouth. Most people in the labour market are thus aware of what different companies are offering. The engineers I interviewed knew that the organisation they were joining did not offer the highest salaries, but had left their previous jobs anyway. They were not attracted to the organisation because of the pay on offer. If they had wanted to maximise their earnings, they could have taken on contract work overseas. Instead, other factors had attracted them and led to their resignations. These were (in priority order):

- an improved role
- a perceived good long-term future for the company
- exciting products to work on
- opportunities for changes in role and development
- location.

If more than three of these factors are satisfactory, engineers tend to accept a job offer. Pay is viewed as almost incidental to the decision to leave one company and join another.

What retention initiatives are likely to meet with most success?

As far as the retention of engineers is concerned, managers must pay attention both to the push and the pull factors identified above. The key is to ensure that as far as possible the push factors do not arise, while at the same time matching or bettering labour market competitors in respect of the pull factors. This should ensure that engineers are not given cause to leave because they are disatisfied or because other employers can offer them a better deal. In my view there are four key approaches which when properly integrated help organisations to retain engineers. They are:

- job sculpting
- structured career programmes
- an open managerial style
- an effective reward strategy.

Job sculpting

This is a process by which an employer designs jobs around the candidates' skills and preferences (see Chapter 7). Introducing it has two major advantages.

One of the strongest pull factors for engineers is the prospect of flexibility in terms of their role. Candidates can be assessed with a number of roles in mind. Consideration of their strengths and weaknesses across different areas can then lead to the creation of a new role for each candidate that accommodates his or her aptitudes and thus ensures that the organisation secures his or her services. Job sculpting formalises this process. It also reinforces a company's reputation in the industry as a flexible employer, thereby attracting more candidates.

Job sculpting is difficult to imitate, particularly in the larger companies where engineers are very highly specialised. It is thus a particularly effective retention tool in smaller and less well-known organisations. Engineers who have experienced this kind of flexibility are unlikely to wish to return to more formal and structured roles. It also allows engineers' jobs to change and develop, and therefore allows the engineers to steer their own careers while gaining new skills. This helps to prevent the boredom factor from having an effect.

Structured career programmes

Perceived lack of career development is a very strong push factor. Meeting expectations in this area is therefore key in retention. Engineers quickly become bored and demotivated if they feel that their career is stagnating and that they are not gaining new skills. Structured career programmes help in three ways:

☐ Opportunities for development are often cited as a reason for choosing a particular job or organisation. If companies can demonstrate that they take employee development seriously and have created a programme to support it, it will impress employees. It need not necessarily be solely a defined route up the promotional ladder. Secondments to other engineering teams, involvement in exciting projects and opportunities to work abroad may provide the engineers with the challenge and development opportunities they need.

☐ The organisation benefits in that its skill base is widened without its having to recruit. Sharing skills and knowledge motivates employees, reduces boredom and minimises the risk of a key activity not being carried out if an employee leaves or is absent.

☐ Engineers who have a goal and are aware of how to achieve it are less likely to leave the organisation before they have reached it. Their hard work will have been wasted and they will be forgoing opportunities to enrich their CVs. For this reason, a development programme must be sufficiently structured so that targets are achievable and clearly defined, yet flexible enough to allow them to be tailored to the individual's work and learning styles.

An open managerial style

Because of the unstable nature of UK industry, engineers are particularly sensitive to rumours of job losses. It is therefore important to emphasise the long-term and future plans of the company during the recruitment process. Any anticipated large-scale investment should be especially stressed. The same messages must be sent to existing staff whenever the opportunity arises. Keeping engineers informed using an open managerial style helps them to feel more secure. If everyone is aware of the situation, rumours are less likely to circulate and will be less credible.

An effective reward strategy

Although engineers are not particularly attracted to a job because of salary, it is important to have an appropriate overall reward strategy in place which serves to prevent dissatisfaction with payment arrangements from festering. Where pay plays a role it is as a push rather than a pull factor. The key is to ensure that reward policy is managed in a manner that is both fair and flexible. There are five key aspects:

☐ internal relativities

During my research it became clear that fairness in reward was a major retention issue. A significant proportion of engineers stated that they would leave the organisation if they discovered that their salary did not match that of their colleagues.

☐ regular increases

Most engineers are aware of their potential earnings because they read the trade journals. They need regular increases to ensure that their salary broadly reflects the increases in the industry generally. It is not necessary for salaries to match the market rate, but increments must be given so that the difference between them does not become too great. Small increases which reflect market movements are better than none at all.

☐ recognition of extra qualifications

Engineers who have gained an extra qualification during their employment will expect recognition, typically in the form of a salary increment. Without it, they will quickly become dissatisfied and begin to look elsewhere for an organisation that will better reward their efforts.

☐ reflection of skills and experience

Job sculpting, as described above, is a process by which jobs are based on the skills an employee possesses. If it is to be successfully implemented, it must be combined with a reward strategy that recognises particular skills and pays accordingly. Individual pay negotiation is a necessary part of this but must be carefully managed to avoid potential internal relativity problems.

☐ flexible pay systems

Flexible pay systems which allow employees to decide how their pay package is formed are ideally suited to an environment in which jobs are 'sculpted'. Employees can select from various benefits those that are best matched to their circumstances (see Chapter 6). Engineers find this a very attractive factor. Because it is not in use in many organisations, especially the larger ones, it is difficult for competitors to match it, and it is therefore a good retention tool.

Conclusions

At the end of the day, employee development is more important than salary for engineers. Their job must be challenging and interesting, preferably with the chance to have an impact on a new product. They will appreciate and be motivated by the opportunity to steer their career and to develop skills in new areas. Career development programmes must be structured yet imaginative to meet these criteria. In combination, an effective reward strategy and an integrated employee development plan should maximise job satisfaction and minimise employee turnover.

16 ACCOUNTANTS AND SOLICITORS

by Claire Redpath

There was a time when turnover among solicitors and accountants was the lowest of all professional groups, reflecting the accepted view that such people remained with the same firm for most (if not all) of their professional lives. As the industry has grown over the past decades and competition between firms has intensified, many more job opportunities have become available. The result has been substantially increased voluntary turnover. In the future there is likely to be more, rather than less, job mobility in the sector as it grows further. In Manchester, where my research was conducted, 50 per cent growth is anticipated over the next decade. There has therefore never been a more important time for employers to investigate the reasons that professional staff move from job to job.

Accountants and solicitors are expensive to recruit and train. The cost associated with the loss of an employee is approximately 18 months of their annual salary. When they leave they take a great deal of knowledge with them which is then no longer at the disposal of their former employers. They also necessarily break up the established individual professional/client relationships that are so central to organisational success. Finally, losing colleagues can act as a blow to morale for remaining employees who are left to shoulder the burden of an increased workload. There is thus a strong business case for firms to take action to combat increasing levels of avoidable departures so that they can better retain their most valuable assets – their staff.

In many organisations incentive schemes and salary increases form the core of retention strategies that are implemented to reduce staff turnover rates. Levels of payment are thought to be the central driving factors in many resignation decisions. My research set out to investigate how far this was true in the case of professional services firms employing qualified solicitors and accountants. I conducted interviews with 28 members of these professions during 2001, asking each to talk to me in detail about their last job move. All my interviewees had resigned from a job voluntarily in the previous two years and had moved to new employment within the sector. They were currently employed in a variety of different firms, both large and small, and represented a good cross-section of their respective professions. All were currently employed in Manchester, but some had moved from London and other parts of the country to take up their posts.

Although different factors accounted for the resignations in different cases, I found that three issues were mentioned again and again by interviewees. These were the prevailing organisational culture in the bigger firms, the poor quality of management that many had experienced, and unfairness in the distribution of work.

Remuneration

Of the 28 professionals I interviewed, only one interviewee (an accountant) stated that the prospect of a salary increase was a major influencing factor in the decision to move. In fact, I found more examples of professionals who had accepted new job offers which offered lower salaries than they had then been earning.

In most cases other factors were a good deal more important than the level of remuneration. The following quotation from one of my interviews with an accountant was typical:

> My decision to leave did not involve the consideration of salary, though everyone wants a comfortable lifestyle. What is more important is self-respect and praise when you have done a good job.

My findings thus supported the view of employee retention held by most occupational psychologists. Pay is only one of the factors that plays a part, and in the case of accountants and solicitors seems to have very little influence on the decision of individuals to leave their jobs. The comparative irrelevance of salary levels to resignation decisions is also highlighted in the failure of incentive bonuses and salary increases to secure employee loyalty. Accounting and legal firms, as is the case in other sectors, frequently make 'buy-back' attempts to dissuade people from leaving. According to a senior legal recruitment consultant I interviewed, 98 per cent of those solicitors who accept a 'buy-back' offer continue to experience job dissatisfaction and leave within six months.

Rather than remuneration, accountants and solicitors are found to place higher value on intrinsic motivators that include quality of work, training and development and the culture of the employing organisation when assessing their levels of job satisfaction.

Organisational culture

A culture of presenteeism seems to be prevalent in the majority of national law and accounting firms. It is believed that you are only 'working hard enough' if you spend long hours sitting at your desk in the office. This only serves to exacerbate the pressure that solicitors and accountants experience in jobs that are already highly stressful. A psychological contract which requires people to work 12-hour days six days a weeks is common in the sector, and accounts for many voluntary departures.

> I was destroyed. I worked solidly for six months five days a week and at weekends ... It was expected of me. I never got away from work, and it began to affect my physical and mental health.
>
> (accountant in a 'big five' firm)

Partners, management and human resource professionals must develop a greater appreciation of the impact that this stress has on both the individuals and their wider families. Greater respect for and encouragement of a proper work–life balance is needed if people are to be retained:

> The continual stress and pressure of the long hours that were demanded of me affected my home life and I ended

up getting divorced. One day I just decided I'd had enough and work wasn't worth the sacrifices I was making.... I downshifted – I had to, or I would have ended up suffering from a heart attack or a nervous breakdown.

The extremely long hours that were demanded from me to succeed and progress in the practice conflicted with my duties as a wife and mother – I found it increasingly difficult to reconcile the two, and had to make a change for the sake of my family.

(accountant in a 'top ten' firm)

When organisations or practices fail to accommodate sufficient flexibility, employees are forced to prioritise (ie choose between home life and their job). Often this results in a decision to quit the firm and seek alternative employment. The provision of flexible working arrangements including flexi-hours, part-time working, the opportunity to work from home, and the implementation of family-friendly policies would help to reduce the stress under which professionals – and especially working mothers – are placed. Increasing flexibility in working practices would thus reduce the level of turnover – particularly among women who leave either to start families or join more family-friendly organisations.

Quality of management

In addition to the introduction of more flexible working practices, human resource departments in professional services firms are well advised to assess their methods of selection and to review the training and development of their team leaders and managers. I was alarmed to discover that in 19 out of the 28 interviews I conducted, a major reason given for the decision to leave was either an unprofessional style of management or an apparent lack of management action in response to problems. It was difficult to avoid concluding that poor management is prevalent in law and accounting firms, and that improvements would lead to substantially improved retention rates:

The quality of work was good, the leadership from the top was not. The way in which the firm was run would not lead you to believe it was an extremely successful global enterprise ...

(accountant)

There were poor people management skills on the part of many of the partners.

(solicitor)

Although excellence in terms of performance should be rewarded with promotion and progression, it is important to recognise that professional expertise is not enough to qualify a managerial candidate for the job. The successful candidate must be able to demonstrate excellence in motivation, communication, delegation and people management, and be capable of offering leadership and support. Many of the professionals I interviewed felt that they had been pushed out of their previous roles by frustration at the lack of recognition they received and/or the absence of praise for their efforts. Quite basic rules of effective leadership and line management appear to be routinely broken, leading directly to a poor retention record:

> I was never given praise or recognition for a job well done – and compliments on the quality of my work, which were made by clients, were never passed on to me. I often felt that good work went unrewarded or unrecognised. All I wanted was respect and recognition for my efforts.
>
> (accountant)

> There were a number of reasons why I would have liked to stay, but the overriding issue was a lack of support. I could not work in an environment that did not offer that and did not foster that kind of approach.
>
> (solicitor)

Quality of work

Solicitors and accountants were particularly frustrated by deficient people management skills in terms of poor leadership and management that also resulted in claims of discrimination and unfair distribution of work. It was explained to me that few managers responsible for the delegation of work tend to do so fairly. Too often, the sort of work people are given is seen to reflect their personal popularity with management rather than their capability:

> Managers and partners had their favourites and work was delegated to them. If you're not a favourite, you don't get the good work ...
>
> (solicitor)

> Because I didn't fit into the clique I got the boring monotonous work and felt that I was never being tested or able to push myself. Consequently, I saw colleagues who had joined at the same time progress and gain broader experience when in comparison my career appeared to have stagnated.

These findings are alarming. After five years of intensive studying to qualify, the subsequent career progression of solicitors and accountants often seems to depend on how much they have in common with their bosses. If their faces do not fit, there is limited opportunity for career development because they get landed with the uninteresting and more routine work. It is unsurprising that people leave when faced with such inherently discriminatory practices.

There is thus a good case for more structured training for managers and partners in professional services firms that incorporates soft people management skills, the principles of effective delegation and employee involvement in decision-making. There is also an apparent need for a review of selection criteria for management positions in many organisations. In addition, the successful reduction of turnover requires the establishment of more open channels of communication. These seem to be few and very narrow in the more traditional, conservative professional services firms. There is a case for the introduction of staff meetings, employee attitude surveys, briefing and debriefing sessions and bi-annual appraisal meetings.

I would also recommend that professional services firms consider adopting rotation schemes for recently qualified professionals where there is a perception of unfairness in the distribution of the type and quality of work. Such schemes help to ensure that each team member gains a broad range of experience, and prevents a situation arising in which some individuals are unjustly fast-tracked while the careers of others stagnate simply because there is a lack of equality of opportunity.

To help to ensure that they are given a sufficiently broad range of experience, solicitors and accountants must also be encouraged to design their own personal development plans. Firms can then use these to identify developmental opportunities and to design and deliver relevant in-house training programmes. Encouraging employees to plan their own career paths helps to ensure that they focus their thinking about future directions on progression in the current firm. This reduces the likelihood that they will look elsewhere, and also encourages more general loyalty and commitment to the firm.

Conclusions

I found little difference between the experiences related to me by the solicitors and the accountants. For each group the factors that influenced decisions to quit were remarkably similar. Both placed importance on the same employment-related issues and neither thought remuneration levels were very relevant. The only significant difference between the groups is the time they seem to take to reach the decision to leave. Solicitors took two to three months on average from the initial assessment of job satisfaction to actual resignation. In comparison, the more risk-averse accountants averaged six months.

My findings broadly support the conclusions of others who have conducted research on turnover and retention, but they also show how particular factors have special resonance in professional services firms. In many cases the solution requires little by way of financial investment – it is a question of altering entrenched management attitudes and long-established cultures which are no longer suited to changed labour market conditions.

My major recommendation is that managers (particularly human resource managers) working in professional services organisations should use the tools that are available to assess current employee attitudes and levels of job satisfaction and dissatisfaction. Carrying out confidential, formal staff surveys provides invaluable information and enhances understanding about the causes of avoidable turnover. It also helps to identify the key issues that must be addressed by retention initiatives in particular organisations. In most cases they should include the provision of flexible working policies and practices, comprehensive tailored individual training and developmental programmes, and managerial training that incorporates core people management skills. Firms that adopt such people-centred measures are best placed to secure competitive advantage in the 'war for talent'.

17 RETAIL WORKERS

by Claire Sweeney

Retailing is a sector which has one of the highest rates of staff turnover in the economy. Turnover averages around 40 per cent in the larger chains, but there is very considerable variation between stores in different localities. It is not unusual to find rates as low as 20 per cent in some places and over 100 per cent in others. In part, the explanation for poor retention lies in the substantial growth that the industry has enjoyed in recent years. With more and more stores opening each year and trading hours continually expanding, employees with the right skills and experience have little difficulty finding new work quickly should they decide to leave their current employment. If people become unhappy in their jobs, they do not need to stay around trying to sort problems out. Instead, they go and work elsewhere.

Aside from its relative fluidity, the retail labour market has other characteristics that make it rather different from others. The most important is the presence of large numbers of second income earners, most of whom are women with children. Many are attracted to the industry by the hours of work that are offered. They are actively looking for part-time work and want hours that allow them to work around those of their partners. Long-term career progression is unimportant for the majority.

My research involved interviewing 25 people employed in a single branch of the large supermarket chain I work for as a human resource manager. All had switched jobs within the sector during the previous year and were interviewed in depth about the decision to leave. Some had resigned from jobs in other large retail operations; others had left smaller employers. They represented a reasonable cross-section of the store in terms of age, department, grade and gender. Twenty of the interviewees were women, and 21 were employed on part-time contracts.

Why do retail workers resign from jobs?

Two major factors stand head and shoulders above the others as explanations for the resignations described in my interviews. The first was a poor (and often very poor) relationship with management, the other was the pattern of hours that people were expected to work. Both these reasons were mentioned at some length by a good majority of my interviewees. Although they made favourable comparisons on both counts between their current and previous employers, it was clear that push factors were at work here rather than pull factors. People left their jobs because they were unhappy and not because they were positively attracted by alternatives. The decision to leave came first in the vast majority of cases, and was followed by a new job search.

Two other issues were raised by a minority of interviewees. These were pay and training opportunities.

Incompetent management

The interviewees almost universally stated that unsatisfactory line management had led either directly or indirectly to their decisions to leave. Many of the stories I was told were astonishing to hear, given the prevailing tight labour market conditions. It almost appeared as if supervisors had gone out of their way to create situations which led to resignations. In retailing, it would seem, there is no question that people leave their managers rather than their organisations. Lack of respect, abusive treatment, a failure to provide support and a refusal to address problems were common themes in my interviews. In every case, the issue had contributed in large part to the decision to leave.

In several cases supervisors appear to have been insufficiently experienced to carry out their roles effectively. Many were poorly paid in comparison with the responsibility they were expected to carry. Others were just unpleasant types who appeared more concerned with establishing and making use of their own authority than providing any form of positive leadership. A failure to address staffing issues was a common theme too. Managers in the retail sector seem fond of saying 'Soon . . .' to people but never actually getting round to tackling the issues.

Hours and shifts

This was the second major issue to account for resignations in the retail sector. Sixteen of my 25 interviewees stated that arguments over hours were in one way or another the source of their decision to leave. In nearly all cases problems stemmed from situations in which hours were changed or extended without the agreement of the employees concerned, often at short notice. In most, the hours that people ended up having to work were different from those that had been agreed when the employment started. For staff who have childcare arrangements to make and who are the second income earners in their households there is a low tolerance threshold in this area. If, over a period of a week or two, they are not able to work the hours they want to, they will start looking for other work.

It was surprising to hear of so many instances in which hours and shift patterns played a major role in the quitting decision. After all, retailing is one of the sectors that is best placed to offer flexible hours and to meet the requirements of staff. That is why so many parents are attracted to work in stores in the first place.

Training

Most retail workers do not enter the occupation with the aim of climbing the management ranks. They are looking for a job rather than a career. However, this does not mean that training and development issues do not play a role in their leaving decisions. The main problems arise when insufficient training is given to enable them to perform their jobs satisfactorily. This appears to happen quite often. Several of my interviewees had left their previous jobs because they were thrown in at the deep end and had found themselves unable to cope. Some had arrived for work on their first days and had been given no training at all, being expected to pick things up as they went along. In one case, not even basic food hygiene training had been given.

The other common situation is one in which people are denied the opportunity to develop skills in a more general sense. They were left, day after day, carrying out the same old tasks when they were keen to learn a wider variety.

For a minority, career aspirations *were* a factor. Here denial of supervisory and management development opportunities are a cause of resignations, especially when they have been promised but never seem to materialise in practice.

Income

It is commonly said in the retail trade that employees are prone to leave jobs in order to gain a slightly higher hourly rate at another store. I found very little evidence of this. Only one of the 25 interviewees stated that the rate of pay offered by the new employer had played a role in his decision to leave his former job. He was a manager and therefore employed on a reasonable salary. But in his case the pay issue was a second-order consideration. The main reason for his resignation was a poor relationship with his immediate boss. Had that not been a problem to him the issue of pay would not have been a factor. The fact that he was paid a below-market rate became an issue because it reinforced an existing perception of being undervalued.

Although pay was not a factor with others, economic factors of different kinds certainly were. In several cases the desire to cut down on childcare costs was the prime motivation for the decision to resign. People found that they could switch jobs and gain a pattern of hours that allowed them to work at times when their spouses were at home. The result was a reduction in the amount of their income devoted to childcare, or even the elimination of childcare costs altogether. These were decisive factors in many resignation decisions.

Measures to improve retention rates

In my view, managers in retailing are often unaware of how far their own individual interactions with their staff account for resignations. They don't know because no one ever tells them. Where exit interviews are conducted, leavers are likely to remain tight-lipped about the extent to which their boss is to blame for their decision to quit. The starting-point for any retailer seeking to reduce turnover must therefore be effective diagnosis of the causes. The best approach involves employing someone from outside the organisation (eg a consultant) to carry out a survey of ex-employees by post or telephone. Provided confidentiality is assured, this should enable reports to be written which set out exactly why people have left in recent months. Alternatively, staff attitude surveys can be carried out, again on a confidential basis, to establish what the major sources of discontent are among current employees. Both approaches provide the basis for action targeted at the root causes of staff turnover in particular stores.

The vast majority of the resignations described by my interviewees could have been avoided, or at least substantially delayed, had managers behaved differently or taken a more flexible approach to decision-making. What my informants told me led me to conclude that retailers could very easily and inexpensively reduce staff turnover rates substantially were modest changes to be made in terms of management style and thinking. This view has been reinforced for me by my experience working as an HR manager in a store which has managed to sustain a turnover rate of 27 per cent – a level well below that of the company as a whole. I have seen, at first hand, that it is possible to achieve both high profitability and high retention rates. The major steps required are:

☐ Rates of pay must be fair. There is little to be gained in staff-retention terms by paying at above the market rate if other aspects of the employment experience are causing people to leave their jobs.

☐ Managers and first-line supervisors must be selected carefully, trained in basic supervisory skills and thereafter appraised on their records as supervisors. A great deal of turnover could be avoided if managers were to take greater care to treat their staff with respect and understanding, to involve them in decision-making, and to give consideration to their basic needs.

□ Retailers should grasp the opportunities available to them to offer hours which suit their employees and which allow them both to work and to manage their domestic lives. In particular, every possible step should be taken to avoid altering or extending individual working hours at short notice.

□ All staff must be given truly effective initial training when they first start. Managers should not assume that their staff will 'swim' when thrown in at the deep end. Many do not, despite outward appearances, leading to ongoing unhappiness and hence to avoidable resignations. Simply making sure that people are noticed and properly communicated with in their first weeks of employment can make a difference.

□ Managers should take more care to investigate whether their employees are becoming bored in their roles. Wherever possible, people must be offered the opportunity to broaden their skills and experience. Job rotation within stores has much to offer here. Not all employees will want to participate in such schemes, but that should not stop the opportunity from being given to those who do.

I would like to conclude by observing that many managers in the retail sector appear unable or unwilling to take the steps that have to be taken to compete for good staff effectively in the current environment. In many cases the styles of management that are adopted are no longer appropriate because labour market conditions have changed. Five or 10 years ago, when unemployment was high and job applicants plentiful, it was possible to get away with thoughtless and autocratic approaches to the management of staff. Nowadays, that is not so. People know that they can find other jobs easily, and will simply hand in their resignations if they are treated in a manner they perceive to be unjust. There is therefore a need for retail managers to adopt a more people-focused approach to their staff than has often been the case historically. Enlightened and respectful management is the key to low turnover in retailing.

BIBLIOGRAPHY

AGR (2001) *Graduate Salaries and Vacancies.* Brighton. Association of Graduate Recruiters/Institute of Employment Studies.

ARNOLD J. *and* MACKENZIE DAVEY K. (1992) 'Beyond unmet expectations'. *Personnel Review.* 21.2.

ARTHUR J. B. (1994) 'The effects of human resource systems on manufacturing performance and turnover'. *Academy of Management Journal.* 37.3.

BARBER A. E. (1998) *Recruiting Employees.* Thousand Oaks, CA. Sage.

BEVAN S., BARBER L. *and* ROBINSON D. (1997) *Keeping the Best: A practical guide to retaining key employees.* Brighton. Institute of Employment Research.

BLAND N., MUNDY G., RUSSELL J. *and* TUFFIN R. (1999) 'Career progression of ethnic minority police officers.' Home Office PRS paper 107.

BRAMHAM J. (1988) *Practical Manpower Planning.* London. IPM.

BRAMHAM L. (2001) *Keeping the People Who Keep You in Business.* New York. AMACOM.

BURTON N. (1996) *The Retention and Turnover of D-Grade Nurses.* Unpublished MSc dissertation. Manchester. UMIST.

BUTLER T. *and* WALDROOP J. (1999) 'Job Sculpting: The art of retaining your best people'. *Harvard Business Review.* September/October.

CAPPELLI P. (2000) 'A market-driven approach to retaining talent'. *Harvard Business Review.* January-February.

CARROLL M., MARCHINGTON M., EARNSHAW J. *and* TAYLOR S.

(1999) 'Recruitment in small firms: processes, methods and problems'. *Employee Relations*. 21.3.

CASCIO W. F. (2000) *Costing Human Resources: The financial impact of behavior in organizations*. Fourth edition. Cincinnati, OH. South Western College Publishing.

CBI (2001) *Pulling Together: 2001 absence and labour turnover survey*. London. Confederation of British Industry/PPP Healthcare.

CHADWICK C. *and* CAPPELLI P. (1998) 'Investments or contracts?: The performance effects of human resource systems under different contingencies'. Unpublished paper. Assessed in R. Richardson and M. THOMPSON (1999) *The Impact of People Management Practices on Business Performance: A literature review*. London. IPD.

CHAO G., O'LEARY-KELLY A., WOLF S., KLEIN H. *and* GARDNER P. (1994) 'Organizational socialization: its content and consequences'. *Journal of Applied Psychology*. 79.

CIPD (2001) *Labour Turnover Survey Report: October 2001*. London. CIPD.

DOLTON P. *and* KIDD M. (1991) 'Job changes, occupational mobility and human capital acquisition'. Mimeo. University of Newcastle.

DOUGLAS PHILLIPS J. (1990) 'The price tag on turnover'. *Personnel Journal*. December.

THE ECONOMIST (2000) 'Labours lost'. 13 July.

ELIAS P. (1994) 'Job-related training, trade union membership and labour mobility: a longitudinal study'. Oxford Economic Papers 46.

ELLIOT-MAJOR L. (2001) 'A degree? Still no job if you're black'. *New Statesman*. 26 March.

ELSDON R. *and* IYER S. (1999) 'Creating value and enhancing retention through employee development: the Sun Microsystems experience'. *Human Resource Planning*. 22.3.

EP-FIRST (2002) *Annual Graduate Recruitment Benchmarking Survey*. Lancaster. EP-First Saratoga Europe.

FAIR H. (1992) *Personnel and Profit: The pay-off from people.* London. CIPD.

FERNIE S. *and* METCALF D. (1996) *Participation, Contingent Pay, Representation and Workplace Performance: Evidence from Great Britain.* Discussion Paper 232. Centre for Economic Performance. London School of Economics.

FIELDS M. (2001) *Indispensable Employees.* Franklin Lakes, NJ. Career Press.

FREEMAN R. B. *and* MEDOFF J. L. (1984) *What Do Unions Do?* New York. Basic Books.

FRIED Y., CUMMINGS A. *and* OLDHAM G. R. (1998) 'Job design', in M. Poole and M. Warner (eds) *The Handbook of Human Resource Management.* London. Thomson Business Press.

FURNHAM A. (2001) 'Catharsis with your cards: exit interviews with departing employees help companies to learn about themselves'. *Financial Times.* 28 August.

GALLIE D., WHITE M., CHENG Y. *and* TOMLINSON M. (1998) *Restructuring the Employment Relationship.* Oxford. Oxford University Press.

GARDNER T. M. (2002) 'In the trenches at the talent wars: competitive interaction for scarce human resources'. *Human Resources Management.* 41.2.

GRAYSON D. *and* HODGES A. (2001) *Everybody's Business: Managing risks and opportunities in today's global society.* London. Dorling Kindersley.

GREEN F., FELSTEAD A., MAYHEW K. *and* PACK A. (2000) 'The impact of training on labour mobility: individual and firm-level evidence from Britain'. *British Journal of Industrial Relations.* 38.2.

GREENHALGH C. *and* MAVROTAS G. (1996) 'Job training, new technology amd labour turnover'. *British Journal of Industrial Relations.* 34.1.

GREGG P. *and* WADSWORTH J. (1999) 'Job tenure 1975–1998', in P. Gregg and J. Wadsworth (eds) *The State of Working Britain.* Manchester. Manchester University Press.

GRIFFETH R. *and* HOM P. (2001) *Retaining Valued Employees.* Thousand Oaks, CA. Sage.

GUSTMAN A. *and* STEINMEIER T. (1995) *Pension Incentives and Job Mobility.* Kalamazoo, MI. Upjohn Institute.

HACKMAN J. R. *and* OLDMAN G. R. (1980) *Work Redesign.* Reading, MA. Addison-Wesley.

HEALTH SERVICE REPORT (2001) 'Recruitment, retention and return in the NHS – still an uphill climb'. *Health Service Report.* Summer.

HILLS F., BERGMANN T. *and* SCARPELLO V. (1994) *Compensation Decision-Making.* Second edition. Fort Worth, TX. Dryden Press.

HOM P. *and* GRIFFETH R. (1995) *Employee Turnover.* Cincinnati OH. South Western College Publishing.

HUSELID M. (1995) 'The impact of human resource management practices on turnover, productivity and corporate financial performance'. *Academy of Management Journal.* 38.3.

HYMAN J. (2000) 'Financial participation schemes', in G. White and J. Druker (eds): *Reward Management: A critical text.* London. Routledge.

IDS (1989) *Labour Turnover.* IDS Focus 51. June.

IDS (1994) 'Reducing staff turnover in the W H Smith Group'. *IDS Report* 661. March.

IDS (1995) *Managing Labour Turnover.* IDS Study 577. May.

IDS (2000a) *Improving Staff Retention.* IDS Study 692. July.

IDS (2000b) *24-Hour Society.* IDS Focus 93. Spring.

IRS (1996) 'Benchmarking and managing labour turnover'. *Employee Development Bulletin* 75. March.

IRS (1998) 'Benchmarking labour turnover: annual update 1998'. *Employee Development Bulletin* 100. April.

IRS (1999) 'Benchmarking labour turnover: annual guide 1999/2000'. *Employee Development Bulletin* 118. October.

IRS (2000) 'Where next for HR?' *Employment Trends* 704. May.

IRS (2001) 'Recruitment and retention'. *IRS Management Review* 23. London. Industrial Relations Services.

JAMES I. (1992) *Graduates in the Metropolitan Police Service and Large Organisations: A comparative study of career development.* Unpublished MA dissertation in Police Studies. Exeter University.

JENNER S. *and* TAYLOR S. (2000) *Recruiting, Developing and Retaining Graduate Talent.* London. Financial Times/Prentice Hall.

JOINSON C. (2000) 'Capturing turnover costs'. *HR Magazine.* 45.7.

KHATRI N., FERN C. *and* BUDHWAR P. (2001) 'Explaining employee turnover in an Asian context'. *Human Resource Management Journal.* 11.1.

KOHN A. (1993) 'Why incentive plans cannot work'. *Harvard Business Review.* September-October.

LABOUR MARKET TRENDS (2001a) 'Length of time continuously employed by occupation and industry'. *Labour Market Trends.* February.

LABOUR MARKET TRENDS (2001b) 'Looking for a different or additional job'. *Labour Market Trends.* February.

LABOUR MARKET TRENDS (2001c) 'Job entry and exit by occupation'. *Labour Market Trends.* April.

LABOUR MARKET TRENDS (2001d) 'How employees obtained their current job'. *Labour Market Trends.* August.

LEAMAN A. *and* BORDASS B. (2000) 'Productivity in buildings: the "killer" variables', in D. Clements-Croome (ed.) *Creating the Productive Workplace.* London. Spon.

LEE T. *and* MITCHELL T. (1994) 'An alternative approach: the unfolding model of employee turnover'. *Academy of Management Review.* 19.1.

LEE T., MITCHELL T., HOLTOM B., MCDANIEL L. *and* HILL J. (1999) 'The unfolding model of voluntary turnover: a replication and extension'. *Academy of Management Journal.* 42.4.

LEIGHTON P. *and* O'DONNELL A. (1995) *The New Employment Contract.* London. Nicholas Brealey Publishing.

LEVIN R. *and* ROSSE J. (2001) *Talent Flow: A strategic approach to keeping good employees, helping them grow and let-ting them go.* San Francisco. Jossey Bass.

MICHAELS E., HANDFIELD-JONES H. *and* AXELROD B. (2001) *The War for Talent.* Boston, MA. Harvard University Press.

MOBLEY W. (1977) 'Intermediate linkages in the relationship between job satisfaction and employee turnover', in R. Steers and L. Porter (eds) *Motivation and Work Behavior.* New York. McGraw-Hill.

MOBLEY W. (1982) *Employee Turnover: Causes, consequences and control.* Reading, MA. Addison-Wesley.

MORRELL K., LOAN-CLARK J. *and* WILKINSON A. (2001) 'Unweaving leaving: the use of models in the management of employee turnover'. *International Journal of Management Review.* 3.3.

PARKER S. *and* WALL T. (1998) *Job and Work Design.* Thousand Oaks, CA. Sage.

PEARSON P. (2001) *Call Centre Rewards.* London. IRS/Call Centre Association Research Institute.

PENDLETON A. (2000) 'Profit sharing and employee share ownership', in R. Thorpe and G. Homan (eds) *Strategic Reward Systems.* London. Financial Times/Prentice Hall.

PENDLETON A., WILSON N. *and* WRIGHT M. (1998) 'The perception and effects of share ownership: empirical evidence from employee buy-outs'. *British Journal of Industrial Relations.* 36.1.

PFEFFER J. (1998) *The Human Equation.* Boston, MA. Harvard University Press.

PHILLIPS J. M. (1998) 'The effects of realistic job previews on multiple organizational outcomes: a meta-analysis'. *Academy of Management Journal.* 41.

PINKOVITZ W. H., MOSKAL J. *and* GREEN G. (2001) 'How much does your employee turnover cost?' www.uwex.edu/ces/cced/publicat/turn.html.

PRICE J. *and* MUELLER C. (1986) *Absenteeism and the Turnover of Hospital Employees.* Greenwich, CT. JAI Press.

PURCELL K., PITCHER J. *and* SIMM C. (1999) *Working Out?*

Graduates' early experiences of the labour market. London. Higher Education Careers Services Unit.

REED A. (2001) *Innovation in Human Resource Management: Tooling up for the talent wars.* London. CIPD.

REEVES R. (2000) 'We should all become time lords'. *New Statesman.* 31 July.

RITZER G. (1996) *The McDonaldization of Society: An investigation into the changing character of contemporary social life.* Revised edition. Thousand Oaks, CA. Pine Forge.

ROBERTS G. (2000) *Recruitment and Selection: A competency approach.* Second edition. London. CIPD.

STEERS R. *and* MOWDAY R. (1981) 'Employee turnover and post-decision accommodation processes', in L. Cummings and B. Staw (eds) *Research in Organisational Behavior.* Greenwich, CT. JAI Press.

STURGES J. *and* GUEST D. (1999) *Should I Stay or Should I Go?* Warwick. Association of Graduate Recruiters.

TAYLOR S. (2000) 'Occupational pensions and employee retention: debate and evidence'. *Employee Relations.* 22.3.

TAYLOR S. (2002) *People Resourcing.* Second edition. London. CIPD.

TOPLIS J., DULEWICZ V. *and* FLETCHER C. (1997) *Psychological Testing: A manager's guide.* Third edition. London. IPD.

UNIVERSUM (2002) *Annual Survey. Main Report, UK.* Stockholm. Universum Communications.

WADSWORTH J. (1989) *Job Tenure and Inter-Firm Mobility.* Centre for Economic Performance, London School of Economics. Working Paper 1187.

WALLACE M. *and* FAY C. (1988) *Compensation Theory and Practice.* Second edition. Boston, MA. PWS-KENT Publishing Company.

WANOUS J. P. (1992) *Organizational Entry: Recruitment, selection, orientation and socialization of newcomers.* Second edition. Reading, MA. Addison-Wesley.

ZARANDONA J. *and* CAMUSO M. (1985) 'A study of exit interviews: does the last word count?' *Personnel.* 62.3.

INDEX